GERMAN LEAVES

German Leaves

Ralph P. Vander Heide, Ph.D.

Copyright © 2012 by Ralph P. Vander Heide, Ph.D.

Library of Congress Control Number: 2012923636
ISBN: Hardcover 978-1-4797-6790-8
Softcover 978-1-4797-6789-2
Ebook 978-1-4797-6791-5

All rights reserved. No part of this book may be reproduced or transmitted in any form or by any means, electronic or mechanical, including photocopying, recording, or by any information storage and retrieval system, without permission in writing from the copyright owner.

This book was printed in the United States of America.

To order additional copies of this book, contact:
Xlibris Corporation
1-888-795-4274
www.Xlibris.com
Orders@Xlibris.com

Contents

Preface vii

Chapter I: Motivation, Atrocities, Concepts, WW II 1
    Personal Experiences with WW II 1
    More Atrocities and Mistreatment of Jews....................................... 4
    A Few Terms and Concepts Defined.. 10
    Other Helpful Common Terms 10
    A Start on Learning German... 14

Chapter II: DB Introduced, Preeminence.. 17

Chapter III: Founders of the DB, Successes, Failures......................... 35
    Representatives Abroad 40
    Working Conditions in Chile.. 41
    Getting Known (Marketing)... 52
    Criticism of the Deutsche Blätter 59

Chapter IV: The German Problem—Historical View 65

Chapter V: The German Problem—New Aspects 87

Chapter VI: New Europe and New World 109

Chapter VII: Nazism, Socialism, Communism 129

Chapter VIII: Religion... 143

Chapter IX: Literature 159
    Literature as Uplifting Fine Art... 175

Chapter X: Travel, Philosophy, Music, Art.. 189
    A Tribute 198

Conclusions 201

Appendices... 207
    A—Alphabetical List of Contributors to the *Deutsche Blätter* with a Chronological List of Articles.. 207
    B—Flier Requesting Financial Aid to Bring DB to POW's an Unsere Freunde Und Leser!... 228
    C—Flier Sent to German POW's... 230
    D—Flier Requesting Financial Aid for Children in Europe 232
    E—Anti-semitism of Hans Fritz von Zwehl and Reaction of Udo Rukser 234
    F—Correspondence... 238
    G—Letter of Appreciation for the *DB* From a German POW........ 244
    H—Letter to Herbert Hoover... 246
    I—*Runder Tisch* at Home of Joseph Kaskell............................... 247
    J—photos: Hitler, Goebbels, Mann Jews, Borkum, Vander Heide, Rukser Theile... 251
    K—Acknowledgments in Original Dissertation 269

List of Sources Consulted 273

Copies of the Deutsche Blätter 281

Preface

Readers will better appreciate this study of one small, but influential resistance effort of World War II, if they first are prepared with some facts concerning the background and reasons for my complete revision of this work. It was born as my Ph.D. dissertation, which I compiled over a period of three years and finished in 1975. For some time, it has seemed to me that the world should be aware of this wonderful little publication, which challenged the Nazis and informed Germans of current truths of the war years, their own history, the humanities and postwar issues. It needs to be universally appreciated for the value of its timeless messages.

It has again taken ten months in 2012 to update, revise, make the reading smoother. Most difficult was the translating of all the German passages, which formed a large part of the original. It was required that I follow policy and keep them only in German in the dissertation. However, it is now my aim to publish a dual language edition so that it can be appreciated by all English speakers in the world today, and not solely by those whose German is adequate. I have made great effort to facilitate comprehension through footnoting, including a glossary, by adding some pertinent information about the Nazis and their victims and by relating personal relationships and experiences with the war years.

Since this is not a weighty tome of history like those produced by the great German historians, Thomas Momsen or Leopold von Ranke, and because the table of contents is rather detailed, I decided against an index. Maybe I simply want readers to read through again and again and…It was my aim to write about a slice of history, which, although heavy in content, is easy to read. I would like feedback from readers concerning my degree of success. In my present biased evaluation, I find the prose to flow smoothly in carefully crafted sentences. It is even novelistic in some parts, for I have never seen the point of dry facts followed by additional dry facts. "Lighten up!" "Get a grip!" "Chill out!" are common utterances of today's younger generation. Perhaps I internalized their advice, although I have not here produced history in novelistic form; that proved to be far too difficult. If that is to be the objective, I found that one must begin with novelistic treatment, and, since my wife and I published the jointly authored, *Chris and Louisa*, I should know better. However, here my style is different, sometimes like a novel, but always I find it to be more exciting than strings of dates and facts. I trust the reader will agree. I have also written more about 1) how I am approaching the task, and 2) about the sequence of explanations that one normally finds in histories or studies of this genre.

Good! let's hope I do not bore anyone. It was my intention to render lighter a heavy subject in part through clarifying concepts and giving background, beginning with the writing itself, which we will consider next. I was tormented concerning how to distinguish between two languages in quotes plus all my text and commentary. Should I use regular script, bold, underline, just what? How to make it easiest on the reader was my overriding concern. I pondered for days and then simply made an administrative decision.

I have decided to modify to some extent the conventions of writing that were pounded into me by teachers from Kindergarten through Ph.D. I decided, for example, as stated above, to make the manuscript completely readable in both English and German. Therefore, I am solely responsible for all translations.

Then, after agonizing over how to use which fonts, size of type and all of that, I concluded that I would keep the German as was, but translate it into English, employing italics for the German and make a sharp contrast to the English by using bold. I can foresee the English-speaking reader being able to go straight to the translation, facilitated by the bold type. Translations longer than three lines are set apart, first the original German, and below it the translation in English bold.

In some places I let readers guess a little, or I think it is more than likely that you know the meaning, and, therefore, render just the essential sense. I know what the grammar books say about italics, bold, parentheses and all, but I believe my approach will assist the readers, and I am writing for them, not for grammar books. I also use the first person pronoun, but that you've already observed.

Hitler inspecting the massive 800mm *Schwerer Gustav* (**HEAVY** or **BIG GUSTAV**) railway gun from afar. It was the largest-caliber rifled weapon ever used in combat, and fired the heaviest shells of any artillery piece.

AND THERE WAS THE STAR !!
(DUTCH VERSION HERE: JOOD)

Dutch were forced to have the star sewed on clothing

Chapter I
Motivation, Atrocities, Concepts, WW II

PERSONAL EXPERIENCES WITH WW II

I WAS A boy only eight years old when the war ended (for me this will always be THE war). Every day I was afraid of Germans attacking the USA, namely me, but as I grew up during those days, I remained safe in Ogden, Utah, USA. Relatives in the Netherlands were not. Years later I was to learn of the following atrocity, an act of gross cowardliness complete with lies and typical Nazi brutality, yes "typical" for it was a recommended tactic

My first cousin was called up to serve in the Dutch army in the defense of the area around the beautiful little city of Rhenen on the Rhein. According to scholars of the war, including Dutch Lieutenant Colonel Eppo H. Brongers, this is a far too little known but major battle of the war and, indeed, the first of this magnitude. Therefore, it is sometimes referred to by those in the know as the first battle of WWII. Few were more important, for the maniacal leader with the poisonous mind had Poland behind him, but was still testing soldiers, equipment, plans. He was exhuberant, prancing around and periodically clapping his hands! At one point Hitler announced that his generals and troops should bolster themselves by reading the novels of Karl May and ape the examples of courage and admirable fighting skills. Who is this May, you ask?

Even today each new crop of German youth read more of his novels than the preceding. May visited the USA only once, but this paragon, born in 1842, of what the Germans term *Trivialliteratur* (**Genre fiction**), this fifth child of fourteen spawned by a poor weaver, turned out seventy-three adventure novels of the American Wild West complete with a kind of knight-errant, Old Shatterhand, who lives in Indian Territory battling desperadoes, and it seems is the example *nonpareil* of the courageous, ethical hero. Now, we should emphasize that Hitler was neither, but at least we know where the source of some of his thinking originated. Did some of the world's most competent generals take the leader's advice? I envision the General Staff soaking up once again these adventure books read in their youth.

Feasibly having Shatterhand in mind, Hitler allowed the commander, Karl von Tiedemann, *General Leutnant,* only one day to crush through and claim victory. Following tradition, the German General Staff had planned well under the direction of Field Marshal General Erich von Manstein, recognized as the most talented field commander in WWII. Well, he probably read Karl May. Representatives of the High Command visited the future battlegrounds several times in civilian clothing or Dutch uniforms to study the area and the ancient, crumbling defenses of the *Grebbe* Line and decided to launch a three pronged attack driving through the Netherlands to France and on to England.

The Dutch had only a small army assessed by military experts as virtually worthless. It was equipped with weapons from WW I, some even dating back to 1878-80 and made up of quickly conscripted, untrained soldiers. Surprisingly, this pathetic rag tag bunch (surely the term, *army,* is incorrect) resisted for several days, yet Hitler allowed von Tiedemann to keep his head. With some help from the British and French, severe damage to the Germans ensued, Including incapacitating hundreds of airplanes (an exact number depends on how many days are included, who is reporting, etc.), which stopped the planned invasion of England due to insufficient air power, but now, please, ponder, envision, for a moment this overwhelming force against the weak.

The officers were acknowledged as the best trained in the world and highly experienced. How shameful, how badly it spoke of von Manstein and the rest to plan a slaughter. Did they, however, have a choice when the deranged supreme commander directed that the carnage begin? At least they had a ready scapegoat for postwar blame, study and discussions. In postwar trials so many muttered about only carrying out orders.

Please stop reading again and conjure up an image, as though viewing a Hollywood blockbuster. The 6th and 18th German armies were drawn up along the Dutch border with a combined strength of more than 24 divisions sporting shiny new equipment, including seventy-five anti-tank guns for each division. The troops were well-trained, and more importantly they were committed. To die for the *Führer* and *Heimat* (**homeland**) would be honorable. The giants of industry, Krupp and Thysen, cozy with Hitler, had given their all as well. The famous nightlife of Berlin was roaring. Here we go again, gang. It's our turn to win. Let's get even! Jubilance reigned.

The loyal generals planned three main attacks with the heaviest advance through the center aimed at the Dutch *Grebbeline* which was to force breakthroughs at the *Grebbeberg* (high point at 52 meters) and at Amersfoort. Then, it would be on to Amsterdam. Precisely at 3:55 am on May 10, 1940, they rolled into the soggy fields of the Kingdom of the Netherlands with all weapons blasting, huge anti-tank guns against what?—peashooters? This will be easier than Poland, they thought.

When my cousin's platoon surrendered, the Germans promised they would be sent to camps, and then marched the men into a depression which ran along the side of the road to Rhenen where they were each murdered (*gesneuveld*, the Dutch say, "**rubbed out**") with a bullet through the brain…fun for the perpetrators I suppose. "Let's kill us some Dutchmen today."

"*Das ist Krieg*" (**That's war**) the German commander told my family, including Dirk's nine siblings. They first told me the details in 1958 and during subsequent visits. Certainly, I can not agree with the commander. No, in my *Weltanschauung das ist **nicht** Krieg*, but rather just wanton murder. The loss was still painful in 2009 when my wife and I last visited. Today, the Great Wheel of History has rolled on. All nine of my cousins have joined Dirk in death, and for those readers who doubt—Yes, the general actually met with them at their request. The *Krauts* (the Dutch call them *Moffen…Rotmoffen* is stronger) felt confident and pesky, for they still had surpluses of both *Butter* and *Kanonen* (more on this later, if you do not know the reference.) even if they had been slowed down a bit. Still, they had not only their 207th Infantry Brigade, but also those wonderful SS troops, a regiment of 5,000 named *Der Führer*, commanded by Georg Keppler. The founders of the anti-Nazi *Deutsche Blätter* knew many such stories.

They were profoundly atuned to the universal mayhem and unraveling of thousands of years of progress that was taking place and of its appeal to that which was the most base in the human psyche. The Dutch, for example, who were being pitied by the world due to German cruelty, as has been noted, and who historically were known to be some of the first to help their fellowmen, were soon becoming all too frequently allies of the enemy. Indeed, they who lost 2,200 (or only 420?—the number now resting in the memorial cemetery—Again number of days, size of the area, etc. alter the figures) of their young men between May 11-14 with another 1,000 wounded, Netherlanders witnessed the volunteering of 25,000 (I have heard 40,000, also 20,000) men to serve in the German regular army (*Heer*) or the *Waffen SS*. Anton Andriaan Mussert was leader of the Dutch *Nationaal Sozialistische Partei*, which remained the only official political party in the Netherlands throughout the war. Jan A. Wolthuis, an attorney, was another committed Nazi leader as were too many more. Traitors are rarely judged kindly in an historical perspective.

Anton was a sycophant among sycophants. This fawning parasite even managed to be summoned to Berlin a couple of times and could spend a whole day awaiting a call from the German High Command, especially Heinrich Himmler, who quickly came to see the need for conscripting as many Dutchmen as possible. The Dutch were, after all, blond and blue-eyed, and Dutch police forces had helped rid the country of Jews. I lived in Amsterdam in 1959 in the Swammerdamstraat (**Swammerdam Street**), which before the war was inhabited principally by Jews. All were forcibly added to the total 105,000 Dutch Jews who were sent to concentration camps. Seventy-five percent died or were killed. I knew of only one family that returned to my street.

Furthermore, too many Dutch women began associating with the German troops or "fraternizing" as is commonly said. The Dutch labeled them *moffenmeiden* (**German maidens,** *moffen* is a derogatory slang term for Germans). Within hours (maybe minutes) following the cease fire, the beatings of these ladies began along with the shaving of heads which when bald were painted with a red cross. When I lived on the Archimedeslaan in Amsterdam East, my Jewish landlord pointed to the flats of former NSB members who lived on the street. In wartime daily existence becomes twisted, different, ugly on all sides. The enlightened reasoning of Goethe or the Netherland's own Hugo Grotius, Joost van den Vondel and other champions of humanism was ignored. "Stop all of this," was the humanistic plea of the *Blätter*. "Come to your senses."

MORE ATROCITIES AND MISTREATMENT OF JEWS

I was to learn of more atrocities as reports came in, historians completed their works and the countless personal stories came to light. We shall never know all of the thousands, but we remember at least the most brutal and outrageous which represent all, including the attempt to create a superrace of Germans through selective breeding. Thousands of German women were inspirited to bear children with SS officers, which may offend the morals of some, but far worse was the practice of kidnapping "racially acceptable" children throughout Europe and rearing them as models of racial purity and teutonic physical perfection, inculcated.with Nazism.

The project, termed *Lebensborn* (**Fountain of life**), was personally set up by Heinrich Himmler, SS chief and *Reichsführer* (**Leader of the Empire**

right below Hitler, but nevertheless **below,** not **Führer,** no, no. One could be executed for using that word, even Himmler. How Hitler's cronies loved their titles!

The *Reichsführer* was possessed with racial war and directed the wholesale abduction of hundreds of thousands of children. Prior to commencing the infamous, abhorrent massacre of all inhabitants of the Czech village of Lidice, a psychotic twist was added. The Nazis quickly examined the community's ninety children, spared eight for Himmler, and, returned to the killings. I swear that when my wife and I visited Lidice on a grey morning with a light drizzle falling, those eighty-two children and the rest of the executed villagers were present. Their cries, their screams or their muted voices and quiet sobs were in the very atmosphere. So many accounts. Why, oh why?

I have visited infamous camps and sites of Nazi killings many times, and each time have observed several persons with tears in their eyes or crying. At Dachau, Auschwitz, Theresienstadt, Treblinka, Maidanek, and all the rest, as well as at the cemeteries, tears gush at thoughts of the brute force, insensitivity, the beastiality of the calculating technicians of genocide. Hitler preached that to be pure, the German, who had sentimentality in his nature, had to free himself from all sentimentality. What impresses, *Der Führer* taught, was cruelty, and that some of his army officers took those teachings very much to heart was nowhere better demonstrated than in the Battle of the Bulge.

Malmédy may be the most depressing site for Americans, for it was there in the gorgeous, deep green Ardenne forest that one of the worst massacres of all time took place. I could term the entire battle as horror in the midst of nature's pulchritude, realizing that on that bitterly cold morning of December 17, 1944, all green was covered with snow, but now in its austere wintriness still beautiful, when at the command of SS Lieutenant Werner Sternebeck, his two remaining tanks fired on the Americans, and so it began.

Sternebeck had lost five of his seven tanks in the advance and his commander, Waffen SS Colonel (*Obersturmbannführer*), Joachim Peiper, was furious, at yet more delay. It has been reported that this up-and-coming officer, always eager to please the higher-ups and longing to be in their presence, was this day in a very bad mood. What did he think? I suppose to improve his mood he decided: "Let's kill us some Americans, even bludgeon some." He had been given great responsibility even though this field officer was the youngest regimental colonel in the Waffen SS. His SS Kampfgruppe Peiper, part of the 1st Panzer Division, spearheaded the Sixth SS Panzer Army.

The American soldiers were deliberately murdered in cold blood by the 1st SS Panzer Division Adolf Hiter commanded by Peiper, which had been responsible for atrocities in Russia and had already shot captured Americans in their advance in the Ardennes Offensive. Nor was this the end, for more were *gesneuveld* after Malmédy. This Division, commonly referred to with pride as *das Lötlampenbatallion* (**The Blowtorch Brigade**), following those murders in Russia, was one of only two allowed to use the Adolf Hitler title, which we encountered in the offensive against the Netherlands. Each carried out murders on prisoners and civilian survivors.

Since Peiper had left the area when the massacre took place and was not at the scene when the shooting started, it is possible that Major Werner Poetschke, who commanded the 1st SS Panzer Battalion, gave the order. Be that as it may, for it makes no difference. The soldiers are just as dead, but champions of the colonel try to mitigate the responsibility of Peiper, who surely gave Poetschke the order to give the order, and Hitler had ordered a slaughter earmarked with fiendish *Unbarmherzigkeit* (**without mercy**). Oral evidence substantiates that on December 12th he had issued an order to take no prisoners while carrying out a wave of terror against the troops struggling to resist the German offensive.

Clearly outgunned by the Germans, the Americans from B Battery surrendered after Sternebeck's attack. Peiper himself went to the Baugnez Crossroads and brusquely ordered Sternebeck to move on. The 113 American prisoners-of-war who had survived the attack were assembled in a field near the Café Bodarwé at the crossroads. This figure included eight Americans who had already been captured by Peiper. A Belgium boy witnessed what happened next.

At about 14.15, soldiers from the 1st SS Panzer Division opened fire on the 113 men who were in the field. The firing stopped at about 14.30. Soldiers from Peiper's unit went around the field and shot at close range anyone who seemed to be alive or— clubbed them to death as later autopsies showed. Incredibly, some prisoners did get away after feigning death. Three of these escapees came across the American, Colonel Pergrin.

Colonel Pergrin had heard the attack by Sternebeck and went to investigate, first in a jeep and then on foot. Near Five Points, three Americans rushed up to Pergrin. It was these men who first alerted the Americans that something had gone on at the crossroads. The colonel took the wounded men to Malmédy and at 16.40 contacted the First Army's headquarters to inform them that some sort of massacre had taken place at Five Points.

Because of the nature of the Battle of the Bulge, neither side could immediately claim the land where the dead troops lay. It was only on Jan. 14, 1945, that the Americans could begin to claim the area and recover seventy-one of the frozen snow-covered bodies, which the freezing weather had preserved.

This made it easier to perform autopsies, especially as some bodies had been covered in snow.

On December 17th, twenty-one survivors of the massacre made statements to the American authorities in Malmédy. Their accounts were remarkably similar despite the fact that they had had little time to discuss their experiences, which gives added credence to their testimonies.

I call your attention once again to the kind of warfare being waged. Once more we see here the most vicious of the commanders. General Sepp Dietrich commanded the Sixth Panzer Army; Hasso Manteufel had the Fifth. Peiper, very much in the loop of the Nazi big shots since age twenty, was for a time First Adjutant to Heinrich Himmler, and, perhaps to ingratiate himself more, murdered with frenzy. He was commanding one of the two dreaded Adolf Hitler *Leibstandarte* (**bodyguard units)**.

The reader has already made connections to the killing of the surrendered Dutchmen, and now we can, most sadly, carry the ties further, since in addition to the 113 (minus survivors), many more persons were murdered at Traves, Haute-Saôn, Bülingen, Ligneuville, Stavelot. Remember, at St. Ordour the whole population was sacrificed to the Nazi Gods.

Not to be left out, General Anton Dostler had American soldiers murdered at La Spezia, Italy. He was executed after a proper trial. *Obersturmbannführer*, Herbert Kappler head of the SS in Rome, wanted to teach the Italian civilians not to rise up again by massacring 335, now known as the Ardeatine massacre, The reader may look elsewhere for information on the numerous executions. I believe the few mentioned in this study indicates the pattern and the mindsets.

For Malmédy a rationalization such as the following may be offered by those who defend the perpetrators. They argue that the sheer number of American prisoners almost certainly sealed their fate. Over 100 prisoners could not be left in the field. But there was no spare capacity for the Germans to guard them as Peiper had ordered the SS units under his command to speed up their advance. Marching POW's back to German lines was viewed as undoable, since Peiper had control of only the single road being used by his unit. Marching in the opposite direction could easily clog up the road. Peiper's other worry was that he might be attacked by American units known to be in the area.

This justifies clubbing men to death? It should turn one's stomach. It seems to me that the only arguable question here asks if this incidence of genocide should be ranked ahead of others. Similar exterminations occurred throughout Europe. I believe it was Hans Frank, Nazi Governor General of Poland, who noted in his diary that he aimed to make mincemeat of the Poles and Ukranians. Occasionally retribution was successful.

Peiper was employed by Volkswagen after wiggling out of punishment for his murders, after all, he wasn't even present, and Hitler personally had presented the boy wonder *Das Ritterkreuz des Eisernen Kreuzes* (**The Knight's Cross with Oakleaves and Swords**). However, he made the mistake of loving France. Go figure! He built a house at Traves Haute-Saône, and was rather mysterioiusly murdered by either former members of the French Resistance or Communists. He was shot in the chest, his house burned, and most fittingly, his charred body found in the ruins. Others too could use *Lötlampen*, it seems. So, we know of at least two instances of revenge.

At Khatyn in Belarus the entire population was burned alive by the German occupation forces. The same occurred at St. Oradour sur Glane in France. Commonly executions of individuals were carried out. Volumes have been written on this demonic, maniacal behavior and more will be forthcoming. Still, the three or four occurrences recounted here indicate the intensity, inhumanity and lust for murder which characterized all, especially those directed at Jews.

A German professor friend counters with accounts of atrocities committed by soldiers of other nations. Apparently as a young boy in Hamburg he witnessed the rape of a young teacher by an entire platoon of Russians, one by one. She was never the same mentally after that, he relates, and wonders even if her life was still worth living. Why did they behave like beasts? If we say the Germans were from the land of Beethoven, we can point out that the Russians were from the land of Tolstoy. Wars and bestiality seem to appeal to *homo sapiens* in spite of their level of so-called culture.

It is now common knowledge that a primary tenent of National Socialism was to rid the world of all Jews. Hitler and followers spoke daily of the *final solution,* which meant extermination of the *Untermenschen* (**subhumans**). The following account of what occurred for many years on the Frisian Island of Borkum stands as a symbol of the anti-semitism espoused by millions of Teutonic racists. Today we might say the German masses (the *Volk*) "bought into it," and quite willingly. *Rassenwahn* (**racial insanity**) was in the air.

Borkum, famous throughout Germany before the *Great War* as "the only spot on earth without a Jew," was also a great German military base. Even prior to WW I it was the most anti-semitic resort on that German North Sea island, it's warped characterization of Jews framed in the *Borkum Lied* (**song**) of which the last verse best reveals its flavor: Those who arrive *mit platen Füßen, mit Nasen krum, mit Haaren Kraus* (**with flat feet, crooked noses and curly hair**)**,** are not only forbidden the pleasures of using the beach, but *der muß hinaus! Der muß hinaus! Hinaus! (***He must get out! Must get out! Out!***)* It became common practice on the island for the local orchestra to play this song at the end of each performance and to invite the vacationers to join in. This was facilitated through the distribution of postcards with the lyrics printed on one side—efficient!

Recall the concept of *Deutsche Genauigkeit* (**German efficiency, precision**). Non-Germans have a little fun when this precision is taken to extremes or it can be sickening in some applications. Indeed, the postcard with lyrics on the other side depicted Germans singing with hands raised and glasses filled, along with a group of *typical* Jews with, of course, *Nasen krum* and all the rest. The postcard depicts a Jewish family being turned away.

I have another question, many in fact, but why did the Jews stay? Was it hope? The decision made that it would all be over soon? Surely Nazis were not committing all those murderous acts and torture. What did they think? How did they think? I am aware of several thousand who did leave, but, still, too many remained, living each day with a sword over their heads, closer to death.

At age twenty-two I lived in Amsterdam in the home of a Jewish diamond merchant and his gentile wife and children. He became a non-person who spent part of the war in a tiny hideaway under the floor boards of his dwelling, one of the lucky, who at age 97 is alive to add his personal tales of the war to the countless stories of the famous and infamous, the rich, the poor, the display of ignorance, pogroms, kindnesses, affect on ordinary life, hunger, suffering, winning a few and, unfortunately losing a few encounters with the GESTAPO or whatever group among the German occupiers.

A Dutch acquaintance, who later joined others in the USA, hid a Jew one evening in Amsterdam. Both were terrified. Each or both avoided possible torture, death or perhaps being left to perish hanging on a meat hook. Later in this book you will read about the torture of several persons, some famous, some Jews, others not, others just trying to do their jobs, and stay alive.

The portrayal of Jews in the Nazi media is offensive beyond words. Just two examples substantiate the accusation: Eric Washneck's *Die Rotschilds* and Veit Harland's vicious spectacle, *Jud Süss*. So many could be added, including the vulgar comedies in which the Jew was a vilivied fool.

In case you need reminding, Jews, who may have been store clerks, business owners, school teachers, physicians, the common man or woman, were dragged into railroad boxcars and from there into camps and/or extermination buildings, and murdered by the same persons who, it is said, were always deeply moved by the Prisoners' Chorus in *Fidelio*. I have never seen evidence that would dissuade me from believing that the killers devised terror with fiendish, laughing brutality. I am not a religious man, but here I make an exception and a wish: May they somehow or other burn in Hell and suffer at a minimum double what their victims experienced.

A FEW TERMS AND CONCEPTS DEFINED

I always find it awkward and annoying to be forced to look up terms, essential dates, names, historical facts, etc. when the writer, supposedly more knowledgeable than I could have supplied a few, and, indeed, I apologize for not listing more, but readers need to work a little. First, let's consider what is in a name? Some scholars and critics of Germany have suggested that the very names of some Germans are responsible for the *German Problem*, since they have meanings related to war. Below are a few. I take no position on the influence of names. I'll leave that up to the psychologists for now.

Gerlinde	elements of *geri*-**spear** and *lind*-**soft, tender, weak** thus also
Gertie,	soft spear and Gertie, pet form of *Gertrude*
Sigis	**Victory,** *Sigieswald-wald*,**victory,** *Sigfried* **many with** *Sigi*
Hadwig	In *Old High German*-**war** or **battle**
Heiko	In *Frisian*—**strong ruler**
Hildegard	*Hild*-**battle** and **Gard—enclosure**
Kriemhilde	**Mask** plus **Battle**
Walter	**Army commander**
Waltraut	**Strong ruler** *(fem).*

OTHER HELPFUL COMMON TERMS

Volk is more than a word; it is a concept. The Literal meaning is **people, tribe, nation,** but there is a deeper feeling, something sentimental, evokes melancholy, **common people, little man on the street, crew, troops, working people, rabble, lower classes, nation.** A *Volksführer* is a very **popular leader (of the people).** Many more combinations with *Volk* are possible connoting a warm, comfortable feeling of home and country, little mother in the kitchen preparing the *Apfelstrudel. Volkswohlfahrt,* **public welfare,** *Volksverbunden,* **rooted in one's home soil,** *Volksverbundenheit,* **national solidarity.** Under National Socialism a *Volkschädling* was an **anti-social parasite** and *völkisch* meant anti-semitic. Concentrate on that one. If you are truly of the people, you are a despiser of Jews. anti-semitic. It tells us something about Germans that *Volk* may refer to a **swarm,** as of bees and to a **herd** or **covey.** *Volksdeutsche* is a term for the pure **German ethnic group,** and *Volksmeinung* translates as **public opinion,** while *Volkstümlich* means **popular** and *Volkseigen* refers to **publicly owned** or **nationalized** and if you are down and out, you may eat at a *Volksküche,* **a soup-**

kitchen. I will stop, but from all of that one can see how the Nazis could play with the word and embrace it as their own.

Geist A word with multiple meanings or senses including **mind, spirit, intellect, intelligence, soul, ghost, genius, essence, wit, brain, imagination, moral, apparition**. Germans are always referring to the *Geist* of this or that. To translate one picks the best sense. The term *geistiger Widerstand* refers to **moral resistance** and is used quite often in discussing nonviolent responses, peaceful commitments, etc.

Stoß aus dem Hinterhalt	Refers to **being attacked from ambush with the harsh** reprisals of WW I and to Weimar Republic days.
Dolchstoß	**stab in the back**—along with the ambush concept refers to being betrayed, cheated, taken advantage of. This conviction of being betrayed after WW I and Lord Vansittart is explained later.

Deutsche Unbezwinglichkeit, Unbesieglichkeit, Unüberwindlichkeit all have the essential meaning of German invulnerability. These terms were repeated ad infinitum in those Nazi diatribes in Nurnberg. When that occurs the *Volk* comes to believe unequivicably at least until all the food is being rationed and the *Butter* is gone (metaphorically), and those who were *unbesieglich* are returning home without body parts or in cheap coffins proving that they were indeed *besieglich*. The *Führer* (the God he became) was wrong. This new God lied to us.

Der Wille des Führers ist recht (**The will of the leader is the law**). All Germans came to understand the full meaning of this phrase during the twelve years that Hitler was wasting their resources of all kinds and precious human lives. Even the great industrial steel baron, Fritz Thysen said Hitler stole a hugh amount of money. Poor Fritz, down to his last few millions, but with his cunning this scoundrel recovered by manipulating the system, conning the Allied Powers and steadfastly pressing on to gain, yet another Phoenix risen.

As I write, the steel company he left behind (after absorbing Krupp) is worth fifty billion dollars. So, to quote the French: *Plus ça change, plus ça meme chose*. Still, one asks what did the war cost everyone involved throughout Europe and the world? It is only now after seventy or so years, that one sees far fewer German men with limbs, eyes or ears missing, but public transportation vehicles and trams still have those seats reserved with a sign for *Kriegsverlezten* to remind us, and what were the economic costs?

HEIMAT also stirs the German soul and is used at least fourteen times in this study. **Home** or perhaps **native land** a dictionary will say, but for the German it conjures up an idyllic scene of "good" (even "the best") people, a buxom young girl dressed in a *Dirndl* strolling across a lush mountain meadow or some elderly gentlemen sipping beer in a half-timbered *Gasthaus* assuring each other that shooting partisans was okay in certain "threatening situations." Quite likely they would know that Colonel Peiper was awarded the *Ritterkreuz mit Schwertern zum Eisernen Kreuzes* (**Knight's Cross with Oakleave and Swords**) for his butcherings and burnings.

I was invited to join this referenced *Stammtisch* (**a regular table of cronies**) of camrades who meet consistently, perhaps once a week, smoke the stinkiest of cigars and cough frequently, requiring that a *Schnaps* or two be added to the beer. *Schnaps* can work wonders.

We can add the domestic affections of family, close friendhips and mother's food. One is comfortable, content and becomes *schwermutig* (also a term with special meaning, **melancholic**, but stronger, **soul touching? maudlin?**) pondering his affection for the *Heimat*, even willing to die for it. And that the world has experienced.

The German finds his *Heimat* to be *gemütlich* (**cozy, snug, agreeable, restful, most satisfying, jovial, genial**), all in all very much to his liking and connected to or overlapping with the terms explained above, i.e. try this: Peter finds his *Heimat, das Volk* and the *Geist* of Germany to be so *gemütlich* that it makes him *schwermutig*.

Or in your mind's eye see a group of Germans aboard a boat on the Rhine. As they get somewhat tipsy and maudlin they join in with some verses such as *Wenn das Wasser im Rhein goldner Wein wär..*(**if only the water of the Rhine were wein**)…then, the ditty continues, **I would so like to be a little fish…** Innocent people out for a weekend outing, but seventy years ago ending the little cruise past the defensive castles of old with a few repetitions of *Sieg Heil* (**Hail Victory**)

This next, final phrase is revolting to today's German feminists, or those from anywhere, but such sayings along with proverbs from the old country do give us insight into traditional ways of thinking: *Kinder, Küche und Kirche* (**children, kitchen and church**). I am never sure of the order of the three terms. No matter, it is the reference to all three in any combination that matters, namely the place of women and their duties.

Military terms may sound similar and confuse foreigners. The *(Schutzstafel, Schutz*=**protection**, *Stafel=a* **group** *or* **squadron***)* is not to be confused witih the *SA (Sturmabteilung*=**storm division***)*, and what are *Brown Shirts*? The SA troops were **strong armers** wearing brown shirts, who "stormed" offensively their military targets or it seems more frequently just battered the unwanted in the civilian population. The other bunch, of double S men, were rather elite, dressed elegantly in black shirts. They were personally devoted to Hitler, especially the *Leibstandarte,* (**body guard**) branch, and many persons had contact with the dreaded *GESTAPO, Geheime Staatspolizei* or **secret police.**

All those **H's** in names are maddening: Hess, Himmler, Heydrich, Hindenberg, Höss, Hitler and more. Names among generals and military personnel may have *Graf, Prinz,* or *von* thrown in (**Duke, Count, Prince**, von—indicating nobility). Perhaps way back when, we copied army ranks from the Germans, since they seem to be very similar with sargeants, lieutenants, generals and such. Of course one can achieve the highest of ranks in the military of Germany in becoming a **Fieldmarshall.**

The above information should be helpful background as we proceed to introducing the *Deutsche Blätter* more formally and read about its founding and how the journal developed and changed focus a bit during its four short years of existence.

Readers should be prepared to understand the grave concerns of the Rukser/Theile team and their irrepressible urgings to do something. Thousands of more incidences such as those described above, gave the impetus to try to stop the Nazis with the written word. The publishers/editors were among those who grew up distrusting their own country, recognizing that since the Franco-Prussian War (1870-71) won by Count Otto von Bismarck's Prussia as the leader of the twenty-one states of the North German Confederation, Germany had been a big trouble maker in Europe. The combination of the "Blood and Iron" policy and Field Marshall General Helmuth von Moltke's brilliant military strategy based on *Blitzkrieg* (**war of lightning speed**—Sound familiar?) was proudly regarded by Germans as proof of greatness. Everyone else in Europe in those days prior to WW II, looked back on that historical period as the beginning of the *German Problem* to which a great part of this study is devoted.[1]

---

1   I would be remiss if I did not acknowledge that changes in military strategy were based on the classic on the subject (still today the "Bible of Military Strategy") written by Karl von Clausewitz (1780-1831), who was indisputably the "Philosopher General" of the whole Prussian lot. He titled his *ouvrage de référence* simply *Vom Kriege*. However, how many ideas are truly original? Napoleon's new way of approaching war formed the basis of von Clausewitz's teachings, for von Clausewitz resigned his commission in the Prussian Army in 1812, fought on the Russian side against Napoleon, then returned to his Prussians where he held various high positions. So...where did Napoleon learn it all? For now we will trace no further back, but write in summary that von Clausewitz taught the advantages of a national defense which is always on the alert and ready to be turned out at any moment into swiftly striking offensive warfare. Being partial to their own theories, the general staffs which came along were unwilling to embrace the entirety of these teachings. They, including the military genius von Moltke, emphasized attack rather than defense and began training troops for *Blitzkrieg*. All agreed, as

Always I have so many questions, and one for us to contemplate here is: Could all of this have occurred without Bismarck leading the way or without von Moltke teaching the military? The brilliant general was still at his desk planning strategy and advising at age 87, slim, trim, fit, all pressed and polished looking no older than a youthful appearing man of 65!

A START ON LEARNING GERMAN

Germans use both *Worte* and *Wörter* to indicate the English plural, **words**, and since the premise of this study is the power of words, a definition is in order as final preparation for the nine chapters that follow. *Wörter* simply refers to a string of unconnected words, a list of terms. Example 1: *Junge, Mädchen, Kind und Frau* are essential German *Wörter*. Example 2: I shall never forget the stirring **words** (*Worte*) spoken by President Obama at his first inaugural. *Worte* renders **expression, saying, promise, pledge.**

All nouns are capitalized. Helping verbs are normally placed at the end of a sentence, example: He says that he can not come=Er sagt, daß er nicht kommen kann. *Tu* is the familiar (friends, family, animals) word for **You** while **Sie** is formal (strangers, teachers, bosses). So, as is the case with other languages, Germans can keep their distance with a word. Recognizable cognates abound. I advise making intelligent guesses.

After all, English and German are closely related as fellow West-Germanic languages; both having descended from the original "Indo-European," and wouldn't you know it? Germans possess it as their own by calling that unknown prototypical, theoretical, ancestral tongue, "Indo-Germanic." You do not have to be perfect at this, but German offers you several words for **The** because all nouns have gender. A masculine, a feminine and a neuter form exist along with "dative forms," **of the** or **to the**, **with the** and others following other prepositons. Examples: The **man** (*Der Man*) or the **woman** (*Die Frau*) or the **animal** (*Das Tier*) is leaving with the **uncle** (*dem Onkel*). More baffling are words that have more than one gender. *Das Band*, for example means **ribbon**

---

do good boxers or street fighters that a victorious outcome may be guaranteed by the first, hard strategic blow. I have heard our own General Collin Powell praise the importance of speed and first strikes as well. However, producers of the *Deutsche Blätter* would ask for no strikes at all, and, surprisingly, for a time the broad humanism of Generals Gerhard Schornhorst, Count August von Gneisenau and Hermann von Boyen, prevailed as exemplified in the formation of the *Volksheer*. They misjudged, obviously, for the mood was not right for accepting a **people's army**. It was short-lived and gave way to the professionalism of the class-conscious military expert and technician, precisely what true humanists and the *DB* renounced.

or **band** on a hat or **tape.** The plural is *Bänder*. A second *das Band* is a **link** or **tie** and pluralized as *Bande*. *Der Band* refers to a **volume** or **tome** with *Bände* as the plural.

That ends the mini lesson. In understanding the subjects covered in the *DB*, it helps to see the whole big picture of what *German, Being German, Speaking German* is, including history, daily existence and all. One can never acquire too much background knowledge which assures better evaluations and understandings.

Chapter II

DB Introduced, Preeminence

The *Deutsche Blätter für ein Europäisches Deutschland gegen ein deutsches Europa* ranks highest among the numerous exile periodicals which were born between the years 1933 and 1945. Robert Cazden, author of *German Exile Literature in America 1933-1950*, recognized that "it was often termed one of the finest of all German émigré literary periodicals" and adds his own categorical appraisal: "The *Deutsche Blätter* represented the best of all German cultural achievement during the emigration..."[2] Marianne Oeste de Bopp pronounced the periodical as being *von hohem Niveau* (**high level**), and found it to be far superior to other German émigré magazines published in Latin America.[3] Indeed it is of great value today in several ways which the reader will observe as we progress. The level of writing and discourse is perhaps the first we should mention in this world of sound bites, vapid television and Internet

---

2   Robert Cazden, German Exile Literature in America 1933-1950 (Chicago: American Library Association, 1970),p. 59. Although Cazden gives a correct evaluation of the *DB*, he did not carefully research some of his assertions. He writes that Karl O. Paetel was the representative for the magazine in the USA but this was only for the last year of publication. Joseph Kaskell was the representative for the first three years and was to some extent responsible for shaping the magazine. Cazden states that Paetel's own publication. *Deutsche Gegenwart*, was an attempt to continue the *DB*. Paetel repeatedly denied this, including a personal denial to me. Paetel initiated several journals.

3   3Marianne Oeste de Bopp, *"Die Exilsituation in Mexico"* in *Die deutsche Exiliteratur 1933-1945*, ed. By Manfred Durzak (Stuttgart, Reclam, 1973), p. 179. Dr. de Bopp reaffirmed her high regard for the *DB* when I interviewed her in July, 1973 at home and at the University of Mexico, where she was chairperson of the German Department. In a letter to me dated September 21, 1973, she once again extolled the periodical.

entertainment and shortcuts accompanied by abbreviations in our speech. The persons who decided to publish this journal did so as a defense against the demonic forces the Allies were combating and to keep the world aware that Germany could and would rise again as the cooperative neighbor and leader she had been in days of yore.

The *Deutsche Blätter* was founded in Santiago Chile by Albert Theile, Udo Rukser, and Nikolaus von Nagel. From its inception in January, 1943, through the last issue of December, 1946, exactly four years, the periodical was published and edited by the two German collaborators. Until August, 1944, the journal was issued monthly; for the remaining years it appeared bimonthly in double-sized issues of sixty to eighty pages. (a little heavy in the briefcase?)

What accounts for the complimentary terms of respect and appreciation that scholars apply to this magazine, i.e. what earns it top billing? It was a product of World War II, the issues it treated reflect the chaotic climate of the times and the spirit of protest against the Nazi infamy. Without National Socialism there would have been no *DB*.[4] From the perspective of their Chilean exile the two anti-Nazi publishers felt obligated to analyze the reasons behind contemporary world events. With articles on culture they hoped to fill a void for readers who for the most part were, like themselves, exiles cut off from the traditional intellectual and cultural stimulation of their native land. Above all, the *DB* was committed to keeping alive what they viewed as the life-enriching German cultural tradition. Its readers and the world had to be reminded that Nazism could not bury the great accomplishments of the past or extinguish the high moral convictions of millions of Germans.

Oeste de Bopp after studying many of the German exile periodicals concluded that *die meisten dieser Publikation waren literarisch erweiterte politische Kampfblätter.*[5] (**Most were just literarily broadened *activist*-or *fighting* publications**.) *Politisch* here means representing a political party. The *DB*, as noted by Karl Paetel was *rechts* (Paetel uses the word **right** to distinquish the *DB* from pronounced leftist publications) and *anti-Hitler*.[6] It was a defender of *das andere Deutschland* (**the *other* German**y) and anti-Vansittart.[7] It too was

---

4   *Deutsche Blätter* will frequently be abbreviated and always treated as a singular noun. In German it is correctly regarded as a plural. To avoid constant repetition, *magazine* and other synonyms, even *Leaves* have been substituted.

5   Oeste de Bopp, op.cit.

6   Karl O. Paetel, "Die Presse des deutschen Exils," *Publizistik*, vol. 4, no 4 (July/August, 1964), p.250.

7   *Das andere Deutschland* refers to Germans who were opposed to Nazism. Anti-Vansittart refers to the harsh proposals for postwar Germany of Robert Gilbert Lord Vansittart. The *DB's* reaction to Vansittart's suggestions are explained in chapter V which treats postwar aspects of the *German Problem*.

a *fighting paper*, but different in that it remained uniquely uncommitted to a political party. Cazden correctly points out that "it was after 1940 the sole nonparty political and literary journal of the German immigration."[8] The editors proclaim their independence in the first issue of the magazine: *Die Deutschen Blätter sind eine politische Zeitschrift (a political magazine) unerbittlich* (**relentless**) *in ihrem Kampfe gegen die Usurpatoren der Macht in Deutschland* (**struggling against those who stole power**), *vertritt sie dennoch keine bestimmte Partei*[9] (**represents no single party**). In a letter to Joseph Kaskel (later he preferred *Kaskell*), representative of the *DB* in the USA, Rukser affirmed his independence: *Nur wenn wir wirklich überparteilich bleiben und nicht eine Gruppe vertreten, können wir dort wirken, wo es ankommt: bei Leuten von Verantwortung und nicht bei geltungsbedürftigen Literaten, die ihre Schlagworte an den Mann bringen wollen.*[10] (**Party affiliations would weaken their effectiveness in reaching responsible persons instead of writers wishing to push their slogans on people**). The principal political purposes of the periodical were to battle Nazism and to advocate democracy. However, in spite of the refusal to be associated with any given party, one discerns in the *DB* a leaning toward Socialism.

The socialistic outlook of the these *Leaves* must not be equated with Marxism, however. Dr. Rukser was by no means about to have control of his properties transferred to the masses. He was disillusioned with Marxism and its effects in Russia and had firmly concluded that its dictates had not and could not produce a better world as he projected it. Although a few contributors deviated, the *DB* objectively sought solutions to human problems within a general framework of conservative socialist thinking. Rukser was known to react sharply to criticism that the *DB* was not sufficiently socialistic as exemplified in these words to his old friend: *Nur Sektierer können uns so interpretieren, als ob wir dem Sozialismus feindlich wären.* (**Only sectarians could interpret the DB as antagonistic**) *Das Gegenteil ist der Fall.* (**quite the opposite**). *Wir glauben bessere Sozialisten zu sein als jene, indem wir nämlich die eigentlichen sozialen Probleme versuchen anzupacken.*[11] (**We are better Socialists than they in that we directly take on the socialistic problems**).

Karl Paetel observed that the Communist journals of the exile period were

---

8 Cazden, op. cit.
9 *Was Wir Wollen*, Deutsche Blätter, 1 (January, 1943), p. 1. **All further references to the DB will be given in the text or parentheses in the text.**
10 Letter from Udo Rukser to Joseph Kaskell, March 18, 1944
11 Ibid. All the mail correspondence as well as other original sources contain typographical errors and/or German mistakes. I have avoided the repeated application of *sic.* but corrected obvious typographical errors.

always preoccupied with representing the party line.¹² They viewed the state throughout history as a device for exploitation of the masses by a dominant class and class struggle as the primary agency of historical change; they had little concern for literature and aesthetics. Rukser would have nothing to do with them. *Wir lehnen es ab, uns ins Schlepptau der Moskowiter zu lassen.* (**We refuse to allow ourselves to be towed by the Moscovites**), he wrote,¹³ and a month later added: *Der vorschlag der Stalinisten Dichter im Exil haben wir abgelehnt.* (**We turned down the proposal of the exiled Stalinist writers**). He advised the Communists to create and pay for their own propaganda.¹⁴

In the editorial referred to above of January, 1943, the editors clarify the conservative, conciliatory and humane outlook of the periodical and the humanitarian goals:

> *Offen für den Meinungsstreit des Tages will ihn die Zeitschrift auf die höhere Ebene der prinzipiellen Auseinandersetzung erheben. Indem sie die so folgenschweren Ereignisse des Tages, mit dem tragenden Strom der Geschichte in Verbindung setzt, will sie den Blick für Zusammenhänge weiten, will sie die fruchtbare Wechselwirkung der Generationen erneuern; in dem sie an das Unvergängliche angeben. Nach unserm Standpunk in der prinzipiellen Auseinandersetzung gefragt, antworten wir am kürzesten mit der Forderung von Pestalozzi:*
>
> *Wir wollen keine Verstaatlichung der Menschen, sondern eine Vermenschlichung des Staates* (p. 1).

TRANSLATION: The magazine is open to differences of opinion on issues of the day which it intends to lift to the highest levels of discussion. While it connects the consequential happenings of daily life with the sustaining stream of history, it intends to broaden the understanding of connections and to renew the fruitful interaction of the generations by stressing that which is everlasting. Concerning our position on principles, we answer succinctly with the challenge of Pestalozzi:

---

12 Paetel, op. cit., p. 242.
13 Letter from U. Rukser to J. Kaskell, January 2, 1944
14 Letter from Rukser to Kaskell, Feb. 1, 1944

**We do not want a nationalization of humanity,
but rather a humanization of the state.**

And on the back cover in Spanish:

*No queremos una estatización del Hombre, sino una humanización
del Estado*, emphasis on **mankind** and **state**.

On some issues of the day the monthly journal was liberal, however. This again attests to its quality and sobriety and few fanatical outbursts. With the exception of five issues in the year 1945, the text by the Swiss educational reformer, Johann H. Pestalozzi was the cover motto of the *DB* throughout the four years of publication. Choosing Pestalozzi's words put the new journal most squarely in the camp of educational reformers of the "pedagogical century," the eighteenth, when the young pietist, Johann himself, was taught (a better term may be *enlightened)* by Rosseau who in that day was awakening new humanistic educational impulses. The goal-setting editorial continues:

> *In einem Bunde freier europäischer Staaten erblicken wir die mögliche Erfüllung dieses Zieles, daher die Erweiterung und Ausrichtung unsere Titels: "Deutsche Blätter für ein europäisches Deutschland gegen ein deutsches Europa." Wir hättten am liebsten den Titel: "Das Deutsche Gewissen" gewählt; er erschien uns aber zu anspruchsvoll. Es ist aber das deutsche Gewissen, das diese Blätter erweckt hat. Tiefe Beschämung und Abscheu über das, was heute im deutschen Namen geschiet lies uns nicht länger schweigen. Wir wollten als Deutsche nicht länger abseits stehen, während unsere Freunden nach einem gerechten Frieden suchen und dabei die deutsche Zukunft in den Mittelpunkt der europäischen Lösung rücken.*
>
> *Durch eine freie, verantwortungsbewusste Erörterung aller der kulturellen, politischen, sozialen und wirtschaftlichen Fragen, die der inneren Erneuerung Deutschlands dienen, wollen wir an der Neuordnung Europas und der Welt mitarbeiten. Wird auch die Zeitschrift in der Hauptsache von Europa handeln, so werden Frage mit den Weltproblemen verknüpfen, wovon sie, eng darin verwoben, doch nur einen Teil bilden.*
>
> *Wir verhehlen weder anderen noch uns selber die Begrenztheit unserer Mittel und die bedrückende Grösse der Aufgabe. Wenn wir uns dennoch an die Herausgabe dieser Zeitschrift wagen,*

geschiet es im Vertrauen auf die moralische Kraft der Ideen, die sie vertritt Indem wir uns mit diesen Blättern um die Klärung einer unhaltbar gewordenen Lage bemühen, wollen wir die Geister scheiden und uns mit den Edelsten unseres Volkes auf die Seite jener schlagen, die der Erde einem neuen Sinn zu geben trachten; auf die Seite jener, die an die Unvergänglichkeit von Ideen glauben, an den Sieg des Güten über das Böse, wie weit auch und ungerundet der Bogen sich spanne in diesem irdischen Kampfe. Als unsere Väter die Dome von Naumburg und Bamburg zu bauen begannen, dächten sie in und handelten sie für Generationen (p. 1).

TRANSLATION: We envision the possible fulfillment of our objectives in a federation of free European states which explains the expansion of our title: *German Leaves Proposing a Europeanized Germany Against a Germanized Europe*. We preferred the title *The German Conscience*, but that seemed a bit too pretentious. However, it is indeed the German conscience that these leaves have awakened. Due to deep shame and repugnance over what is today happening in the name of Germany we could no longer remain silent. As Germans we did not want to stay on the sidelines while our friends were seeking a just peace and thereby making the future of Germany central to a European solution.

The inner renewal of Germany will require a free conscientious debate of cultural, political, social and economic issues through which we wish to collaborate to reorganize all of Europe and the world. The magazine will primarily deal with Europe, but there will be no absence of articles which connect the German and European questions with world-wide problems. No matter how tightly intertwined, they will form only a part. We don't conceal the limit of our financial means nor the crushing weight of our task from ourselves or others. Nevertheless if we dare to publish this periodical, it will happen through trust in the moral power of the ideas that it represents... While we trouble ourselves through these *Leaves* with the clarification of a situation which has become untenable, we wish to separate minds and, along with the noblest of our people, join those who believe that ideas are everlasting and that good will ultimately triumph over evil, no matter

how far and wide it stretches in this earthly fight. When our ancestors proceeded to construct the cathedrals of Naumburg and Bamberg they thought of and acted for generations.

The above passage should be classified among the finest of its genre, for It best shows how powerfully the *DB* pen could be employed against the Nazi sword. Please recall here the political rallies of the Nazis and the inquiry to the people of the German Minister of Propoganda, Dr. Paul Josef Göbbels, who posed to crowds the choice: *Butter oder Kanonen* **(butter or cannons)?**

Messieurs Rukser and Theile did not equal the persuasive powers of Demosthenes, whose fellow Athenians cried out *To arms! To arms!* following his bold and rousing call to rise up and take action against Philip of Macedon, but, here in their beloved *Blätter*, they were very close in their own eloquently articulated plea. Churchill's *We shall fight on the beaches...* quickly comes to mind or the youthful John F. Kennedy's inaugural invitation: *Can we forge against these enemies a grand and global alliance, North and South, East and West, that can assure a more fruitful life for all mankind? Will you join in that historic effort?*

Franklin D. Roosevelt's first inaugural also motivated by first assuring the nation that we had only fear itself to fear and then reminding that... *in every dark hour of our national life a leadership of frankness and vigor has met with that understanding and support of the people themselves which is essential to victory. I am convinced that you will again give that support to leadership in these critical days.*

Recognized essential elements of the best hortatory speaking/reading are evident: primarily words, so inspiring that they create an atmosphere of action. Readers will repeatedly observe in this analysis of the *DB* that the publishers remained true to the principles, objectives and purposes expressed in this first editorial. Look for the consistent commitment and keep it in mind.

The opening editorial of the second issue continued the spirit of the first by emphasizing the true German spirit to which Hitlerism was anathema. *Vielleicht* (**Maybe**) *the editor hopes, kann so diese kleine Zeitschirft helfen...* (**can this little magazine help...**) to save the true German spirit from the destruction which is threatening it from within. A just peace was the subject of several editorials composed by the two rather unlikely collaborators.

The highly regarded lawyer from Berlin and the accomplished professional journalist didactically repeated, reinforced and expanded all of their humanitarian concepts in each issue of the periodical. At the end of four years of reaffirming their beliefs, they expressed satisfaction that their expository skills had been successful. On page sixty-four of issue thirty-four in 1946 they thank their helpers, contributors and all others and assure them that their ... *gemeinsame vier jährige Arbeit nicht vergeblich gewesen ist* (**four years of working together had not been in vain**).

The concepts of *humanitarianism* and *humanism* referred to above are a key concern of the *DB*; therefore it is essential that we understand the precise use of these terms as applied to the periodical and its editors. As is either clearly stated or strongly implied in the first editorial and in many that followed, Rukser and Theile sincerely hoped for a future brotherhood of all mankind. Equality of opportunity, civil rights, just treatment before the law, and freedom of religion were basic principles.

Furthermore, the editors believed that individual lives could be improved through humanization of the state, an objective proclaimed on the cover of most issues.

Classical idealistic humanism as taught by Wolfgang von Goethe, Friederich von Schiller, and all the great German *literati* of the eighteenth and nineteenth centuries was blended with the practical message: *Be thy brother's keeper.*[15] Throughout the years of publication the classical idealists were referred

---

15 The period of classical humanism in the cultural history of Germany lies between the birth of Gotthold Ephraim Lessing (1729) and the death of Goethe (1832). Believing that the nineteenth and twentieth centuries had turned away from the humanistic tradition, the *Leaves* longed to reawaken it. Representative of the classical humanistic tradition include Lessing (1729-1781, Johann Gottfried von Herder (1744-1803), Schiller (1759-1805), Goethe (1749-1832), Immanuel Kant (1724-1804), and Ludwig van Beethoven (1770-1837). The writers and thinkers of this epoch emphasized the significance of the *human* element in history and the dominance of man's reason. Accepting this concept some one hundred years later, Udo Rukser was confident that potentially man's reason was the key to understanding his inclination for war.

The century represented a cultural revolt against pettiness, intolerance, and philistinism; the poetry and philosopy of the period reflect the ideals of *Entsagung* (**self-denial**), thrift, duty and service. Lessing was known as the " Voltaire of Germany" because of his sharp criticism of intolerances; Goethe's *Sturm und Drang* play *Goetz von Berlichingen*, was a similar protest. Schiller's *Die Räuber* and *Kabale und Liebe* exposed injustice and oppression. Herder stressed the human and moral element in Christianity while Kant undermined the supernatural foundation of the traditional world outlook in his *Kritik der reinen Vernunft*; he encouraged *homo sapiens* to trust his own reason instead of being guided by others. *Sapere Aude*, he exhorted, *Habe Mut, dich deines eigenen Verstandes zu bedienen* (**Have the courage to follow your own reasoning**))

The classical humanistic tradition was characterized by a veneration of man as an individual and of collective man or humanity. For both Goethe and Schiller the meaning of life was to develop the individual. Goethe taught that every individual bears his own law within himself, and the highest realization of humanity was to form one's own life out of inner laws. According to this cultural concept of humanity, each individual "becomes" man through education. Theile and Rukser agreed that humans could be educated for both intellectual and moral improvement. Kant's ethics teach that a free man is autonomous; he exists only as an end unto himself. Freedom for Kant (and for Rukser and Theile) is to have the cause of one's self-determination within oneself.Goethe and the others found their own generation lacking

to and quoted. In addition, much of the literature printed in the periodical reflected humanistic thinking. Education to develop an individual to his fullest potential was advocated; lofty ideals for the betterment of mankind were put forward. Some contributors proposed the idealistic Kantian concept that *homosapiens* should strive for moral perfection for its own inherent rewards, and although the editors never specifically supported such a proposal, the number of clues in their writings indicate that each was sympathetic to the suggestion.

Unquestionably they longed for a rebirth of the ideals of the eighteenth and nineteenth centuries. After Nazism Germans would do well to refresh their understanding of Goethe, Schiller, Kant and even Rosseau, although his exaggerated faith in the intrinsic goodness of *mankind* in the raw was never recommended. Such faith in humans was perhaps a bit too optimistic, especially in a time of war, torture and concentration camps. Insistence on basic goodness? . . difficult indeed! Yet, articles which plead with the nations of the world, especially the Allied Powers, to have compassion for the defeated German people further exemplify the humanitarian outlook of the *Deutsche Blätter*. An objection could be raised that mercy was sought only because the publishers were German, but a careful perusal of the magazine quickly quiets this criticism. It is obvious to the reader that the call for compassion would be just as strongly voiced for any country because it was rooted in a principle: only through sincere cooperation among nations could mankind improve.

Additional evidence that humanitarian thinking was a favored editorial principle is the persistent championing of a cooperative *new Europe* and *new world* in which nations would unite to work peacefully for the benefit of all mankind. The periodical examined various proposals for creating a kind of *socialistic humanism*. In the revitalized states individual rights would be guaranteed, and large nations would not take advantage of small ones. The *DB* echoed fifteenth century humanism, especially as expressed in Thomas Moore's portrayal of the perfect state in his *Utopia*, and nineteenth century humanism as reflected in Kant's essay, *Zum ewigen Frieden*.

The following characteristics of the classical humanistic tradition permeate the pages of the *DB:* optimism, humanitarianism, tolerance and

---

in the ideals they cherished and were, therefore, almost entirely nonpolitical. They viewed the state with hostility, suspicion and fear. Neither patriotism nor nationalism was esteemed; rather they thought of themselves as world citizens. The comprehensive concept of universal peace, world citizenship and brotherhood was one of the most deeply rooted ideals of the classical humanistic tradition, and it permeates the pages of the *Blätter*. Kant's essay *Zum ewigen Frieden* (**On Eternal Peace**), is often referred to, and the basis of much *DB* thinking was derived from Kant's plan for the elimination of war and dream of a world order.

cosmopolitanism, including the establishment of world peace, as well as the all-important self-reliance and individualism. As Kant would have expressed it, man must free himself from his self-imposed *Unmündigkeit i.e.* **his dependency or inability to speak for himself.** The journal evolved; its emphasis shifted, but throughout the years of publication the above characteristics remained constant and will be pointed out in the analyses of individual articles.

The devoted publishers launched the *Blätter* with concentration on the evils of war, the *German Problem* and details of Nazi atrocities as related to Hitler's miraculous rise to complete usurpation of dictatorial power. Some of those articles were shrill and unpolished, yet already in the magazine's infancy, editorial concern with aesthetics and excellence was firmly established. Most of the pieces were setting the high standards in quality and variety that quickly became the hallmark. Rukser made his exacting requirements known in a letter to Joseph Kaskell, his friend since infancy:

> *Wir können nur hoffen durch die Samlung einer gewissen Elite etwas abzuwirken. Darum müssen wir immer wieder vom Zeitungsniveau vom Schlagwort und auch von der Kriegspropaganda und—Psychose fort auf die tieferen Gründe hinstreben. Das klingt anspruchsvoll—aber wenn wir uns kein anspruchsvolles Ziel stellen, dann lohnt, es nicht diese Mühe und Opfer.*[16]

TRANSLATION: It is only through reaching an elite group that we can hope to achieve anything. Therefore, it is vital, if somewhat pretentious, that we avoid newspaper claptrap or war propaganda—And psychosis...that we strive for deeper ground. That sounds pretentious—but if we have no demanding objectives all our fuss and sacrifice is worthless.

The *DB* did reach an elite.... PauL Tillich, Bertolt Brecht, Arnold Brecht, Ivan Heilbut, Julius Bab, Erich Kahler, Wolfgang Stresemann, Berthold Viertel, Fritz Karsen and many more distinguished names were among its readers and contributors. Typical of the early writing referred to above is the *Deutches Pantheon* of issue one. Written in passionate language, the article tells of five Polish women who were sentenced to six years imprisonment for the crime of helping Jewish children.

Another article, *Polnische Mädchen,* of issue four gives an account of four

---

16   Letter from U. Rukser to J. Kaskell, March 16, 1945.

Polish girls who rebelled in different ways against Nazi rules and were so severely punished that one died. *Aus dem dritten Reich* (**From the Third Reich**) in issue nine announces the mobilization of all German women between the ages of seventeen and forty-five. *Gewissensnöte (***Moral Dilemas***)*, of issue, five cried: *Entweder mit den Nazis oder gegen sie. Der eine Weg bedeutet den Untergang unsrer Heimat der andre die zukunft Deutschlands Europas, der Welt!* (**Either with the Nazis or against them. One way means the fall of our homeland, the other the future of Germany, Europe, the world.**) Similar excoriations and admonishments were frequent. In addition to such ardent and emotional writing, creative literature began to appear in the first year of publication, along with discerning essays on political subjects and world problems. Authors, some no longer living at the time, included the established and distinguished names of Hermann Bahr, Claude G. Bowers, Hermann Hesse, Stefan Zweig, Pablo Neruda, Edwin Dwinger, Thomas Mann, Albert Schweitzer, Thomas Wolfe and Gabriel Mistral.

In subsequent years essays on highly accomplished persons, literature, art, music, philosophy, travel, science, economics and politics were published along with poetry, short stories and reviews of magazines, newspapers and books on sundry subjects with miscellaneous quotations and relevant news items sprinkled in. Frequently the subject matter dealt with postwar Germany. Readers could voice reactions in the feature, *Der Leser schreibt* (**The Reader Writes**).

Finally, on page sixty-seven of the last issue of 1945, the welcome announcement appeared: *Die kulturellen Themen werden in Zukunft die politischen überwiegen.*[17] (**In future issues cultural themes will be preferred to political subjects.**)

They were true to their promise; the zealous intensity abated as the *Thousand Year Reich* experienced an early, crushing demise some 988 years short of a full term, forcing the German expatriate publishers to ask themselves how great their role had been in bringing the Nazis to their knees as well as: "…And… now, what do we do?" The decision was to continue the *Deutsche Blätter* as long as possible for now all the proposals for the humanization of Europe and indeed all nations could begin to be executed via Pestalozzi's *europäisches Deutschland* (or we might say *Pestalozzied or Rukserized Germany).*

Essays on great cultural figures included Goethe, Albert Schweitzer, Thomas Mann, Thomas Jefferson, Walt Whitman, Friedrich Hölderlin, Ernst and George Jünger, Romain Rolland, Carl Schurz, Max Barth, the Danish

---

17 Concerning *Kulturellen Themen* the respected influence of Joseph Kaskell must be acknowledged since from the beginning, he urged Rukser to give this aspect greater emphasis.

patriot Kaj Munk, the German socialist Carl Mierendorff, and more of equal reknown, representing a cross section of disciplines The *DB* praised the specific accomplishments of these persons, but for the publishers their significance as champions of peace or humanitarianism was often more important. As these names attested, not all Germans were warmongers.

Enough *belles-lettres* were printed to justify the growing reputation of the *DB* as a literary periodical of distinction. Much of the poetry and some stories were written by well-known German authors, some of whom were contemporaries of Rukser and Theile living in exile; other literature was submitted by relatively unknown German émigré authors. A salient objective of the journal, at least partially achieved, was to bring the best Latin American men and women of letters to the attention of its readers. However, it was not solely the intrinsic beauty of this literature that attracted the editors. Much of it either overtly or subtly supported their favored objectives and commitments.

Art music, philosophy, and science were not granted the attention devoted to politics and literature although a keen interest in these subjects is evident. Several articles on art inform readers of both its history and practice. Reviews of musical performances in London and New York were periodically printed; in addition a few perceptive and informative essays on music and musicians were scattered throughout the pages and even a few articles dealing with scientific subjects.

Considerable space was alloted to travel where some articles were accounts of Theile's travel experiences and residencies in several countries.Writers described exotic parts of the earth such as Bali and India as well as writing on better known places in Europe and Australia. All accounts were most informative and added to the variety of the *DB*, while preventing a metamorphosis into one more single-minded *Kampfblatt*.

The *DB* devoted many pages to religion, and to the Catholic and Protestant churches. Some authors examined the historical effectiveness of organized religion in improving the moral character of mankind and concluded that it had been of little value. But, others asked, how could religion be replaced? Some writers analyzed to what extend Catholicism and Protestantism had historically tried to prevent war and/or probed the issue of what political positions the churches espoused during both world wars. Others were attempting to determine what the future tasks of the eclesiatical forces would be. The monthly justly presented strong criticism as well as justification and rationalizations of the positions of the churches. For the most part readers were left to form their own conclusions.

Greatest emphasis even in the postwar years of publication was still given to politics and economics. Many proposals were made for a *new Europe* and a *new world* in which nations should cooperate and unite for the betterment of all. A most important means for firmly establishing world peace would be a world bank. Indeed, the editors assured readers that war was to become a thing of the past for permanent world peace could and would be established by merely following the precepts put forth in their exiled journal.

A service greatly appreciated by *DB* readers was the initiation of book reviews. Principal reviewers included Rukser Theile, and KarI O. Paetel in New York. Others lived throughout the world. Books with political subjects were favored; postwar Europe, postwar Germany, the rise of Hitler, the history of Germany and economics were common topics. Works of fiction were also critiqued. A few of the political books became the subjects of lengthy articles or were frequently recommended. Rukser favored Edward H. Carr's *Conditions of Peace* since for him it presented optimistic plans for a revitalized postwar Europe. He lauded the book in a letter to Kaskell:

> *Scheint mir das bedeutendste Buch zu allen europäischen Fragen überhaupt zu sein. Vor allem, ist es der erste der sieht wie riesenhaft die Produktionsmögichkeit gewachsen ist und daß die Organization nicht mehr von der Produktion sondern nur vom Verbrauch auserfolgen kann.*

TRANSLATION: It seems to be the most important book covering all questions on Europe. Above all, it is the first to perceive that production has risen to gigantic capabilities and that organization no longer can be based on production potential, but rather on actual consumption.

Did Peter Drucker read Carr? The above reflects current thinking of the manangement gurus, so venerated in recent years. Did the *DB* beat them to the punch?

Rukser extolled The *Next Germany* written by a group of English Socialists as *wirklich wichtig—bisher die beste Denkschrift über die künftigen Verhältnisse, Von tüchtigen Leuten geschrieben.*[18] (**It is truly important—up to now the finest researched prediction on the future situation, written by some competent persons.**) Beardsley Ruml's *Tomorrow's Business,* Hermann Rauschning's *Die Konservative Revolution,* Wilhelm Röpke's *Die Gesellschaftskrisis der Gegenwart,* Oswald Dutch's *Economic Peace Aims,* and Heinz Pol's *The Hidden Enemy* also drew high respect.

---

18   Letter from U. Rukser to J. Kaskell, April 24, 1944.

The *Blätter* was the first German language journal published outside the U.S.A. to be allowed in prisoner of war camps for Germans in the USA. This was in part due to the help of Thomas Mann.[19] In a letter to Theile of June 27,1944, Mann pledged assistance:

> *Für die Zulassung der Deutschen Blätter zu den amerikanischen Gefangenlagern werde ich gern alles tun was in meinen Kräften steht... es geht gleichzeitig mit diesem Brief eine Äusserung an Dr. Kaskel ab, in der ich für das War Department die Wunschbarkeit dieser Zulassung nachdrücklich betone.*[20]

Mann promises to do all within his power to assure the distribution of the *German leaves* in the camps. He promises to immediately send a letter to Kaskell in which he will beseech the Department of Defense to allow it.

Meanwhile, the editors exhibited little hesitation in soliciting funds from readers in order to meet the increased demand for the periodical. The response was gratifying. On page sixty-three of the January/February, 1945, issue we read: *Durch unsern Redaktionsvertreter in den USA, Dr.Joseph Kaskel, wurden bis Ende Januar über 1.1 OO Hefte in 75 verschiedenen Lagern verteilt* (**As of the end of January, our *USA representative*, Kaskel, had distributed *1,100 copies in 75 camps*)**. By April,1945, three thousand copies had been sent from Chile and Kaskell had distributed two thousand copies in the camps (24, 1945).

Since many of the young soldiers in the camps had known only Nazi teachings, The *DB* informed them of a Germany of which they were almost totally ignorant. *Kriegsgefangene und Wir* (**23, 1945, POW's and Us**) and *Der Führer denkt für Uns* (24, 1945, **The Leader Thinks for Us**) reveal how serious this condition was and point out that it could be alleviated by quickly getting inro the hands of these victims of Nazism the kind of information found in the *DB*. In short reports and letters from the prisoners, readers were kept posted on the warm reception given to the periodical by the Germans in the camps. Eberhard Ulbrich's assessment of the *DB* is typical: *Welchen Wert die Deutschen Blätter für uns Kriegsgefangen, vor allem auch für die Antinazis unter uns, hatten, brauche ich Ihnen wohl kaum auseinanderzusetzen. Auch in*

---

19   In the correspondence among Kaskell, Rukser and Theile many references are made to their desire to get the *Blätter* distributed in the camps. Kaskell made trips to Washington D.C. wrote USA authorities and worked tirelessly.

20   Letter from T. Mann to A. Theile, June 27, 1944

unseren politischen Arbeitsgemeinschaften lieferten sie uns wertvolles Material zu anregenden Diskussionen.[21] (**What value the DB had for us prisoners, above all for the ant-Nazis among us, I really need not clarify. Also it provided worthwhile material for stimulating discussions in our political discussion sessions.**)

The publishing team hoped to continue publication after the war with the purpose of bringing their humanitarian views to the millions of Germans who had never heard of the periodical. *Die Deutschen Blätter in Mengen nach Deutschland zu bringen, schien uns sehr notwendig"* (34, 1946, p. 64). (**It seemed vital to us to bring the monthly to Germany in greater numbers**). Rukser solicited help from Thomas Mann who agreed that the *DB* could give moral help to postwar Germany and in one of his supportive letters, Mann tells Rukser of his faith in the its comforting message:

Ich beeile mich, ihnen zu versichern, daß ich das ernsteste Interesse daran habe, daß es Ihrer Zeitschrift gelingen möge, in Deutschland Eingang zu finden, weil ich überzeugt bin, daß die Deutschen Blätter vielen Menschen in dem leidvollen Lande tröstlich und geistig und moralisch hilfreich sein können.[22]

TRANSLATION: I hasten to assure you that I have great interest in your magazine being introduced to Germany because I am convinced that it can be comforting—spiritually and morally helpful in that sorrowful country.

A few hundred issues were sent to Germany in 1945 and 1946. *Seit einigen Monaten* (**For a few months**), the editors wrote, in the first issue of 1946, *gelangen Unsere Hefte nach Deutschland und aus Deutschland erreichen uns Briefe, die um mehr Hefte bitten* (p. 66). (**For a few months our issues have reached Germany and we are receiving letters from Germany requesting more**). However, Lamentably due to merely exiguous income, the *DB* ceased publication in *December,1946.*

Upon hearing of the demise of the journal, Thomas Mann expressed his disappointment in a Letter to the expatriate editors. *Mit Bedauern habe ich Kenntnis genommen von der Einstellung Ihrer schönen Zeitschrift, an der ich so oftmals meine Freude gehabt habe* (**It is with sadness that I received the news of the discontinuation of your wonderful magazine which I have so often**

---

21   Letter Eberhard Ulrich to Theile and Rukser, September 15, 1946. The entire letter appears in the appendix. It makes a strong appeal for continued publication of the *DB*.
22   Letter from T. Mann to U. Rukser, December 11, 1946.

enjoyed.) Mann comforts the publishers that theirs is not the first quality periodical to perish, his son's *Sammlung and Decision* and his own *Mass und Wert* knew the same fate. He gives the following final word of sympathy:

> *Ich habe die Melancholie dieser Sterbefälle immer sehr lebhaft empfunden und empfinde sie wieder in diesem Fall, der mich so beschäftigt hat. Sie können sich damit trösten, daß ja auch in früheren Zeiten hochstehende Zeitschriften, auch die Goethes und Schillers, immer nur einige Jahre bestanden haben. Der historische Wert der Jahrgänge der Deutschen Blätter wird bestimmt nicht gering sein und nicht nur Ihnen sondern der ganzen Emigration zur Ehre gereichen.*[23]

TRANSLATION: Mann assures that the entire emigrant population will be honored by the *DB* and the magazine will have historic value. After all, he and his son experienced the short lives of periodicals as did even Goethe and Schiller whose magazines lasted only a few years.

The judgment and consolation of the dean of the German exiled writers may have been welcome to Rukser and Theile, but they were unable to resume publication. It is regrettable that the *DB*, which from the beginning suffered from too little financial support, couldnot bring its inspirational humanitarian message to Germany after the war and continue to help in the formation of thinking in the *New Germany*.

Since this positive future was not to be, the question arises: To what degree was the intellectual monthly, plagued by various difficulties throughout its existence, successful? were the noble objectives proposed in *Was Wir Wollen* **(What We Want)** of the first issue realized? Two statements by Albert Theile give a partial answer:

> *Die Wirkung der Zeitschrift? Dort wo sie verbreitet wurde in der ganzen von den Achsenmächten nicht eroberten Welt, war die Resonanz beträchtlich. Politisch ist sie am stärksten unter Nichtdeutschen gewesen. Die meisten Auslandsdeutschen die uns oft eher eine literarisch als politisch gute Note geben wollten blieben bei ihrem Right or Wrong Standpunkt. Carl Schurz, des grossen Deutsch-Amerikaners, kluge Ergänzung zählte für sie nicht: If right*

---

23 Letter from T. Mann to U. Rukser, March 1, 1947.

to be kept right, if wrong to be set right.[24] Theile tersely expressed to Dr. Vander Heide: *Die DB hatten Erfolg auf Politik aber eher ausserhalb Deutschland.*[25]

TRANSLATION: The effect of the *DB* was significant in the parts of the world that had not been conquered by the Axis Powers. Political influence was strongest among non-Germans, and most of the expatriate Germans viewed it as a literary rather than political journal and stuck to their right or wrong point of view. It appears that they paid no attention to the addendum of Carl Schurz: If right, to be kept right, if wrong to be set right. Theile periodically confirmed his view that the political influence was greatest outside of Germany.

Some of the political and economic proposals of the magazine that have today become reality will be pointed out in the following pages. Joseph Kaskell attributed significant influence of the journal to an elite group of readers who promulgated its humanitarian position. The *DB* was unquestionably successful in helping to keep German culture alive, if only for a small group. During the years of publication many exiled German readers expressed appreciation similar to the exhuberance of Julius Bab:

> *Seltsam aber wahr: Weder in London noch in New York, noch an sonst einem Ort der Erde erscheint heute eine deutsche Zeitschrift von so hoher geistiger Haltung und so reichem kulturellen Gehalt wie die Deutschen Blätter in Santiago de Chile. Für uns alle die wir in der deutschen Sprache aufgewachsen sind, sind sie eine grosse Freude und ein grosser Trost* (23, 1945, p. 63).

TRANSLATION: Strange but true: neither in London nor New York, nor any other place on earth does there exist a German language newspaper of the high intellectual level and rich cultural content as the *DB* of Santiago, Chile. For all of us who were reared with the German tongue it offers great joy and comfort.

---

24 Letter from A. Theile to R.P. Vander Heide, June, 7, 1974.
25 Albert Theile, "Vorwort zur Reprint-Ausgabe" (Neldeln/Lichtenstein: Kraus Reprint a Division of Kraus-Thomson Organization Limited, 1970), p. 5.

In Chapter III we will learn about the backgrounds of the German founders and how they decided to publish and share their *Weltanschauung* (**world view, outlook on life**), love of their homeland and unfathomable detestation for the calamitous *Führer* and his loyal teutonic myrmidons.

Chapter III

Founders of the *DB*, Successes, Failures

Albert Theile and Udo Rukser, both experienced in publishing, met for the first time in Chile. Neither, as stated in *Was Wir Wollen* (1, 1943), could sit idly by and refrain from taking a stand against National Socialism. They shared the conviction that German culture had to be kept alive, and Germans everywhere encouraged to become better Europeans. The *Deutsche Blätter* was a logical outgrowth of their common interest in publishing and similarity in thinking.

Theile maintained that he and Rukser chose Chile for their exile because it was the only country in South America that had remained neutral.[26] Indisputably, Chile's neutrality was a major consideration in the choice, but there were additional reasons. Rukser decided to flee to Chile after the events of the notorious *Kristallnacht* (**night of the broken glass,** November 9, 1938) because he could make a living in agriculture and transfer his considerable fortune to Chile, much of which was invested in his art collection. Readers are reminded of Rukser's modified definition of *socialism*. He well understood that money could assure comfort and contribute to power. With Nikolaus von Nagel, who had been living in Chile for twenty years, this lawyer from Berlin purchased a huge sheep ranch stretching from the *cordillera* (**mountain chain, here, the Andes**) to the sea in Quillota, Chile.

Rukser was born in 1892 in Posen, obtained his *Abitur* (**school leaving examination in German academic high schools**) in 1910 and followed the profession of his father and grand-father in studying Law. By the time the

---

26 Letter from A. Theile to R.P. Vander Heide, June 7, 1974.

Nazis were gaining power in the early 1930's he was a respected lawyer in Berlin specializing in international law and had established a reputation as publisher of the *Zeitschrift für Ostrecht* (**Journal on east European law**). His wife was Jewish as were many of the couple's acquaintances and his professional colleagues. Rukser witnessed harassment of these Jews by the Nazis, including an order he received to forbid Jews to work on his *Zeitschrift*. Rather than to become an accomplice of the Nazis by complying with the order, he resigned from the bar and his editorship of the magazine in 1933 and moved from Berlin to Lake Constance where he managed the farm and orchard he owned there until fleeing to Chile in 1938.[27]

Joseph Kaskell described his good friend, Rukser, as an intelligent and generous person who always defended right causes. Courage, according to Kaskell, was an integral element of Rukser's nature. Ana Steurwald-Landmann used almost the same words.[28] Indeed kindness and humanitarianism are evident in much of Rukser's correspondence in which he offers help to Germans before and after the war. In later life, after the demise of the *DB*, Rukser, always the gentleman farmer, remained in Chile, attending to his farm and ranch and writing on Goethe, Nietzsche and José Ortega y Gasset. He published *Goethes Einfluss in der spanischen Welt* (**Goethe's influence in the Spanish World**) and *Nietzsche in der Hispania*. Kaskell helped him obtain a Guggenheim grant to research a book on Ortega y Gasset which he was writing at the time of his death in 1971.

Rukser's co-founder, Albert Theile, was born in Hörde, Germany, July 31 1904. He studied in Münster, Munich and Berlin. In the 1920's he was well-acquainted with a fellow citizen of Hörde, Berrnhard Hoetger, the sculptor, and in 1928 became the editor of the *Böttcherstrasse* (**Böttcher Street**), a magazine inspired by Hoetger. Theile rejected Nazism as soon as it appeared, and in 1933 he began a journey that took him to Norway, the Soviet, Union, India, China and finally in 1940 to Chile where he made the acquaintance of Rukser. Because of his experience as editor of the *Böttcherstrasse* Theile was able to get

---

27 Rukser was horrified and enraged at the fanatical anti-semiticism of Hans Fritz von Zwehl, his superior at the Court of Appeals in Berlin. Rukser wrote von Zwehl on May 26, 1933 in behalf of a fellow attorney, Elfriede Cohnen, who had lost a leg in World War I while serving with the Red Cross. Because she had defended communists and received a citation from the Comunist Party, she had been forbidden to practice. Rukser assured von Zwehl that Miss Cohnen was pure Aryan, but von Zwehl refused to help. Some of the correspondence between von Zwehl and Rukser appears in the appendix. It exemplifies the kind of prejudice that Rukser faced as an attorney, gives cause for his resignation and is the beginning of his ever deepening loathing of the Nazis.

28 R.P. Vander Heide, interview with Anna Steuerwald, August 26, 1974.

work on the editorial staffs of various magazines during his seven years of wandering. He was well-prepared to help Rukser launch the *Blätter*.

From 1952 until his death Theile lived in Switzerland, writing and publishing. In addition to numerous articles on art and literature he translated Spanish, Latin American and North and South American Indian poetry and prose into German. Theile is perhaps best known today for his editorship of *Humboldt -Zeitschrift für die Luso-brazilianische Welt*; *Fikrun wa fann— Zeitschrift für die islamische Welt*; and *Duemila—Revista Italo-tedesca*. Briefly translated **as a magazine for the Brazilian world, another for the Islamic and the last a magazine for the Italians /Germans.**

The third founder of the *DB* was Nikolaus Freiherr von Nagel who through fear of appearing as a *Junker* (Theile insisted that it would be most unjust to apply this label to von Nagel) refused to be named as a co-publisher.[29] Although he had been in South America for twenty years, von Nagel had remained in close contact with happenings in Germany and abhorred Nazism from the beginning. His help was primarily financial.

Theile worked with the printer and on technical aspects of publishing, in addition to writing and editing. Rukser devoted himself almost exclusively to editing and writing. Both men carried on an extensive correspondence with contributors, representatives of the journal, politicians subscribers and friends. Theile has described the division of labor between himself and Rukser as follows:

> *Dr. Rukser besorgte fast ausschliesslich die Korrespondenz, nachdem wir uns über die Richtlinien für die Briefe verständigt hatten,— was stets leicht war. Ich selber besorgte alles redaktionelle Aufbau der Hefte,—nach Absprache mit UR, Einrichten der Mss..Lesen der Fahnen, den gesamten Verkehr mit der Druckerei wo niemand Deutsch verstand. Ferner die Finanzierung der Zeitschrift durch eigene und gespendete Mittel.*[30]

TRANSLATION: Dr. Rukser took virtually exclusive care of the correspondence after we agreed upon the general content of the letters, which was always easy. I personally handled all editorial construction of each issue, following

---

29 Albert Theile, "*Vorwort zur Reprint Ausgabe* (Nendeln/Liechtenstein: Kraus Reprint Division of Kraus-Thomson Organization Limited, 1970), p. 3. Junker=aristocratic landowner in the Prussian territories, a squire, associated with Pan-.Germanism, Bismarck, wealth, pomposity

30 Letter from Theile to Vander Heide, June 7, 1974.

discussion with UR: arrangement of the manuscripts, reading the galley proofs, the entire relationship with the printer where nobody understood German. Then, further, the financing of the journal through private and donated means.

Theile's contribution to the magazine was considerable and invaluable his energetic devotion commendable. Rukser lacked his organizational talents and his abiity to deal with practical routine matters, but in spirit the *DB* was Rukser's periodical. This is obvious from the journal itself and from Rukser's correspondence. In recent years Theile has been lauded as the publisher of the *DB* by newspapers in Hörde and Dortmund, with almost no mention of Rukser. In fact, financially and intellectually the magazine was Rukser's and Theile himself always acknowledged his indebtedness to Rukser.

Two women played significant roles in sustaining the *DB*, Rukser's wife, Dora, and Anna Steuerwald-Landmann. Theile paid Mrs. Rukser the following tribute:

> *Es war Ruksers Frau Dora Rukser, die für den Ambiente sorgte, der entscheidend war für die geistige Arbeit in einem politisch explosiven Klima wie dem der Deutschen Blättern. Dora Rukser war unsere einzige redaktionelle Hilfe, Sekretärin, Archivarin, Ubersetzerin in einer Person denn wir mussten sparen für das Sichtbare, das neue Heft.*

TRANSLATION: It was Rukser's wife, Dora, who was responsible for the ambience which was crucial for the intellectual work in a politically explosive climate like that of the DB. Dora was our sole editorial help, secretary, archivist, translator in one person, for we had to save for the sake of the visible, the new magazine.

In calling Mrs. Rukser *the einzige redaktionelle Hilfe* (**only editorial assistance**) Theile is either forgetting the indefatigable work of Anna Steuerwald, or stressing Mrs. Rukser's work in translating and editing, in which Mrs. Steuerwald was somewhat less involved.

Anna Steuerwald-Landmann, retained her maiden name throughout her married life, perhaps as a sign of her strong independence and liberal *Weltanschauung* (**outlook on life**). She was a feisty little lady who very much belonged to the *avantgarde*. Anna and her physician husband, Dr. Richard

Steuerwald, escaped to Chile in January, 1939, after having been victimized by the Nazis in Nürnberg. She was born in Fürth in 1892, studied at the universities of Erlangen and Cologne and received a degree in welfare work. Anna practiced her profession in Nürnberg from 1919 to 1923 and served as editor of the *Wohlfahrtsblätter* (**Welfare Notes**) published by the *Wohlfahrtsamt* (**Welfare Bureau**) In addition, she was politically active in the *Sozialdemokratische Partei Deutschlands* (**Social Democratic Party of Germany- SPD**). The Steuerwalds continued to enjoy great respect in the SPD in Nürnberg after their return to Germany in 1947. Anna Steuerwald volunteered to work for the *DB* after reading the first issue, as stated in her own words:

> *Die Begegnung mit dieser Zeitschrift bedeutet für mich weitaus das stärkstegeistige Erlebnis meiner Exilzeit. Die Begegnung mit den Herausgebern und meinem Mann und mir wurde bald echte Freundschaft, die auch die Gattin Dr. Ruksers einschloss und bisheute nicht endete.... Im Januar 1943 brachte mir mein Mann das erste Heft. Nach kurzem Überblick sagte ich: Da muss ich mittun; ich schreibe einen Aitikel. Mein Mann war skeptisch; werden sie dich dort brauchen? Ich wagte es und hatte das Glück, daß mein Beitrag angenomen wurde, daß weitere Mitarbeit gewünscht ja, daß sie ständing intensiviert würde. Hier konnte, ja sollte ich meine politischen Grundsätze vertreten: überparteilicher Pazifismus, Toleranz und besondere Betonung des Fraulichen, obwohl ich nie Frauenrechtlerin war.[31]*

TRANSLATION: Mrs. Steuerwald stresses how the magazine changed her life. It was, she writes, the high point of her expatriate (or exile period) to work for the *DB* and along with her husband to get to know the publishers. They all became fast friends. Dr. Steuerwald brought Anna her first copy in January, 1943. She was immediately hooked and expressed a need to write for it. Her husband wondered if she would be needed and proved to be skeptical. She chanced it and states (modestly) that she lucked out in having her piece accepted which led to a job where she could represent her pacifism and tolerance especially as reflected in feminine issues, although, she points out she was never heavily involved in women's rights.

---

31 Anna Steuerwald-Landmann, "Erlebnisse im Exil" (Chilli 1939-1947), *Fürther Heimat Blätter*.

REPRESENTATIVES ABROAD

The publishers needed representatives throughout the world who would be responsible for promoting the magazine and stimulating sales. They found such highly gualified individuals as Joseph Kaskell and Karl O. Paetel in New york, Paul Zech in Buenos Aires, José Antonio Benton in São Paulo, Philipp Berlin in Mexico City and Georg Berger in Australia.

Paul Zech, the representative in Argentina was also a frequent contributor to the periodical. He and all the other representatives were staunch supporters of its aims. Because many prominent and even moderately wealthy refugees from Germany were in the USA and predominantly on the East Coast, Kaskell and Paetel had greater success than any of the other representatives in finding subscribers for the *DB* and soliciting financial assistance. along with Zech they were also influential in shaping the program of the journal.

Joseph Kaskell was born the same year as Rukser (1892) in Posen and both studied at the same Gymnasium. Kaskell too became a lawyer; the two men remained life-longfriends,and Joseph was another who perceived early that he could not live under National socialism. In 1939 the Kaskells moved briefly to England and then to New York City. He decided it might be difficult to find employment as a foreign lawyer in the big city; therefore, in his mid-forties he enrolled in Columbia University Law School in order to become a properly credentialed lawyer in his new homeland. Kaskell graduated near the top of his class and received his second law degree. In addition to his studies he worked energetically for the *DB*. Kaskell practiced into his eighties in New York City where he was of great assistance to German emigrants for whom his efforts were commonly *pro bono*. In fact he advised this writer on a small legal matter, also gratis. The expatriats learned well the value of mutual assistance.

While digging out my old files from the 1970's to update this study of the *Blätter*, it was a pleasure to come across letters, notes, articles that I had completely forgotten. How delighted both my wife and I were to find a Christmas card signed "Liselotte and Joe Kaskell." My mind immediately flooded with memories, including "Joe"'s generosity with Karl Otto Paetel, a truly tragic figure among the expatriates.

Known as KOP, Karl worked with Kaskell almost from the beginning and during the last year of publication was the sole representative of the journal in the states. He was born in berlin on november 23, 1906. From 1928 to 1930 Paetel studied at the university of Berlin and the *Hochschule für Politik* (**high school**— university level— **for political studies**) in Berlin. He was forced to end his doctoral studies due to lack of finances (one example of his bad luck). Early in his student days KOP was chief editor of *Das Junge Volk* a monthly journal of the youth movement; in addition he edited the weekly, *Die Kommenden*, and published the *Politische Zeitschriftenschau*. In 1932 he published the *Antifaschistische Briefe* and from 1930 to 1933 *Die Sozialistische Nation*. Then came the Nazis and lots of trouble ("real bad luck," if you will).

In 1933 Paetel was questioned by the SA for three days and in November, 1934, held by the *Gestapo* for nine days. Soon thereafter the Nazis forbade him to publish. Therefore, in January, 1935, he fled to Czechoslovakia. Later travels took him to Denmark, Sweden, back to Czechoslovakia, then to France, on to Spain, Portugal and finally to the USA. Following his work with the *DB* Paetel continued to reside in Forest Hills, New York with his devoted wife, Elizabeth, although he frequently returned to Germany, including a speaking tour in 1949 and several visits to Ernst Jünger, a friend from their student days, who was an existentialist and disciple of Nietzsche and one of the strongest literary talents of his era.

KOP published many articles, most of which dealt with youth groups, and immediately after the war, edited and published the little read and virtually unknown magazine, *Deutsche Gegenwart*. he never received the recognition he deserved due, it seems to both to not being in the right place at the right time or his own stubbornness in clinging too long to his passé views on Socialism. He never moved beyond his beloved *Wandervögel* (**the Wandering Birds**) days.[32] He lived in a cramped apartment in Forest Fills, NY surrounded by stacks of old newspapers in German and English. his wife, Elizabeth, loyally sustained this man with such a fine mind whose eyesight worsened by the day as he chain smoked while reading those saved newspapers. I shall never understand how he avoided self-immolation nor what he continued to discover in the papers.

WORKING CONDITIONS IN CHILE

Working conditions in Chile were by no means optimum, and Rukser frequentry complained of a lack of help. *Wir machen alles alein* (**we do all alone**) became

---

32   The *Wandervögel* movement, was established in Steglitz in 1896 by Karl Fischer, a student who became disgruntled with the artificiality and moldiness of his middle class existence. He found it to be stale, hackneyed, vapid and advocated that the children of the well-healed patricians of the Berlin suburb return to the forests, fields, meadows and streams. These wandering birds, who wanted to feel the snow on their skin, sleep in haystacks after a day of hiking, avoid trains, and cook their own simple meals in the great outdoors (not known to admit it wasn't all that wonderful all the time), formed the first formal organization of German youth, destined one day to become the *Hitlerjugend*, a turn for the worse. of which Paetel, of course, did not approve, for he was a "true *Wandervogel*" and despiser of Nazis.

an "in" slogan. the office of the *DB* consisted of one corner of a warehouse in Santiago. in the main part of the single, huge room a German emigrant sold clothing. in a third section fresh eggs were vended. Anna Steuerwald managed the office practically singlehandedly, and later recounted humorously how she thought it more sophisticated and official to say, "office of the *DB*," when she answered the telephone rather than "fresh eggs and the *DB* sold here."[33] At times she did sell eggs; other times she dusted. more important was her daily reading of manuscripts which arrived in increasing numbers from around the world and her labor in finding quotations for her beloved journal, either from the ciry library in santiago or her husband's personal library which, surprisingly, the Nazis had allowed the Steuerwalds to take to Chile. The staff were successful in convincing Luis Aguirre Ruiz, manager of the University of Santiago Press, *Imprenta Universitaria*, to print the *DB* even though the only thing typesetters, binders and other workers understood were the few words of the Spanish summaries at the end of each issue. It is no wonder that there are typographical errors in the periodical; in fact a small miracle that the number is not higher. A story recounted by both Theile and Anna Steuerwald deals with the gravest, yet most amusing, typographical error of the four years of publication.

it seems that one of the most sensitive of the contributors, concerning even minute errors was Kurt Hiller, and, as we may expect from Murphy's laws, somehow a "**t**" had been substituted for the first "*l*" in his name which appeared in the table of contents as *Kurt Hitler*. Theile worked throughout an entire night correcting the mistake in two thousand copies with a pen.[34]

Added to the poor working conditions and problems with the printers was a persistent sobering concern: insufficient funding. Rukser appreciated and was an early defender of the modern art of his day. he had accumulated pieces by Chagall, Malewicz, Archipenko and other moderns as well as paintings by Lehmbruck Sisley, Corinth, Liebermann and Hofer. Much of his collection was sold, primarily in the USA to finance the *DB*. Joseph Kaskell was soliciting funds in New York and elsewhere in the U.S.A. and Nikolaus von Nagel was contributing generously. Other monetary assistance drifted in in small amounts so that publishing with insufficient funds continued while the group in Chile shared the hope that maybe, things would pick up.

Then the death blow struck: von Nagel suddenly withdrew his primary support of the magazine following the appearance of Joseph Kaskell's piece on Vansittart. It seems that the three founders had agreed to his stipulation that no article critical of allied policies and proposals would be published by

---

33   Interview, August 26, 1974.
34   Theile, *Vorwort*, op. cit. and Steuerwald in interview of Aug, 26, 1974.

their non USA based magazine, and this gentleman, who once feared the term *Junker*, insisted that the article by Kaskell, a naturalized citizen of the USA, but nevertheless a German emigrant, violated the agreement. The enlightening German anti-Nazi publication, although it continued for another three years, financed chiefly by Rukser's farm, art collection and modest investments, was from that moment, doomed.

As a result of this financial shock and von Nagel's withdrawal from all association with the *Blätter*, Fritz Siegel, part owner of the Schoken-Verlag (**Schoken Publishing Co.**) who sometimes wrote for the magazine under the pseudonym, Fritz Meyning, worked more closely with the publishers. He did not, however, possess the means to replace von Nagel's support.

Much of Theile's and Rukser's correspondence both before and after von Nagel's action reveals monetary concerns. Joseph Kaskell even in the first year of the magazine's existence hoped for much help from von Nagel's in-laws in New York; however, they never donated generously. Kaskell wrote to Rukser:

Ich hatte eine ausfürliche Besprechung mit Mrs.Vischer und Stresemann. Mrs. V. ist voll guten Willens zu helfen. Leider sagte sie mir bald am Anfang, daß ihr Mann keine weiteren Opfer bringen wolle. Später aber stellte sie in Aussicht, daß sie doch von Zeit zu Zeit kleine beträge von $5 bis $10 würde zur verfügung stellen können, was ich mit Dank annahm, Büchersendungen zu finanzieren.[35]

TRANSLATION: (essence) She says her husband is not willing to give more, but she will donate five to ten dollars now and then to help with the cost of sending books.

Later in 1944 Kaskell wrote:

Damit sind wir wieder bei der Geldfrage. Erstklassige Leute sind nur einmal in der Regel nur für Geld zu haben .Auch ein anderes Problem wird nur mit Geld zu lösen sein,nämlich die Verwaltung hier. Mir sind die Geschäfte dermassen über den Kopf gewachsen, daß ich für nichts Anderes mehr Zeit habe. Ich muss aber irgendwie zurück zu meiner Berufsarbeit und auch meine Mitarbeit an den DB glaube ich fruchbarer gestalten zu können, wenn ich mehr Zeit habe um zu lesen und alten und neuen Kontakten nachzugehen. wenn ich nir nur eine sekretärin nehme, so ist dies eine Ausgabe von

---

35 Letter from J. Kaskell to U. Rukser, October 1, 1943.

$35.00 bis $40.00 die Woche, also weit über unseren erschwingbaren Budget, Paetel wurde da er zur Zeit arbeitslos ist, gern bereit sein, seine zeit zur Verfügunq zu stellen, Wenn ich ihm wenigstens soviel bezahlen kann, das sein Einkomen zusamen mit den Einkünften seiner Frau, seine sehr bescheidenen Ansprüche an Unterhalt deckt. Ich glaube, daß er halb soviel kosten würde, wie eine sekretärin und dabei mehr leisten könnte.[36]

TRANSLATION: There we go again, the question of money. First class help, for the most part, can only be secured for cash. We also have another problem here that can only be remedied with additional funds, namely, the administration. Tasks have increased so greatly that the whole thing is simply over my head and I have no time for anything else. However, I now simply must get back to my profession and also I believe I could be more productive with the DB, if I had more time to read and go through all my mail. If I simply get a secretary, it will cost $35 to $40 per week…far above our affordable budget. Because Paetel is unemployed at the moment, he would be pleased to put his time at the disposal of the DB, that is, if I could pay him enough that his income combined with his wife's, covers the expenses of his few demands and modest way of life. I believe that he would cost half of what a secretary would need and notably, would accomplish more.

The pattern continued, Paetel destitute, Kaskell trying to help. Of course we already know that not all expats were forced by circumstances to count their pennies. They included movie stars, authors, attorneys, business persons and prominent Jewish families, Some of whom could have financed the whole show for years to come. One such family, the Vischers, are mentioned in several letters even after von Nagel's refusal to contribute. Hope had not died…not quite yet anyway.

Ich berichtete lhnen wohl schon, daß Mrs. Vischer Herrn von Nagel den Vorschlag gemacht für einige Zeit hierherzukommen. Ich halte für möglich, daß sich hinsichtlich ihrer Finanzen einiges tun liesse, wenn er auf den Vorschlag eingeht.[37] (**I am already notifying you that Mrs. Vischer approached Mr. von Nagel with the proposal**

---

36 Letter from Kaskell to Rukser, Feb. 15, 1944.
37 Letter from Kaskell to Rukser, Jan. 17, 1944

that he come here for a while. I take it is possible that in hindsight their finances would allow them to do something...if he takes up the proposal.)

Juan Gildemeister, the owner of sugar plantations in Peru, was another possible Maecenas for the sick publication. Even when he had refused help, Rukser persisted, hoping that Kaskell could persuade Gildemeister's daughter in New York to convince her father. Letters were flying back and forth, even without computers! Financial need is a driving force, which challenges us to find solutions.

> *Fall Gildemeister: durch Vermittlung traten wir an Juan Gildemeister heran und bekamen eine saublöde Absage. Das geschriebene Wort sei jetzt zwecklos, jetzt müsse man die Kanonen sprechen lassen usw. Könnten Sie nicht die Tochter veranlassen, an den Vater eindringlich und aufklärend zu schreiben und ihm klar zu machen, daß er dafür etwas tun muss, auch finanziell. Diese Leute ersticken jetzt in dem vielen Geld, dass ihnen USA für Zucker zahlt: und ausserdem würde es sehr grossen Eindruck machen, wenn dieser Mann in Peru sich für uns einsetzte, wo wir wenig Echo haben.*

TRANSLATION: The situation with Gildemeister. Through intermediaries we approached Juan Gildemeister and received a stupid refusal. The written word has no purpose, now one has to let the cannons speak, etc. Couldn't you encourage the daughter to write the father in a forceful and clarifying way in order to make it obvious to him that he must do something financial. Right now these persons are choking on the large amount of money that the USA is paying them for sugar, and furthermore, it would make a great impression if this man in Peru would join our cause where we have little influence.

Because Gildemeister refused to consent, Rukser urged Kaskell again to work through the daughter, but Gildemeister never cooperated. Advertising in the *DB* was a possible way of raising money. butthere was never enough advertising to help significantly. Kaskell happily reported in a letter dated February 15, 1944 that Karl Nierendorf, owner of art galleries in NewYork and Hollywood, had taken a quarter page advertisement at fifty dollars for a half year. Kaskell tried to get others to advertise with little success

The financial situation continued to worsen until late 1946 when all the strongest supporters launched a final vigorous struggle for the journal's life. None fought harder than Otto Klepper, former Prussian Minister of Finance, who lived in exile in Mexico. He clarified his reasons in a letter of August 15, 1946, emphasizing that the *DB* was vital for the development of future politics in Germany:

> *Einerzeits müssen die Grundlagen einer zukünftigen deutschen Politik schon jetzt gedanklich entwickelt werden. Andererseits ist das in Deutschland selbst und—auch darin stimme ich Dr. Rukser zu—in Europa zur Zeit unmöglich, Gegenstand der künftigen deutschen Politik muss die Zurückwinnung der Freiheit sein; d.h. die Frage, wie das zu geschehen hat. Schon wegen der Besatzung kann man darüber in Deutschland kaum sprechen, und andere Länder wie z.B. die Schweiz, würden die Unbequemlichkeiten scheuen die das Erscheinen eines unabhängingen deutschen Organs natur notwendig mit sich bringt. Davon abgesehen sind die Deutschen Blätter soweit ich sehe, die einzige Publikation, die qualitativ den Anforderungen entspricht, die Ernst und Schwere der Situation stellen. Die New Yorker Staatszeitung ist ein harmloses Organ für das deutschamerikansche Herz, die Volkszeitung ist sozialdemokratisch. Die neuerdings in Schweden herausgebrachte Neue Rundschau des Bermann-Fischer Verlags ist, begreiflicherweise, nicht frei von dem jüdischen Ressentiment. Sind die Deutschen Blätter eingegangen, so können wir, Gott weiss, wann, mit neuen Opfern und neuem Lehrgeld einen, abermaligen Versuch machen. Gelingt es dagegen die gegenwärtige Krise zu überwinden, so wird man im Laufe einer, wie ich glaube, allerdings längeren Zeit gelingen die Zeitschrift auf die eigenen Füsse zu stellen. Ich nehme das deshalb an, weil sie notwendig ist.... Nun Weiss ich ja, wie die situation hier ist. Dr. Berlin, mit dem ich gesprochen habe, weiss keinen Rat. Er sagt, gewiss mit Recht, in den ihm bekannten jüdischen Kreisen sei für einen deutschen Zweck kein Pfenning zu finden. Ich meine nun, so viel Mumm müssten die Deutschen noch haben, um für einen solchen lebenswichtigen zweck sieben-tausend Dollars aufzubringen. Finanziel kann ich ja leider nichts beitragen. Wenn Sie so wollen habe ich selbst viel geopfert. ich bin aber bereit in jeder Weise als Zwischenglied zu dienen sei es als Unterstützungsempfänger, Kreditnehmer oder in welcher Form auch immer. Auch wenn Sie meine leibhaftige Mitwirkung bei einem erneuten Anqriff für notwendig halten, stehe ich zur*

Verfügung, Unternehmen Sie also bitte den neuen Effort. Ich habe schon einmal scharfer gesehen, als die meisten Deutschen und glauben Sie mir bitte, daß ich auch jetzt auf dem richtigen Wege bin. Es kann gelingen weil es gelingen muss.[38]

TRANSLATION: On the one hand it is vital that the basis for the future political Program for Germany be developed now. On the other hand it is impossible to do so in Germany itself and in Europe at this time (on this point I agree with Dr. Rukser). The objective of future German politics must be the regaining of freedom, i.e. the question of how that can be achieved. Due to the occupation, one can hardly speak about this in Germany and other countries, Switzerland, for example, will avoid the discomfort which the appearance of an independent German agency would naturally bring. That aside, the DB are, in as far as I can see, the only publication that qualitatively meets the challenges and presents the seriousness and gravity of the situation. The *New Yorker Staatszeitung* is a harmless publication for the German-American heart, the *Volkszeitung* is social-democratic. The recent *Neue Rundschau* brought out in Sweden by the Bermann-Fischer Company is, understandably, not free of Jewish resentment. If the *Deutsche Blätter* ceases publication, God knows when we can make another desperate effort with new offerings and learning the hard way. If it works, however, to overcome the present crisis, one will have, in my opinion, during the course of a quite long time success in setting the magazine on its own two feet. I assume that because it is necessary. I know what the situation here is. Dr. Berlin, with whom I have spoken, offers no advice. He correctly says that in the Jewish circles with which he is familiar, there is not a single penny to be found for supporting German aims. I think that the Germans must still need a lot of guts to cough up seven thousand dollars for such a purpose so important to life itself.

I have shared with readers what I know about the treatment of Jews and the strong support of the *Rassenwahn* that possessed the very souls of Germans, a loathing directed even against Jews whose families had long lived and prospered

---

38 Copies of this letter were sent to prospective supporters.

in Germany and contributed so much to their common country. We should all quickly comprehend that these Jewish families had no intention of financing persons who, in their view, wanted only to slaughter them.

Klepper hoped epecially for help from Thomas Mann. He wrote to Mann explaining sone of the problems in raising money, why he wished to aid the *DB*, and asked Mann to help:

> *Bitte erlauben Sie mir, Ihnen eine Anregung zu unterbreiten. Es handelt sich um die in Santiaqo de Chile erscheinenden Deutschen Blätter, wie die Herren Rukser und Theile schrieben, sind sie über die fortgesetzten finanziellen Schwierigkeiten, mit denen die Zeitschrift zu kämpfen hat, unterrichtet. Nunmehr scheint die Situation besonders kritisch geworden zu sein. Für den laufenden Jahrgang besteht ein Defizit von 2000 USA-Dollars, und für den nächsten ist ein solches von 5000 Dollars zu erwarten.... In Verbindunq mit dem hiesigen Vertreter der D.B., Dr. Berlin, habe ich mich seit Längerem bemüht, neue Mittel flüssig zu machen. In betracht kommt hier für praktisch nur die alte deutsche Kolonie. Die Emigranten verfügen entweder nicht über grosse Mittel, oder sie wollen mit Deutschland überhaupt nichts mehr zu tun haben; Im Durchschnitt ist beides der Fall, die alte, ingesessenen Deutschen sind nicht durchweg Anhänger des Nationalsozialismus gewesen. Unter den fünftausen in Mexico lebenden Deutschen hatte die Partei nur etwas über zweihundert Mitglieder. Aktive Gegnerschaft hat man allerdings auch nicht entwickelt; im allgemeinen beschwichtigte man den zweifel nach dem Satz right or wrong my country. Nun sind die Leute bestrebt, eine neue Orientieruirq zu qewinnen, und die Frage ist, ob sie in die richtigen oder wiederun in die falschen Hände fallen. Daher stammt mein, wenn ich so sagen darf, lokales Interesse an den Fortbestehen der Deutschen Blätter...Unter den hier lebenden Deutschen befindet sich Herr Rudolph Groth. Er stammt aus Lübeck, hat daßelbe Gymnasium besucht, wie Sie, und bewahrt hieran, wie er mir erzählte, wache Erinnerungen. Groth war einer der hier erfolgreichsten deutschen Kaufleute, und er verfügt auch jetzt noch über Mittel die ihm erlauben würden, die qesamten siebentausend Dollars allein zu geben. Er ist auch auf allen möglichen nicht geschäftlichen Gebieten interessiert und, wie das zu sein pflegt, geltungsbedürftig; ich möchte ihn als einen der Leute bezeichnen, die zu Mäzenen der Deutschen Blätter prädestiniert sind. könnten Sie sich wohl dazu entschliessen,*

ihm ein paar Zeilen zu schreiben und ihm nahe zulegen, eine grösseres Opfer zu bringen? Er erzählte mir, seine in Kalifornien verheiratete Tochter habe Sie kürzlich besuchen können und habe sehr sehr entzückt darüber berichtet. Ich bin überzeugt, daß ein solcher Brief das wunder bewirken würde, das herbeizuführen wir hier kaum imstande sind.[39]

TRANSLATION: Please, allow me to support you with some encouragement. It concerns the Deutsche Blätter which is published in Santiago de Chile. According to what Mr. Rukser and Mr. Theile are writing, you are informed about the problems with ongoing financial concerns that the journal has to combat. By now the situation appears to be most critical. The current issue has incurred a deficit of 2,000 US dollars, and a shortfall of 5,000 is anticipated for the next. The present representative, Dr. Berlin, and I have for some time tried to make new means readibly available. Practically almost the entire German colony here comes into consideration. The emigrants either do not have great means or they want nothing to do with Germany anymore.

On the average both are the case. The older well-situated Germans were generally not followers of National Socialism. Among the five thousand living in Mexico the party had only a little more than two hundred members. To be sure active opposition also did not develop. In general people appeased their doubts with the concept of "right or wrong, my country." Now people are striving to gain a new orientation, and the question is whether they will fall into the correct hands or once again into the wrong ones. My, if I may say it this way, local interest in the continued existence of the *DB* is based on that.

Mr. Rudolph Groth is included among the Germans living here. He comes from Lübbeck, attended the same Gymnasium as you, but has only vague memories. Groth was one of the most successful German businessmen here and still today has control of sufficient funds to allow him alone to give the entire seven thousand. Furthermore, he also has all sorts of nonbusiness interests, which it seems

---

39   Letter from Otto Klepper to Thomas Mann, Aug. 22, 1948.

are worthwhile; I would like to designate him as one of the persons who could be a Maecenas for the *DB*. Could you please bring yourself to write him a few lines and encourage him to make a larger offer? He told me that his married daughter in California visited you not long ago and was most enthralled. I am convinced that such a letter would work the wonder for which we here do not have the means.

Klepper was incensed when Mann evasively refused help:

Er hat auf meinen Brief albern ausweichend geantwortet, he wrote to Rukser, es lohnt sich nicht, eine Abschrift zu machen, zumal der Brief noch langatmig ist . . Hinter der Ablehnung steckt m.E. la Señora, die den Fischer-Bermann Verlag näher steht. Wenn der Kaiser, Wie ihn Dr. Berlin nennt, Verstand und Humor hat, schwenkt er um. Ich wäre sodann bereit, zu revozieren. Vamos a ver.[40]

TRANSLATION: He answered my letter in a stupid evasive way. Making a copy is pointless, especially since the letter is long-winded. The Señora, who is closer to the Fischer-Bermann Publishing House, is behind this refusal. If the Kaiser, as Dr. Berlin calls him, had any sense and humor, he would turn around. I would then be ready to retract. Vamos a ver (Let's see— in Spanish).

Mann did not change his mind, although paradoxically, as has been noted in the introduction, he too desired continued publication of the *Blätter*. Then, too, in 1944 he made the much praised statement to Julius Bab: *Hitler ist ein unvergleichliches Schwein (***Hitler is an incomparable swine**—a very strong term in German. We should add that the leader was unquestionably maniacal and indowed with demonic intuition). Somehow plain old *swine* is better.

Anyway, the good patrician author continued lunching with famous guests on that large patio/balcony in Pacific Palisades, California and enjoying the gorgeous view of the Pacific. But he did not like Hitler! ...and would we want T. Mann on the front lines in his fine wool suit with vest?

Opposition from Germans living in South America to editorial positions of the *DB* also plagued the editors; strongest antagonism came from local Nazis. In a Letter to his brother-in-law, the film director Hans Richter, of

---

40   Letter from Klepper to Rukser, Sept. 5, 1946.

January 5, 1944, Rukser tersely portrayed the Nazi opposition: *Im übrigen wird es euch wichtig sein zu hören, Mitteln aufs skrupeloseste gegen uns arbeiten, weil wir ihen nämlich jetzt sehr unangenehm werden.* (**Furthermore, you should know that the most unscrupulous forces are working against us because we are becoming irksome to them.**)

One attempt by Chilean Nazis to thwart the effect of the *DB* had comic elements. They planned to buy up all copies of the first issue but were roited by the alertness of Pablo Gompertz, a Jewish emigrant from Essen. According to Theile:

> *Don Pablo erwiderte auf die Frage eine vorgeschickten Agenten, ob sich der Kauf von einigen hundert Exemplaren nicht, billiger stellte mit einem ermunternden ‚Ja.' Als dannnach der Auflage gefragt wurde setzte er erheblich übertreibend mit ironischem lächeln hinzu: Im Augenblick fünftausend, aber bei der Nachfage, müssen wir die Auflage bald verdoppeln. Der Agent verschwand, und der überaschend hohe Einzelverkauf der ersten Nummern hörte bald auf.*

TRANSLATION: A Nazi agent was sent to ask Don Pablo if it was not cheaper to purchase a few hundred copies. He replied with a resounding *yes*. He was then asked how many were on hand, to which the exaggerated answer was 5,000 at the moment, but due to this inquiry we'll have to double that. The agent vanished.

Rukser sometimes wrote to Kaskell about defamation of the *DB* by Germans living in south America who were **not** Nazis:

> *Hier gibt es schon genug Verleumdungen aller Art gegen uns. Das ist wie Flohstiche—und ebenso lästig und wiederwärrtig. Dabei machen sich alle diese Leute lächerliche Illusionen darüber, welche Rolle sie etwa nach dem Kriege spielen werden—als ob man sich um unsereinen dann überhaupt gross kümmern könnte.*[41]

TRANSLATION: There is all kinds of slander of us here, like stings of a flea and no more bothersome. All these persons make themselves ridiculous figuring out what

---

41 Letter from Rukser to Kaskell, Nov. 23, 1943.

role they want to play after the war—as if one could bother himself about us at all.

GETTING KNOWN (MARKETING)

Authors in general agree that marketing is a repugnant, but vital, labor intensive endeavor, for no one having any self-respect and pride in his "intellectual property" wants to imitate a circus barker and hawk his research and years of composing, rewriting, editing. He expects to be recognized and be sought after, not the reverse. but the primary task of the publishers and representatives was to get the *Leaves* known and to increase subscriptions. in Spite of problems several schemes were tested. Kaskell engaged the services of the book seller, Friedrich Krause, who sold the *DB* in New york city for a commission of ten cents per copy. Rukser urged Kaskell to persist in trying to get the review mentioned in the *Reader's Digest* as well as in other magazines and leading newspapers in the USA. However, it did not cooperate. Several other magazines were willing to exchange subscriptions with the *DB* and carry reports of its existence, and a few newspapers published reviews. Kaskell solicited subscriptions from several universities, which brought a measure of success, and fliers describing the *DB* were mailed to emigrants in North and South America.

In the summer of 1944 Rukser encouraged friends of the *DB* to organize discussion evenings, *Runde Tische* (**Round Tables**). The discussions were to stimulate interest in the issues presented in the *DB* and emphasize the value of the magazine. Thousands of miles away from Chile, Kaskell held some of these gatherings in his large and well-appointed apartment on Riverside Drive in New York City. An elite group of German émigré intellectuals augmented by a few distinguished Americans attended; some of this group also wrote for the journal.[42] Ein *Runder Tisch* in Mexico or Chile took place under humbler circumstances, but was dominated by the same idealistic enthusiasm. Anna Steuerwald described the meetings as follows:

> *Der Runde Tisch…so nannte sich ein Kreis von Freunden der DB, den wir Mitte 1944 gründeten. Natürlich hatten wir nicht die Prominenz der deutschen Emigration, wie sie uns von Freundeskreis der DB aus New York gemeldet wurde. Ich hatte die sogenannte Leitung dieses RT. Das heist: Ich durfte Einladungen*

---

[42] See the appendix for the guest list of a discussion evening held at Joseph Kaskell' s condominium, March 10, 1945.

schreiben und relativ oft das einleitende Referat halten Unseren RT fingen wir mit wenigen Freunden an, hatten bald mehr als 30 Mitglieder, die sich meist in unserer höchst einfachen Wohnung trafen, manchmal auch bei andren Freunden im Turnus von drei Wochen. Man sass zum grossen Teil auf zwischen Stühle gelegten Brettern und diskutierte bis nach Mitternacht über je ein vereinbartes Thema.[43]

TRANSLATION: Anna emphasizes that the meetings were far different than in NY, since at most 30 Round Table members met in most humble circumstances in a tiny apartment where they sat on planks placed on chairs and discussed whatever subject they agreed upon until past midnight. They took turns about every three weeks. She was frequently the leader which meant she gave the first lecture or was the one who addressed envelopes and organized.

Surely, being a German gathering there was plenty *Kaffee und Kuchen...* We will let the reader translate, no help here!

Kaskell thought it vital for spreading the *DB's* message that Rukser travel to New York where he could meet or renew acquaintances with the intelectual émigrés and Americans who could be influential in a marketing scheme (my modern term). Perhaps his friend's magazine could even be published in the USA. *Alle meine Hoffnungen klammere ich daran, daß Ruksers im Mai soweit sein werden, um eine Reise planen zu können.* (He hoped with all his heart that the Ruskers would plan a May trip.) However, Rukser saw no possible way to Leave his work in Chile.

Kaskell's plan for increasing readership was to fail, for the *DB's* founder replied: *ausgeschlossen* (impossible) and added: Who ever brought up the idea?)

Kaskell's eagerness to have Rukser travel to New York was in part selfish. He was interested at the time in the *Tillich Committee* from which he later withdrew, and hoped to use the *DB* as a German voice of the committee. Kaskell tried to impart his enthusiasm for this group to Rukser:

Ich schrieb Ihnen vor einiger Zeit darüber, daß der Plan eines Committees unter Thomas Mann gescheitert ist. Das Projekt ist jetzt wieder aufgenomen worden und zwar hat Prof. Tillich diesmal die Chairmanship. Tillich ist, wie sie wissen Sozialdemokrat und zwar

---

43 A. Steuerwald, *Fürther Heimatsblätter*, op. cit., p. 116.

gehört er zu der Gruppe der betont christlichen Sozialdemokraten. Er ist seit 1933 hier, eingebürgert und lehrt an Union Theological Seminary, das Columbia University angegliedert ist und einen grossen Ruf als Theologenschule geniesst. Niebuhr, der von Geburt Amerikaner ist und an derselben Schule lehrt, steht in engen Beziehungen zu dem Unternehmen. Der innere Kreis setzt sich aus früheren Politikern und Schriftstellern verschiedenster Richtung zusamen, bisher etwa 20 an der zahl. Alle antinazi parteien sind vertreten. Nur die hiesige Gruppe der Mehrheits-Sozialisten hat Mitarbeit abgelehnt und polemisiert in der Neuen Volkszeitung gegen die Gruppe. Mehrere Sozialdemokraten, wie Staudinger, Gerzinski u.a. treten der Gruppe aber trotzdem persönlich bei. Auch Hagen hat sich angeschlossen. Das State Department steht der Gruppe wohlwolend gegenriber. Als Mitglieder ohne politische Vergangenheit sind Haussmann und ich eingeladen worden und auch Paetel werden wir wohl mindestens in den äusseren Ring und in einige Spezial Kommissionen hereinbringen können. Ich habe erklärt, daß ich nicht persönlichdnlich, sondern nur, als Vertreter der DB mich beteiligen will. Es besteht der Gedanke, die Beziehungen der Gruppe und den DB auszugestalten trotzdem die räumliche Entfernung einige Schwierigkeiten bereiten wird. An die öffentlichkeit sind wir noch nicht getreten. Meine Information ist daher nur für Sie persönlich bestimmt.[44]

TRANSLATION: I wrote you some time ago in relation to the failure of a plan proposed by a committee under the leadership of Thomas Mann. The project has been taken up again with Professor Paul Tillich as chairman. Tillich is, as you know, a Social Democrat, in fact a strong Christian Social Democrat. He has been here since 1933, a naturalized citizen who teaches at the Union Theological Seminary, which is connected to Columbia University and is held in high repute as a liberal theology university. Niebuhr, who by birth is an American and teaches at the same institution, is closely involved in the undertaking as well. The "inner circle" is made up of former politicians and writers of various persuasions, to date some 20 persons. Every anti-Nazi party is represented. Only the local group of majority socialists has rejected representation and campaigned against the group

---

44   Letter from J. Kasell to U. Rukser, February 15, 1944.

in the new *Volkszeitung*. Other Social Democrats, however, including Staudinger and Gerzinski among others, belong to the group personally. Hagen too has joined. The state department wishes the group well. As members with no political past, Haussman and I have been invited and we can bring Paetel in, at least as a member of the "outer ring" and special commissions. I declared that I shall not take part personally, but only as a representative of the our *Blätter* The thought has been expressed that arrangements should be made for a connection with it. Nevertheless the great distance between us would cause difficulties. We have not yet gone public. Therefore, this information is for "your eyes only."

To the same letter he added the following, written one week later:

Ich schrieb Ihnen vorige Woche über die Gruppe die hier unter der Führung von prof. Tillich bildet und daß ich an ihr namensrs der DB teilnehme. Am liebsten wäre es mir, wenn Rukser persönlich als Mitglied der Gruppe geführt werden würde, während ich als sein Vertreter an Sitzungen und dergl. teilnehme, solange er nicht hier ist. Es bestehen allerdings Bedenken gegen die Einbeziehung von mir lieb, wenn Rukser mich ermächtigen würde, in seinem Namen zu handeln.

TRANSLATION: Kaskell explains that he would be most pleased if Rukser were appointed to the prestigious committee with power to act in his name granted to Kaskell which would mitigate being exposed to misgivings the group exhibits about accepting persons who live in South America.

It seems Kaskell doesn't know what he wants here since Rukser would continue living in Chile! One did not jet around the world back then, especially in the middle of a world war. Only Roosevelt and Churchill sneaked off to strategize in some exotic port. That's fine. The Allies had to make certain that those two were safe!

A great effort was made to solicit the help of men of letters and other leading intellectuals in getting the *DB* known. The following three excerpts from letters to Hermann Hesse, Aldous Huxley, and Carl Gustav Jung are typical examples of the appeal.[45]

To Hesse, November 1, 1944

Wir möchten sehr gerne etwas von Ihnen bringen, neuere Gedichte, eine Erzählung, jedenfalls eine unveröffentlichte Arbeit. Ich liess Ihnen Hefte unserer Zeitschrift schicken; es wird weiter regelmässig geschehen. Hier lege ich einige Urteile bei, obwohl ich weiss daß sie auf dergleichen wenig oder kein Gewicht legen. Ich Weiss dies aus fruherem Briefwechsel mit Ihnen; beim Lesen vom „Glasperlenspiel" wurde es mir bestätigt.... Unsere Zeitschrift, die durch ihren Kampf gegen den Nazismus eine betont politische war, wird im neuen Jahre vielseitiger werden, weltweiter. Wir hoffen mit unsren Mitarbeitern unser Teil zum geistigen Wiederaufbau unsrer Heimat beitragen zu können. Werden Sie uns bald antworten?

TRANSLATION: All letters to the "intellectual elite" are asking for help with both the solicitation of funds to keep the *Blätter* going and for help in fighting the cause or causes. Then too they point out that essays are welcome. **This begins: We would like so very much to bring something from you, latest poems, a story, in any case some work not yet made public. I have asked that copies of our magazine be sent to you; it will happen regularly from now on. Herewith I am including some evaluatons although I know you that you put little important such. I know this from earlier exchanging letters with you. After reading *Glasperlenspiel* it was substantiated...Our magazine, which due to its fight against Nazism, has been distinctively political, will in the new year contain several more pages and world wide content. We hope along with our co-workers to due our bit in contributing to the moral reconstruction of our country. Will you kindly respond soon?**

To Aldous Huxley, April 2, 1943 (the English has been left in the original.)

---

45 Copies of more retyped complete letters are in the appendix.

This is to tell you how deeply I am impressed by your work and how much I feel obliged to you. Really, I want to thank you for all you wrote and for all I owe to you… Recently with my friend Albert Theile I started an anti-nazi monthly on a humanitarian basis.This review "Deutsche Blätter" is published in german with the intention to fight back Nazi-Propaganda from the German people living here. I will try to send you some copies of the first 3 numbers and hope you will not be afraid to find the illustrious name of yours in some pages. We dare not hope that there may be a possibility to have some contribution of yours for this paper. But if you mean, that, our efforts are not entirely unworthy of your appreciation and you would send us some lines about, this would mean a lot for us. We are going on now to form an honorary comitee for the review and invited Thomas Mann, Hermann Hesse C.G. Jung to give us this support. Is there any hope, that in some future you could allow us to inscribe your name too in this comitee?? We hope that those lines will find you in good health, with all ways better eyes! We apologize duly for our poor english and bag you to receive the expression of our thanks, sympathy and admiration!

To Carl Gustav Jung, April 4, 1943

Unterm 9. November 42 habe ich mir erlaubt Ihnen laut Anlage zu schreiben. Ich füge die Abschrift meines damaligen Briefes bei, weil man heute ja nie weiss, ob Briefe ankomen. Die Zeitschrift, über welche ich Ihnen damals berichtet habe, ist seit Januar dauernd erschienen. Die bisherigen 3 Hefte werden wir Ihnen auf mehrfache Weise, die wir für sicher halten, zusenden wie auch bisher schon Versuche derart gemacht worden sind. Da die Zeitschrift hier eine wirkliche Mission zu erfüllen hat, wie bei allen Urteilsfähigen anerkannt wird so hoffen wir unsere Arbeit ständig weiter zu führen und zu vertiefen. Daß uns dazu ein Beitrag gerade von Ihnen unschätzbar wäre, werden Ihnen verehrter Herr professor die bisherigen Hefte zeigen. Denn nicht nur der uns so ehrwürdige Name Jung erscheint dort immer wieder, sondern wir bemühen uns, wenn auch unter schwierigsten Verhältnissen, in der Leitung der Zeitschrift im Jungschen Geist zu handeln. Freilich möchten wir dem jezt gern sichtbareren Ausdruck verleihen und zwar Folgendes vor: Wir möchten eine Anzahl von wirklichen Europäern, denen wir uns besonders verpflichtet fühlen, Verfügen bitten sich für ein Ehren-Komite unserer Zeitschrift zur Verfügung zu stellen. Wir denken dabei an Sie, an Thomas Mann, Hermann Hesse, Aldous Huxley F.W. Foerster, Alexis Carrel um nur die Wichtigsten zu nennen an die wir uns jetzt wenden. Daneben würden einige der massgebenden hiesigen Humanisten treten, deren Namen Ihnen kaum etwas sagen werden.

TRANSLATION: Dated November 9, 1942, I took the liberty of writing you according to plan. I am including here a copy of that letter since these days one never knows if letters arrive. The magazine which I wrote about has continued to be published since January. We will send you the 3 published to date by different means which we consider to be secure as has been done with other trys of this sort. Since the magazine has a true mission to fulfill here which is recognized by all who are capable of judging, we hope to take our work further and to deepen it. For this purpose a submission from you would be invaluable, which the issues published to date will show you. For not only does the honorable name, Jung, repeatedly appear there, but we are struggling, even under the most trying circumstances to direct the magazine in a Jungian spirit.

 Clearly, we would like to lend the name, which is so gladly seen, and indeed we have the following plan: We would like a number of true Europeans to whom we feel ourselves to be particularly obligated, to offer service on an "Honor Committee" of our magazine. We are thinking for example of you, Thomas Mann, Hermann Hesse, Aldous Huxley, F.W. Foerster, Alexi Carrel, to name only the obvious to whom we are now turning. Along with them we'll include some current humanists whose names are not well known.

The English is a bit quaint, but nevertheless impressive. Having been a student and teacher of languages, I am quick to give kudos to Mr. Theile before considering some negative aspects, disappointments and other concerns regarding the struggling little magazine.

CRITICISM OF THE DEUTSCHE BLÄTTER

Expectantly, the *DB* received criticism, since all humans as we and P.T. Barnum know, can not be pleased all of the time. Let's start at the top with Rukser himself who was disappointed that not all contributors wrote like Emerson whose style, in his opinion, should be imitated. My personal response: No, we do not really want to, Udo. We Americans do appreciate your admiration of one of our great countrymen, but we too, as do Germans, develop our own writing styles. Karl Paetel wished for more polemics; he thought the journal's political positions should be more clearly defined and more forcefully defended. Rukser was adamantly opposed to his suggestions. Theile thought the translation of the motto by Pestalozzi on the back cover should be exchanged from Spanish to English. Kaskell frequently complained that the *DB* often failed to cite the original place of publication of a translated article. This criticism is truly justified; failure to cite sources was a most unfortunate oversight by the editors.

Criticism of style was sometimes rather vehement as evidenced in the following:

> *Mit seiner Kritik scheint Ranshofen mehr Theiles Anteil zu treffen. Theile wird nicht nur Ästeticismus vorgeworfen, sondern auch ein snobistischer Unterton und eine Art von oben her zu belehren. Als Gegensatz wird dann zuweilen die Natürlichkeit und schlichte Menschlichkeit lhrer Diktion erwähnt. Entmutigen Sie ihn nicht, aber wenn Sie zustimmen, lenken Sie seine Aufmerksamkeit gelegentlich darauf.*[46]

TRANSLATION: Theile's position. Theile is charged not only with aestheticism, but also with a snobbish undertone and an aloof manner of instructing. In direct opposition the naturalness and commonness of your way of writing is sometimes mentioned. Don't encourage him, but if you agree, periodically direct his attention to it.

Concerning criticism of the magazine in general, Kaskell later had the following to say:

> Theiles Aufsatz über skandinavische Volksschulen lässt auf jeden Fall die Bescheidenheit des Authors vermissen. Rukser hat in dieser Beziehung den Ton nie verfehlt. Ihm

---

[46] Letter from J. Kaskell to U. Rukser, January 17, 1944

wird vorgeworfen, daß er nur moralisiert ohne Probleme fest ins Auge zu fassen. Ganz allgemein kann man sagen, fest jeder Politiker uns gern in seine Richtung hin einziehen will, während die nicht-politiker uns eine reine Literatur Zeitschrift machen möchten. Zuweilen höre ich auch Urteile wie nicht interessant genug oder falsches Pathos. An fast jeder Kritik ist irgend etwas Richtiges dran, Sie zeigt uns gewissermassen die Klippen, die wir versuchen müssen zu umschiffen. Absolut genommen, halte ich die Aufgabe nicht einmal für schwer, nämlich die Aufgabe interessant, literarisch wertvoll, politisch und doch nicht parteipolitisch zu sein. Die wichtigsten Hindernisse scheinen mir zu sein: 1. Die berwindung Distanz zwischen Chile als dem Platz der Herstellung der Zeitschrift und den vereinigten Staaten, die einerseits im Brennpunkt der Ereignisse stehen, und andererseits einen bedeutenden teil des Leserkreises liefern sollten. 2, unsere finanzielle Begrenztheit.... Ich schickte Ihnen kürzlich die Stilkritik eines Freundes. Nehmen Sie bitte Heft 11 Seite 9 Satz 3 "Die Sicherheit dieses Satzes ist es… Auch die Wendung bewusst und tiefeingreifend… miterlebt" im nächsten Absatz ist nicht schön. Was Theile über den Einfluss der Beschäftigung mid fremden Sprachen auf den Stil sagt, ist sicherlich richtig. Es weist aber auch gleichzeitig darauf hin, daß die Fähigkeit zu stilreiner Sprache durch Übunq wieder erweckt werden kann, Oft getadelt wird übrigens auch unsere Beschäftigung mit so "ollen Kamellen" wie "Incorporationen Staat." So nun ist es aber genug über Kritik. —Ich hofe, Sie werden mir wieder schreiben, daß die "anderen es erst einmal besser machen sollen." Das ist durchaus kein Einwand, sondern eine unsachliche Erwiderunq. Erwidern ist überhaupt nicht wichtig, denn die bestmöglichen Antworten wissen wir im allgemeinen zu geben. Wichtig ist lediglich die ständige Verbesserung des Blätters, die Heranziehung der besten Köpfe in Literatur und Politik.[47]

TRANSLATION: In any case Theile's article on the Scandanavian folk schools lacks modesty. Rukser never let that happen. He is accused of only moralizing instead of facing problems square on. In general one can always

---

47 Letter from Kaskell to Rukser, Feb. 15, 1944.

say that every politician wants to pull us in his direction, while the non-politicians want to make us a purely literary magazine. Sometimes I also hear evaluations like "not interesting enough" and "wrong sentiment." Virtually every critique has something correct in it. In a sense they show us the cliffs which we should try to circumnavigate. In an absolute sense, I don't regard the task as difficult. It is namely interesting, of literary merit, political but not of a single party. The most important negatives appear to be 1. the insurmountable distance between Chile, as the production center and the United States, which on the one side is the focus of activities and on the other side should deliver a significant readership. 2. Our financial limitations…Soon I'll send you the critique of style of a friend of mine. Kindly take issue 11, page, 3rd sentence: "The reliability of this sentence is …" Also the idiomatic expression, "experienced… conscious and reaching deeply" in the next paragraph is not good. What Theile had to say concerning the influence on style due to working with foreign languages, is correct. However, it also indicates that at the same time the ability to use stylistically correct language can be regained thorough practice. Frequently we are faulted for concerning ourselves with such "old camels" as Incorporation State. So now that is enough about criticism.—-I hope that you will never write me again that first the "others should do it better." That is in no way an excuse, but rather a subjective reply. Replying is absolutely not important, for in general we know the best possible answers to give. The only thing of importance here is the ongoing improvement of the leaves, the attraction of the finest minds in literature and politics.

The *DB* sometimes unknowingly misinformed its readers which, understandably, brought consternation and quick responsive criticism in those tense times. Günther Lederer, who lived in Valparaiso was among those who were incorrectly informed about the death of Romain Rolland in 1943. The *DB* had stated that Rolland died in a concentration camp a victim of the Nazis. After learning that Rolland actually died on December 30, 1944, the incensed Dr. Lederer wrote the following to Theile:

Wenige Stunden nach unserem Gespräch über Romain Rolland

brachten die hiesigen Zeitungen die Nachricht von dessen am 30. vor. Mts. Erfolgten natürlichen Tod, und zwar mit so unverkennbaren Merkmalen der Echtheit, daß die im September 1943 publizierte Meldung wohl als widerlegt gelten kann und ich nicht mehr daran zweifle, daß Sie trotz aller Nachforschungen damals das Opfer einer ganz gewöhnlichen Greuellüge geworden sind. Das ist umso schmerzlicher, als die in ihr enthaltenen Anschuldigungen eine besonders verabscheuungswürdige Untat zum Gegenstand haben, die gerade bei dem geistig höher stehenden Leser (der aber leider keineswegs immer zwischen Nazis und Deutschen schlechthin einen Unterschied macht) unverschönlichen Hass zu nähren geeignet ist. Vielleicht mag man darüber diskutieren können, ob es Sache der "D.B."sei, den Hass gegen die Nazis zu schüren —durchaus undiskutabel wird dies aber, wenn es mit Hilfe von Greuellügen geschieht, wobei die Gutgläubigkeit in die Echtheit derartiger Meldungen keine Rolle spielt. Nicht aIlein, daß solches nun in der Tat dem sonstigen Niveau der "D.B." nicht entspräche, sondern es müsste auch die Achtung vor dem übrigen Inhalt und seinen Verfassern beeinträchtigen, wenn der Eindruck entstände, die Zeitschrift bediene sich bedenkenlos verächtlicher Propagandamethoden, wie sie heutzutage leider zu den überall gebräuchlichen Mitteln der Kriegsfürung gehören.[48]

TRANSLATION: A few hours after our conversation about Romain Rolland the local newspapers brought the news of his ensuing natural demise on the 30th of last month. And, indeed, with such unequivocal characteristics of authenticity, that the announcement published in September, 1943, can unquestionably be regarded as refuted, and I will cease to doubt that inspite of all the research at the time you were the victim of a common detestable lie. It is even more painful since the subject of the accusations is a loathesome outrage, which with more intellectual readers (This unfortunately in no way always only makes a difference between Nazis and Germans) tends to nourish unmasked hate. Perhaps we can dicuss this, If it is the role of the *DB* to incite hatred against the Nazis—This becomes completely nondebatable, however, if it takes place with the help of detestable lies, where the believability in the truth of this

---

48 Letter from Günther Lederer to A. Theile, January 3, 1945.

kind of announcement plays no role. Indeed it is not only that such does not correspond to the level of the *DB*, but also it must influence the attention given to the rest of the contents and the writers if the impression occurs that the magazine thoughtlessly employs loathesome propaganda methods which unfortunately today belong to the common methods of conducting war.

The *Deutsche Blätter*, as has been observed, was genally well-received by discriminating readers; in spite of criticism and the other problems subscriptions increased. According to Theile the number of monthly issues grew from a beginning 2,OOO to approximately 5,000 during the last years, depending on the number requested by prisoners of war in the USA.[49] These figures are disputed. Joseph Kaskell has stated that the total number of subscriptions in the states never exceeded 1,000[50]. The Verzeichnis der Bezieher (subscription list) has approximately 1,600 subscribers including many universities, magazines and instutions in the USA. Unless the number of subscribers among the POW's was unusually high, it seems that the figure of 5,000 is exaggerated.

---

49 A. Theile, "Vorwort," op. cit., p. 5.
50 R.P. Vander Heide's Interview with Joseph Kaskell, April 6, 1974

Chapter IV

The German Problem—Historical View

SEVERAL YEARS AGO, while studying and teaching foreign languages, I came across a perceptive comment on being German in John LeCarre's *The Little Drummer Girl*. Alexis is speaking of various countries and cultures. Below I offer you her words, which I have shared with students since that day:

> In my next life I shall be a Jew or a Spaniard or an Eskimo or just a fully committed anarchist like everybody else, Alexis decided. But a German I shall never be—You do it once as a penance and that's it. Only a German can make an inaugural out of a dead Jewish child.

The above is not quite accusatory of warmongering; however, one primary element of the lust for war is expanded—the constant lambasting of the Jew. The Dutch hint at another aspect when occasionally they describe their fellow tribesmen of northern Europe as *Kuddevolk* or *Herrenvolk* (both refer to **herd people** who, like sheep, follow the strongest among them). The *Deutsche Blätter* scrutinized all elements (as determined by the co-publishers and contributors to the magazine) of the universally recognized *German problem*, which can perhaps best be defined as Germany's responsibility for repeated disruptions in Europe between the era of Bismarck and World War II.[51] The *DB* viewed

---

51 Friedrich Wilhelm Foerster, an adamant critic of his native Germany, has defined the problem concisely in *Europe and the German Question* (New York: Scheed and Ward, 1940), pp.3-4. Foerster refuses to accept rationalizations of Germany's behavior. He explains that because he loves her, he must be realistic and hard. "Prusso-German responsibility for the

the problem as complex with no single solution; therefore, different possible explanations of the problem and ways to deal with it were examined.[52] Articles

---

present state of Europe began about 1866," he writes, and continues:

> Certainly the other nations are not better than the Germans, but their defects and vices are of another order. Nor do all nations reach their moral nadir contemporaneously. The vice of modern Germany is militarism, a deification of war and its supposed blessings, unqualified belief in force, and contempt for international law. And for this reason Germany was guilty of the World War. That guilt can be questioned by no one who sincerely seeks the truth, has genuine knowledge of pre-war Germany, and has studied the relevant documents. Germany's guilt strikes us in the face. The proofs of it are clear and convincing. Indeed they are so plain that to cover them up has required the determination to lie at all costs and a crusade of lies financed by millions of marks. Other nations besides Germany have sinned. But Germany has made of her sin a new biology, a new religion, or as an American writer has expressed it, "a philosophy of the earth spirit," which cynically rejects all the achievements of the past two thousand years."

The *DB* was too conciliatory to accept fully Foerster's harshness. Rukser quoted in the first issue of the journal, which brought a quick reaction from Joseph Kaskell. Rukser and Kaskell exchanged letters concerning Foerster's views on June 1, 1943, June 24, 1943; and May 10, 1943. They feared that Foerster might hinder constructive postwar progress of Germany toward democracy. The correspondence does not mention other works on Pan-Germanism such as Roland G. Usher's *Pan-Germanism* (New York: Grosset and Dunlap, 1914) or Mildrred S. Wertheimer's *The Pan-German League 1890-1914* (New York: Columbia University, 1924).

52 The *DB's* broad definition of the *German Problem* is similar to the concept of Koppel S. Pinson as clarified in his *Modern Germany , Its History and Civilization* (New York: The MacMillan Company, 1954), pp. 1-2:

> Germany has been a problem not only for the world at large; it has also been a problem for Germans themselves. Among no other people, with the possible exception of the Jews, has there been so much speculaton, so much painful thinking on the why and wherefore of being and on the "essence" of Germanism. "It makes me miserable," said Goethe, "to think of the German people. They are valuable as individuals, but hopeless as a whole."...Germany has become a world problem particularly during the last century. Today (1954) it is still destined to occupy a central role in the politics of Europe and the world for generations to come. The advent of National socialism in 1933 in particular made the problem of Germany one of universal concern and gave rise to varied and conflicting theories regarding German mentality, German national character, and German social structure. Cataclysmic and magical interpretations of German history have been particularly abundant. The Marxist-Leninist theory of the "last stagesof capitalism," the Freudian interpretation of a nation of paranoiacs; the "fruits of Versailles," all have been invoked to provide oversimplification and monistic explanations of the so-called German Problem. While these theories have much to offer in highlighting certain aspects of German behavior, none are adequate without the long-range factor of historical, mental, biological

concerning the subject fall into thematic groupings, three of which will be considered below.

One group of articles emphasizes the historical cultural contributions of Germany to the civilized world or points to the impeccable moral character of many Germans now trapped in Nazi Germany. Many quotes by eminent Germans remind readers that "good" Germans are in abundance and argue that the so-called evil in the German could be eradicated by proper channeling of the innate good.

A second group of articles analyzes Germany's apparent predilection for causing wars, examines the rise of Hitler, or seeks to explain why National Socialism arose in Germany. It speaks well of these writers at least that they were early on incredulous that a fanatic with a dazzled mind could come to rule their homeland.

A third group of articles examines the educational system of Germany from its beginnings through the nazification and presents plans for a better system in the future; proper education is seen as a means for moral and ethical improvement of the German. In attempting a penetrating study of the *German Problem* the *DB* endeavored to examine all facets of the essence of what had historically comprised both Germany and *Germanness*.

Udo Rukser's *Right or Wrong —My Country* (1 , 1943) is the best of several articles which treat the historical contributions of German culture to the world or emphasize the existence of *good* Germans. *Der Nazistaat ist nicht der Staat der deutschen Menschen* (**The Nazi state is not the country of the German people,** p. 16) the editor writes and argues that the fight against Nazism means the preservation of German spirit and traditions as the basis for a future political solution. One year later an editorial in the first issue of 1944 reminded readers of a principal goal of the *DB: die deutsche kulturelle Überlieferung zu vertreten und lebendig zu erhalten* (**to represent the German cultural traditions and to keep them alive,** p.1). In 1945, in reaction to the harsh decisions of Potsdam, the editors posed the following question which clearly limplied that Germany had a redeeming side to her character: *Glaubt man wirklich, daß ein Volk, das die Weltgeschichte mitgestaltet hat, nur nach seinen dunkelsten Schattenseiten, nur nach seinem letzten Abschaum verurteilt werden darf?* (**Do people really believe that a nation, which helped create the history of the world, should be judged solely by its darkest shadow side, only by its last dregs of society?** 27,1945, p. 4)

An editorial written jointly for the third issue of the *DB* of 1943 states that the just solution of the *German Problem* is the central problem for the future

---

and historical evolution. Physical, environmental, biological and psychological factors all play their role, but the chief reason for Germany's being what she is lies in her history.

of Europe, but the exiled collaborators quote Wolfgang von Goethe to remind readers that evil does not predominate in Germany: *Wo viel Licht* (**light**) *ist, ist auch starker Schatten* (**shadow,** p. 2). On the one hand the Goethean sentence as applied to the Germany of 1943 could be interpreted as a rationalization for Germany's misdeeds. On the other hand, it could serve as a suggestion to the world that Germany was a paradox. she had indeed brought *viel Licht* as evidenced in her enlightened leaders of culture. The editors are emphasizing the importance of a fair solution of the *German Problem* fearing that injustice could lead to more *starke Schatten*.

In addition to such direct references to German contributions to culture, the publishers continually made use of a subtler means of reminding the world of Germany's intellectual and artistic achievements. They published in each issue numerous quotations from famous Germans or essays about them. Goethe was most frequently singled out; Friedrich von Schiller; Friedrich Hölderlin, Gotthold Ephraim Lessing, Wolfgang Amadeus Mozart and many others were also given voice or eulogized. Many names whose talents and deeds will be mentioned as we continue. However, the world need not judge Germany only by her most accomplished and talented citizens; accounts of moral acts of numerous common people also proved that the German conscience still lived.

One of these accounts is a short article, *Brief einer Deutschen* (**Letter from a German Woman** 4, 1943), which recounts the experience of one Gertrud Grünwald with acquaintances who became Nazis. Gertrude courageously rejected their increasingly forceful efforts to convert her to their political persuasion. Who could justly say that all Germans are evil when even average citizens like Gertrud exemplify morality?

Similar accounts of altruism, righteousness and acts of conscience were featured in early issues of the *DB*. Anna Landmann-Steuerwald insisted that equating the German people with Hitler did them a grave injustice, and she listed the actions of several "good doers." Her article *Nach der Verbrecherliste die Gutäterliste* (**Afer the Criminal List, the List of Gooddoers,** 6, 1943) suggests that a List of all good actions by Germans, including the hiding of Jews, be compiled.

In 1946 Steuerwald was still reaffirming her belief that *anständige* (**decent, upstanding**) Germans existed and stuck by her strong position when I met her in 1974. In *Die in der Heimat und Wir* (**Those in the Homeland and Us,** *31,1946)* she argues that there were not only citizens in Germany who exemplified integrity but also a strong resistance movement.

It would be fatuitous to doubt the existence of so-called "good" Germans or to question that Germany had made contributions to civilized culture.

Beethoven, Schiller, Mozart, Kant, Goethe and a couple of Mendelsohns are household words. What probably troubled the reader of the day much more was the image of Germany as a destroyer of culture as a nation unable to live with her neighbors in peace in spite of its music, literature, philosophy, and its good Germans. Gustav Mana in issue seven of 1943 expresses this fear in the following words: *Es ist aber eine Tatsache, daß Deutschland im letzten Jahrhundert wiederholt das Zentrum und der Ausgangspunkt von Angriffskriegen gewesen ist (***It is, nevertheless, a fact that during the last century Germany has repeatedly been the center and initiator of aggressive wars,** *p.4).*

In agreement with Mana, both German and non-German readers had many questions including these salient four: Why did Nazism arise in Germany? When once stamped out could it be reawakened? Can Germany cease to make war and become a properly functioning, peaceful democracy? What is the connection between German industrialists and militarism? How can Germany best be reeducated? Such questions were being discussed earnestly in intellectual circles throughout the world of the war years and were stressed in the work of Theile and Rukser.

The Pan-German question was a hotly disputed issue to which more than one contributor to the *DB* turned his attention, including Friedrich Ballhausen who studied *Die all-deutsche Gefahr* (**Danger of Pan-Germanism**) in the eighth issue of 1944. In a careful delineation of Pan-Germanism, Ballhausen sketches its rise, its goals and its use of Adolf Hitler, whose own party worked according to the principal precepts of Pan-Germanism; he cautions about its possible future buildup. Ballhausen begins by agreeing with Heinz Pol's *The Hidden Enemy* that the background and roots of Nazism have their source in Pan-Germanism, the "most despicable" of the varied manifestations of imperialism and "the breeding pen of Nazism." Pan-Germanism not only gave direction to the development of Prussian militarism, but stood at the head of all nationalistic and chauvinistic tendencies in Germany. The jingoism of the German-Austrian and the German-Bohemian was combined in Pan-Germanism with that of the *Junker* and the magnates of industry and finance. Bismarck kept this latter group in check and during his time it remained without great influence. After his power waned, Pan-Germanism grew, favored by the circumstances of the time. The method of the Pan-Germans was to rule indirectly, to remain behind the scenes. Ballhausen well describes its adherents, who had connived with *Genauwigkeit.*

> *Der alldeutsche Verband war nur eine kleine Elite, die sich hauptsächlich aus akademischen Kreisen rekrutierte, zu denen viele pensionierte Offiziere und Industriele stiessen. Die einen sorgten*

für die Finanzierung und Propaganda, die anderen stellten die Verbindung zum Generalstab, zum aktiven Offizierkorps und wichtigen Ämtern her. Diese aktiven militärischen Kreise haben es sich zum Gesetz gemacht, nicht direct zu regieren, sie wollen die Entwicklung aus dem Hintergrund heraus lenken, ohne öffentlich dafür verantwortlich zu sein (p. 12)

TRANSLATION: The Pan-German organization was only a small elite, who were recruited primarily from academic circles comprised of several retired military officers and industrialists. Some took care of financing and propaganda; others established connections with the general staff, to the officer corps and other important offices. They made it a fast principle, not to rule directly. They wanted instead to develop ties from the background without being official responsible.

At the beginning of the 1920's the Pan-Germans were looking for someone who could stir up and lead a mass movement which could serve their purposes. They flirted with others before finding their man in Hitler, who had confessed his Pan-German inclinations in his autobiography, *Mein Kampf* (**My Struggle or Fight**).

In fact he always highly praised one of his teachers at the Linz Realschule, Dr. Leopold Pötsch, who professed ardent German Nationalism. He was, according to Hitler himself, responsible for Hitler's interest in history. The two of them were aflame with enthusiasm for things German as they sat there in Austria discussing the subject, the rabid professor and the student who could not manage to graduate with an *Abitur* (**school leaving examination**). Instead of earning the "leaving exam," he left the school, and as the saying goes: "The rest is history." Readers who like me have taught high school students will pause a moment to ponder the character and the psyche of Adolf, the teenager, who to me appears to have been a true psychopath.

In order to show that only the agreement of goals and methods gives conclusive proof of what he has explained, Ballhausen cites various quotations from Pan-German sources such as the following from the *Grenzboten* **(Border Messengers)**, a literary magazine of 1896:

Wir lehren, daß wenn das Wohl unseres Landes eine Eroberung, Unterjochung, Verdrängung, Vertilgung fremder Völker fordern

*sollte, wir uns davon durch Christliche oder humanistisches-
gedenken nicht dürfen zurückschrecken lassen.*

TRANSLATION:We teach that if the well-being of our country requires the conquest, suppression, dislodging or expulsion of minority groups, we shall not allow ourselves to be deterred by Christian or humanitarian thinking (p. 13).

That seems pretty clear to me! Such thinking could, also curiously be connected with Christianity, as seen in the following statement by Wilhelm Stapel:

Wenn nun der Germane, der nordische Mensch, seinen Fuss auf den letzten Streifen eroberten Landes gesetzt hat, so nimmt er die Krone der Welt und legt sie Gott zu Füssen, um sich von ihm damit krönen *zu lassen* (p. 13).

TRANSLATION: When the German, the nordic human being has set his foot on the last strip of conquered land, he will take the World Crown and lay it at the feet of God in order to be crowned by Him.

Ballhausen agrees with those who emphasize that the Pan-Germans were a very small group, but he is dismayed, even horrified, that so few could wield so much power. He notes how after World War I the Pan-Germans cleverly worked from two premises. First, they passed the blame for defeat to others; secondly, they immediately began preparing for a new war. Typical of many admonishments given in the *DB*, Ballhausen cautions that, only through awareness of these facts can repetition be avoided. Lest the movement rise again the author recommends *die endgültige Zerschlagung der alldeutschen Zentren im Grossgrundbesitz, in der Schwerindustrie und der Finanzbürokratie (* **The complete destruction of pan-german centers in gross estates, heavy industry and financial burocracy, p. 14)**. The *DB* was still warning about the old evils when Hitler was defeated and the time came for the establishmentof the utopian *new postwar Germany*. In issue twenty-nine of 1946 *Aufruf der S.P.D. für ein neues, besseres Deutschland* (**Call of the German Socialist Party for a New and Better Germany**) by Kurt Schumacher appeared. Here, once again, Germans and readers of the *DB* were admonished that never again in Germany should *Grosskapital* be allowed to have political influence. Clearly meaning the

Pan-Germans and their sympathizers, Schumacher refers to the evil of the *Verderber Deutschlands* (**spoilers of Germany**) and the guilt they must bear, in poignant words:

> *Zur moralischen Gesundung unseres Volkes ist es nötig, ihm zu beweisen, daß jedem Frevel die Sühne folgt. Darum müssen die Verderber Deutschlands vor allen anderen die Folgen des grossen Weltvernichtungskrieges tragen. Niemand von ihnen darf in Staat und Wirtschaft, in Kultur- und Geistesleben eine stellung von Bedeutung einnehmen. Niemand soll aus dem Nazi-deutschland reicher herauskommen als er hineingegangen ist* (p. 60).

TRANSLATION: To achieve the moral health of our people it is necessary to prove to them that every crime is followed by punishment. Therefore, the corrupters of Germany, above all others, have to bear the consequences of the great world-wide war of destruction. None of them may hold a position of significance in government or business, in cultural nor intellectual life. No one should emerge from Nazi-Germany richer than when he entered.

By printing articles such as the above the journal was defining dangers within Germany which could overshadow its cultural contributions. The intellectual German twosome in Chile wrote constantly, and were reading, studying, editing when they were not grinding away at their desks. They went from one subject to another with equal skill and knowledge. They seemed to always be atuned to uncovered sources and potential contributors. At some point they recognized that subtle psychological factors could also play a role in creating a German problem and published articles dealing with the German character and psyche.

What had been the affect of tales of mythical heroes and stories of greatness? Not to mention the frequently referred to *Weltanschauung?* Just the grim tales so diligently collected by The Grimm brothers should give one pause.

What is the psychological composition of the German? How can his behavior best be understood and explained? In *Der Mythos deutscher Unbesiegbarkeit* (**The Myth of German Invincibility** (April, 1944). Major Erwin Lessner elucidated the myth of German invincibility. According to him this myth is worse than the legend of the stab in the back post WW I, and has an insidious affect on the German mind. Thomas Mann, who was appreciative of the *DB* and in agreement with its goals, sent his well known essay *Schicksal und Aufgabe*

*(***Destiny and Task***)* to Kaskell for publication in the *DB*, which Kaskell then forwarded to Chile where it was evaluated as being in harmony with their own conciliatory feelings; it appeared in the seventh issue of 1944. In a letter to Rukser Mann revealed his reasons for writing it:

> *Das Gefühl, daß ich mich über die deutsche Frage wohl nicht auf die Dauer in still schweigen werde hüllen können, sondern daß ich über kurz oder lang mit einem Bekenntnis hervortreten muss, ist mir auch nicht fremd. Ein Anfang in dieser Richtung ist ja gemacht mit der Rede, die kürzlich auf Deutsch als Aufsatz bei Ihnen erschien.*

TRANSLATION: I have a feeling that I can not continue to hide in silence my feelings concerning the German question, but rather sooner or later have to come forth with a statement. I made a beginning with the speech which recently appeared as an essay in your magazine.

In his analysis of the German question Mann considers the responsibility of Germans for the Nazi government as well as the historical political and sociological makeup of Germany. He asks: *Wie weit ist das deutsche Volk in seiner Gesamtheit verantwortlich zu machen für die Untaten der Nazis?* (**To what extent are the German people as a whole responsible for the misdeeds of the Nazis?** P. 3). He answers that the responsibility for Nazi doings cannot be denied because human beings are held responsible for their actions, but Mann ascribes Germany's problems not to crime but to misfortune, error and a historical curse. Germany's case is confusing, he writes, because it is a paradox: *Gutes und Böses, das Schöne und das Verhängnisvolle vermischen (***Good and bad , the beautiful and the fateful intermix** (p. 5). Wagner's art revolution gives us a key to what is German. Wagner, according to Mann, was conerned only with *das Ur-Epischer, das Erste und Einfachster das Vor-Konvenionelle und Vor-Gesellschaftliche* (**the ancient, original epic, the first and most simple, that which is prior to the conventional and the societal**). Only this was proper for art. For the German as a type, he writes: *Das Ungesellschaftlich-Ur-Poetische ist ja sein eigener Mythus, seine typische und grundgegebene nationale Natur, die ihn von anderen europäischen National-Geistern und Typen unterscheidet* (**The unsocietal-original-poetic is indeed its own myth, its typical and national nature which gives it the basis that separates it from other European national identities** (p.6) Mann further explains that the German *Geist* (**intellect,spirit,mind**) is socially and politicaly disinterested. National Socialism is for the German a *mythisches Surrogat* (**mythical surrogate**). Unfortunately the German seeks surrogates instead of solving problems of the times, and he thinks it necessary to throw all morals and humanity overboard when he becomes political. the German misunderstands politics because they are strange to his spirit as a world of absolute cynicism and ...Machiavellianism. In short, Mann sees National Socialism as an example of this overcompensation and the German's ineptness for politics.

The foregoing seems to prove that the German character and National Socialism are inherently and inextricably entwined and Mann reminds us of the humanistic and democratic tendencies operative in German life which have always resisted folksy barbarism and which bind Germany to the western Christian World. We must not forget, he writes, that the Hitler party gained control only through intrigue and terror. Hundreds of thousands of political opponents were placed in concentration camps. It is not the German people who should be destroyed or sterilized Mann advises, but the alliance of *Junkertum, Generalität und Schwerindustrie*. (see p. 29 **aristocratic landowner, German body of generals and heavy industry**) Here Mann is in complete agreement with Ballhausen or Schumacher and the editors of the *DB*. He views National Socialism as a negative, distorted and perverted manifestation of the universalism unique to the character of the German. Basically the German wants to dominate the world, and in earlier times he gained the admiration of the world through dominance of a higher, purer and nobler kind; Mann is referring to intellectual, artistic, and cultural leadership. The author is optimistic and forsees a new humanism rising from the ashes of World War II. Take note of his summary:

> *Ich gIaube, daß aus dem Leiden und Kämpfen unserer schweren Übergangszeit ein ganz neues, gefühlsbetontes Interesse am Menschen und seinem Los, seiner exzeptionellen stellung zwischen den Reichen der Natur und des Geistes, seinem Geheimnis und seiner Bestimung geboren werden wird, ein humanistischer Impuls, der heute schon überall in den besten, der zukunft verbundensten Herzen und Geistern lebt und tätig ist (p. 12).*

TRANSLATION: I believe that from the suffering and fighting of our difficult transition period a completely new interest in mankind and his lot will be born based on sensitivity and recognition of his exceptional position between the richness of nature and of spirit, of his secret and his destination...a humanistic impuls, which these days

lives and is active in the best hearts and spirits bound with the future.

Mann's S*chicksal und Aufgabe* (**Destiny and Task**) is similar to another of his essays, *Deutschland und die Deutschen*, written in 1945. In both he insists that the German is an "inward person"..really? One of my most respected professors insisted that the German functioned best under foreign hegemony due to this "inwardness." So, other students of Germany would agree with Mann. I find it to be true at least for those who come from northern Germany as did Mann himself, who ventures deeper analysis in claiming that his people are more fit for music than for understanding politics.

The German longs for companionship. Therefore, after the war he could become a diligent worker for the cause of European cooperation. There were those who felt that Mann was far too severe with his own people in some of his utterances and speeches including *Schicksal und Aufgabe*. Again, I believe readers should decide that for themselves, but when considering his California days, I always conjure up an image of Mann dressed in a three-piece suit sitting on his patio in Pacific Palisades, California, pen in hand, gazing at the Pacific Ocean toward all those military forces thousands of miles to the West who were being killed as representatives of their governments, while this patrician gentleman was about to join whatever dignitaries and celebrities who were on hand for lunch.

Herbert Lehnert has shown that Bertolt Brecht repeatedly attacked Mann for his lack of compassion for the Germans. However, careful perusal of Mann's essay reveals hope for the future of Germany and the Germans. Perhaps Lehnert is correct in deciding that Brecht's scanty reading of Mann led to a misunderstanding.

Karl O. Paetel, who frequently wrote for the *DB* contributed a further analysis of the German soul. He too sought reasons for German susceptibility to Hitler's ideas. In *Der Führer* (8, 1944) Paetel observes that historically the German has proved himself to be endowed with a peculiar affinity for subjective truths. He neither carefully studies two sides of an issue in the manner of the Anglo-Saxon nor possesses the realistic political cynicism of the French. *Der Deutscher*, we are told *nimmt alles tierisch Ernst, was ihm mit Intensität nahegebracht wird* (**The German takes with extreme earnestness everything that is intensively brought close to him p. 16**). Paetel sees this as the real source of conflict in the German soul and observes that Hitler recognized this trait in his countrymen. The ambiguity of his politics and his *Weltanschauung*, were resolved in *Intensität*.

In *Die Wollust des Gehorchens* (**The Joy of Obeying**).Werner Bock, writing from Buenos Aires for the March/April issue of 1946, examined the German joy in obeying which, he says, may lead the average German to accepting rule by evil as was the case with the Nazis. Bock believes that finding pleasure in obeying has always been a characteristic peculiar to the German and quotes Gustav Freytag's observation that the first word of the German language was brought to Germany from Rome some two hundred years B.C. It was the old Germanic word for *Beamter* and connoted a friendly, servile attitude to the Romans, that of the servant to his master. Bock writes that the sense in which the German has been bound to this word is significant for his *Gemüt* (**disposition or well-being**), and his history. He lists various versions of the word; including *ambactus*, Gothic *ambahts*, meaning **follower**, *anbahti, ambet, Amt*, thus hoping to prove that the German has always been a good servant. Discussions and debates could be motivated by the above food for thought.

Bock made a good choice in quoting Gustav Freytag who in living from 1816 to 1895 experienced the growing strength of his homeland which he chronicled in a lengthy novel, *Soll und Haben* (**Debit and Credit**) published in 1855. In this well-known novel Freytag acclaims the enterprising spirit and perservering dedication of North German merchants. The work deserves our attention because in glorifying the *deutsche Bürgertum* (**bourgeoisie, middle class**) and even the *Spiessbürgertum* (**the raw elements of the bourgeoisie**) this novelist of "artistic realism" has given us an interesting and useful picture of the culture of the early nineteenth century which is the all important background for this study of the *DB* because Dr. Ruckser and his associates perceived that these traits could lead to what indeed was to come.

Freytag's middle class folk, strong, honest and growing in power are ripe and ready to launch WWI. Perhaps they were bored with fighting just against Europeans and neighboring countries. This war stuff was getting to be more and more fun when more literary foreshadowing came In 1862 in *Bilder aus der deutschen Vergangenheit* (**Pictures from the German Past**) at the time when Germany was focusing on the establishment of a Second Reich, Freytag undertook to collect historical and literary works to which he added commentary and published, resulting in word paintings of the good German folk and their *raison d'etre*, admirable and wholesome like no others.

Hopefully, our occasional digressions and tangential commentary lead to deeper understanding of the big picture and the happenings which resulted in launching the admired periodical. History could be defined as connected connections. This event caused that event which in turn is related to or an outcome or cause of another war, crash of a government leading to….on and on; all change changes. Let us now return to the insights and information of the *DB* pieces.

However biased and over-simplified they may be, the articles outlined above represent a sampling of psychological studies of the German and explanations of his behavior. The *DB* thus gave its readers some perceptive insights into the German character; the thesis emerges that understanding is a prerequisite to change. It is logical that educational reform was recommended by many intellectuals of the day as the ideal means for effecting amelioration.

Education is examined historicaly, compared to the systems of other countries, and proposed by some writers as the solution to the German Problem. Young Germans could be molded to work for peace and harmony among nations; older Germans could be reeducated to strive for similar ends. Glorification of military feats, insistence on the subordination of Europe to Germany, and ethnocentric worship of the German should be eliminated from the schools.

The position of the *Blätter* concerning education and the responsibility of the state is proclaimed in the first issue of the magazine. A quote on *Erziehung* (rearing, education) by Adalbert Stifter is compared to a note entitled *Erziehung im dritten Reich* in the *Kulturchronik* (**cultural chronicle**) section of the periodical in a letter to Joseph Türk of April 26, 1849, Stifter observed that nations too often neglect proper education: *Das arme Erziehungswesen! Der Sündenstuhl seit zweitausend Jahren!* (**poor old education! the dunking chair for 2,000 years.**) The Nations have no money for preventive education against war, but there is plenty of money for war itself, which costs much more. Stifter expresses the following heartfelt conviction; *daß nämlich Erziehung die erste und heiligste Pflicht des Staates ist* (**namely education is the first and holiest duty of countries p. 26**).

As I wrote above, to give background information on the many contributors to the *DB* is daunting and, of course, beyond the scope and purpose of this study, but Adalbert Stifter (1805-1868), another writer too often neglected in his day, continues to receive too little attention. Yet, these perceptive sentiments on education are typical of his insights and understanding of the human condition. It is not an exaggeration to label this lover of nature, instructed in his early years by Benedictine Monks, as the "Genius of Austria," whose body of work reflects his pious devotion to God and man, sentiments fostered by communication with nature when he contemplated the pulchritude of his native Bohemia in its humble forms of minerals, plants and animals, lush mountainsides, meadows, rivers and lakes. Far from Nazism was Stifter, the incarnation of God lay all around him in the nuances of weather, in the shapes and colors of minerals, in the changing blue of a rushing river, in an animal mother nurturing her offspring. For Stifter these simple manifestations of life, beauty and nature became an observable incarnation of the Godhead. No wonder our *DB* personnel were eager to include pieces by him.

Wallace Deuel's account of Nazi judges removing children from the jurisdiction of their parents and giving them to the state for a so-called proper education contrasts sharply with Stifter's ideas, According to one Nazi judge children must be taken from parents who fail to teach their offspring responsibility to the state and subservience to its authority. As distasteful as this article is, the reader learns that the Nazi state was aware of its duty to educate the young; it knew the importance of controlling minds. The *DB* was implying that postwar Germany should be equally concerned with education for peaceful ends,stressing the thought that *nicht alle probleme lasen sich durch Erziehung Lösen, aber keins ohne Erziehung,*(**not all problems are solved through education, but none is solved without it.**) Theile recounted his personal experiences with Danish *Volkshochschulen.* in issue eight of 1943 as a substantiation of thoughts on education written by Rukser for the fourth issue of the same year; he had expressed a conviction that a *Volkshochschule* could contribute to a victory over Nazism.

Theile begins by explaining that the first Scandinavian *Volkhochschulen* established by the Dane, Nicolaj Frederick Severin Grundtvig, after Denmark lost a war to Prussia and Austria in 1864. Grundtvig convinced his nation that the only way to overcome the defeat was through *geistige Mittel.* (moral—educative means) His goal was to achieve political and social equality through moral and intellectual education. The editor writes that there is much to be learned for the future of Germany through study of the Scandinavian experience. Henotes, however, that some lessons may also serve as a warning. *Man tat alles, die persönliche Neigung, die unterschiedliche Begabung zu entwickeln, doch musste sie, entfaltet, der Allgemeinheit dienen* (p. 2 **One tried everything to develop personal inclinations and unique talents; however, once developed they were required to serve the public**). There were parties and festivities, but here also the *Kollektive Wirken* (**collective outcome**) was most important. Theile notes, obviously very much aware of the sobriety of the German schools of his day, that in the future reform of the educational system in Germany this *unterhaltende Seit*e (**the non-academic side, "entertaining"**?) must be considered.

The warning for the Germans mentioned above lies in noting the splits which developed in Denmark. Grundtvig based his schools on two sources: Christianity and Danish Nationalism. Followers of Rudolf Steiner's anthroposophy emphasized only the Christian aspects of Grundtvig's schools and established their own *Volkshochschulen.* Another group in Denmark favored purely humanistic schools. In further splinter developments, international schools were established to oppose Grundtvig's nationalism.

Theile himself founded a *Volkshochschule* with the help and advice of Norwegian friends. His kind of wirklich freie Schule seemed to him most suited for working youths, such as are found in Germany, because it meets the needs of the student for a well-rounded orientation and deepening of his education without taking him out of the working force and so removing his source of income. How different are the methods of free discussion and spontaneity of the Volkshochschulen from the forceful suppressive ways of the Nazis. A variation of the school suited for Germans could be an important tool of reeducation. The editor sees much value in using this type of school for the fifteen to thirty age group which had suffered most *from Nazi-Erziehung*. He emphasizes that he views *diese skandinavische Volkserziehung für einen der wichtigsten Bausteine des künftigen Europas. für Deutschland ist diese Methode wie keine andere geeignet denn sie, und ich glaube nur sie kann etwas fördern, was die Nazis bewusst unterdrückt haben die schöpferische Spontanität.* (**this Scandanavian folk education as one of the most important building blocks of the future Europe. For Germany this method, like no other, is suited to accomplish something which Nazi educators have purposely omitted, creative spontaneity, p.4**)

A change in the teaching of history in Germany was advocated by Heinrich Berlin writing from Mexico for the May/June issue of 1945. In his article, *Gedanken zum Geschichtsunterricht* (**Thoughts on the Teaching of History**), he explains that history, as normally taught in Germany, stresses that the nation experienced its greatest territorial expansion under Henry III and then slowly watched it shrink. Germany's lowest period came after the humiliation by Napoleon. Berlin remarks that during the period after Napoleon, Goethe and Beethoven were making contributions to culture which would last even if Germany were destroyed. This fact, he states, is ignored in history classes in Germany.

Berlin asserts that extolling territorial gains and stressing past humiliations can only lead to the most harmful nationalism. Quoting Jakob Burckhardt and Wilhelm von Humboldt, he asks for a new writing of German history which would teach world history with the proper perspective on Germany within the greater world picture. If world history were taught first, and then German history, no dangerous nationalistic thinking would result, Berlin informs us, because Germany would simply fit into the existing *Weltbild* (world view). Such a method of presenting history would lead Germans to think of a European humanity and act according. It would also be good for other nations that are teaching history from a nationalistic point of view.

Rukser's sympathy with Berlin's evaluation is evident in a letter he wrote to Ernst Alker in 1946 in which he expands the said report to include an international alignment of all university courses: *Wird es möglich sein, in absehbarer Zeit zu einer mehr internationalen Ausrichtung des Universitätslebens zu kommen? Oder wird man mehr auch den Jammer der Autarkie erleben?*[53] (**Will it be possible in the forseeable future to take a more international direction with universities? Or will we experience more wailing of autarchy?**)

Anna Landmann-Steuerwald was convinced that assurance of world peace lay in education for nonviolence. In issue twenty-nine of 1945 she opened her article, *Erziehung zur Gewaltlosigkeit* (**Education for Nonviolence**) with the following idealistic premise: *daß durch Erziehung—und nur durch diese—der Weltfriede gesichert werden kann, daüber ist man sich einig"* (**Everyone agrees that world peace can only be assured through education—and only education**, p. 27). In building her case for educating people for nonviolence, she confronts the counterargument that it is only through force that the spirit of barbarism can be successfully supressed. Steuerwald believes that only a new war can arise from such *militanter Pazifismus*. How, she asks, can a warlike. generation rear a new peace-loving generation to follow it?

Steuerwald has some discerning insights; she insists that education for change must begin before birth and alerts readers to the importance of toys, games and forms of punishment administered in German schools. Observing that *nomen est omen*, she writes that pacifist parents would not choose war-like names such as Sieghart and Gerlinde for their offspring. She would abolish lead soldiers and tanks from children's play and would have us follow the example of both Montessori and Rudolph Steiner schools which had banned toys considered to be psychologically harmful. Steuerwald is most opposed to toy guns and the war games which take place under the Nazi system of education. Games such as the storming of fortresses not only glorify violence she warns, but also have resulted in dead children.Continuing her argument for nonviolence the author censures one of the worst sins of the German schools, the *Prügelstrafe* (**corporal punishment**...administered with teutonic intensity) which can only teach violence. German educators seemed to delight in administering such!

In her appeal for a general reform of the school system Steuerwald championed "*die Wiederherstellung des sozial-ethisch wertvollen Einflusses von Familie, Jugendpflege und Jugendbewequng*" (**the reestablishment of worthwhile social-ethical influence of family, care of youth and a youth movement**, p. 29).This is just as necessary, she writes, as the purification of the schools from the "*Ungeist des Nazismus*" (**intellectually lacking Nazism**). She closes her article with a reminder that education for nonviolence must not be interpreted

---

53 Letter from U. Rukser to E. Alker, November 19, 1946.

as education for spiritlessness, but as education for self-responsibility and self-discipline; the emphasis on *self* is vital.

From Richmond, Virginia, Curt Bondy added more thoughts on education in *Erziehungsarbeit im neuen Deutschland* (**The Task of Education in the New Germany, 31, 1946)** in which he expresses satisfaction at the appearance of Hermann Nohl's magazine, *Die Sammlung* (**compilation or collection**), in Göttingen in the British zone. Nohl stated the purpose of his periodical succinctly: "*Unsere Zeitschrift will dem Wiederaufbau unseres Volkes dienen, seiner Kultur und insbesondere seiner neuen Erziehung*" (**Our magazine will serve the reconstruction of our people, their culture and especially the new education**, p. 23). Several leading educators welcomed the journal as a vehicle for contributing their ideas for reforming of education in Germany.

Bondy feared what might happen if the liberal and democratic forces in Germany were not successful in effecting the drastic school reform measures being debated. Two salient problems this reform advocate recognized were, first, the weakness of Germany and secondly, the advanced age of many German educators. Much help from the Allies will be needed, he says, in order to aid destroyed Germany in the improvement of its educational system. He was cognizant, of course, at the time of writing that proper nutrition and adequate shelter were more important to the German people than education. Furthermore, it had already become evident that youth did not wish to be led by older people. For Bondy proof of this was the rejection by students of pastor Niemoeller's appeal that all Germans accept responsibility for the evil deeds of the Nazis. He insists that reform must come from within Germany, led by the young and assisted by the Allies. Repeated ad infinitum by others in the German *Blätter* was Bondy's goal, *Erziehung zum Weltbürgertum*, (**education for worldwide citizenship**, p. 27).

Friedrich Ballhausen's discussion of *The Next Germany* referred to earlier (6, 1944) focuses much attention upon the theme, *Education for a New Society*. He observes that *neutrale Erziehung*, is neither fish nor fowl; the educator must have in mind a goal to which he is committed. The book advocates a system of education founded on social justice. For Ballhausen such a utopian thought is not hopeless if German youth will become aware of it and accept it. Fritz Meyning (pseudonym of Fritz Siegel) in *Das deutsche problem von England aus gesehen* (**The German Problem seen from England**, 8, 1944) reviews a private report on Germany published in England. The hope of the British report is to effect a change in the German mentality and argues that Germans must learn that political leaders who know no scruples in dealing with foreign nations will also have fewer scruples in dealing with their own people. The report calls for punishment as part of the postwar reeducation without forgetting that the very best factor for effecting change is cooperation with other nations.

Rukser was also interested in *Arbeitsdienst* (**work [community] service**) as a means for change. He was, of course, familiar with Nazi use of *Arbeitsdienst* and knew such service would have to be cleansed of Nazi influence. He wrote to Kaskel On June 11, 1943: *Vom international Labour Office bekam ich einen sehr freundlichen Brief mit einer guten Broschüre über den Arbeitsdienst in Bulgarien. Man teilt mit, daß bisher kein anderes Land den obligarischen Dienst eingeführt habe ausser den Totalitären.* (**He received a brochure on work service projects in Bulgaria and informs that only the totalitarian states have this obligatory service**). And where it exists, he adds, it is nothing more than a form of taxation for the construction or repair of roads. Well, we could observe, so far so good for he continues:

Daraus kann man ja nach dem Krieg genug brauchen. Nur muss man der Sache, das Nazi-Aroma nehmen. Also, es wäre gut, darüber bald etwas Konstruktives zu bringen. (**OK, after the war enough of such service will be needed. It is just that one has to take the Nazi-aroma out of the program Furthermore, it would be good to bring something constructive out of this right away**) The *DB* never carried much on this topic in spite of Rukser's urging. However, as always in the exiled publication, quality and depth were appreciated as was the writing which warrant some final thoughts on the foregoing analyses of the aspects of the *German problem* published in the *DB*.

Already, we have noted that the editors did not underestimate the complexity of the problem. They emphasized that there were *good Germans* and never ceased to remind readers of German cultural accomplishments. Essays, articles, and short quotations which delved into the history of Germany and explored the depths of the German psyche tried to account for outbursts of violence and war. Leading German intellectuals as well as foreigners considered sociological, historical ard psychological factors in an attempt to explain the paradoxical light and dark sides of the nation's character.

Contributors to the *DB* pleaded for understanding for the problems of Germany, and warnings were voiced concerning possible vitriolic reprisals. Education was viewed as a solution to the *German Problem*, but the question of education itself was many-faceted. Re-education of Germans of the day was deemed vital, and programs for the education of future generations of Germans proposed. The magazine could not have been more diligent in its search to understand the German problem thoroughly, groping for *just* solutions and pleading with all nations to reject *unjust* proposals. They looked to Dr. Fritz Karsen to lead the educational reform.

Karsen, who was born in Breslau in 1885, began his educational career in

Berlin as a secondary school teacher. He drew attention to himself as a potential national educational leader and reformer when in 1920, at the National School Conference in Germany, the young Karsen presented a paper, outlining his concept of the *Einheitsschule* (**unified primary school**), which proposed the mixing of social classes, and advocating self-paced learning. Both changes were at the most revolutionary and at the least challenging eye-openers in this nation where students stood when the teacher entered the classroom. Notably, in today's democratic Germany, behaviors of teachers and students have been virtually reversed. Now, it seems students are in charge.

Karsen was promulgating these changes at a time when Germans were becoming increasingly disgruntled with their new Weimar Republic and wondering how they would find the funds, some thirty-three billion dollars, assessed by the Allied Reparations Committee, to cover the costs of WWI. Any thinking person should have found the demands strangling. Fortunately Karsen could continue with his reforms aimed, really, at producing a new kind of German who would be kind and love all mankind. Well...The Weimar stipulations did not foster the same. Karsen ploughed ahead. He could not know where the *Kapp Putsch* and all the other distruptions were heading, although he got the point along the way, leading to the hour when the Nazis dismissed him. He immediately fled to France to be principal of a boarding school.

Dr. Karsen was the father of Sonja P. Karsen, a scholar of languages and the department of languages chairperson at Skidmore College, who hired me as the replacement for Ernst Waldinger, another of the exiled Germans. These individuals, who were uprooted so suddenly and violently, were happy just to be away from the control of true evil. They helped each other willingly, ignoring the formal norms of the homeland society with its different social levels and establishing friendships and associations that never would have taken place had their lives continued in the cultural patterns they were accustomed to. Joseph Kaskel, for example, helped Karl Paetel with finances for years. In the USA even the most well-known among the emigrants commonly were unable to have household help, secretaries and other assistance. Was this the beginning here in the states of the democratization of Germany?

The lure of diverging is tempting and informative; so many stories can be told. Any single individual among the uprooted Germans warrants a book detailing his life. It is difficult to resist. However, for now Dr. Karsen merits further attention..

His major achievement during this period was the organization and direction, 1921–33, of a school complex (from kindergarten through secondary school), the Karl Marx School in Berlin-Neukoelln. He introduced various new procedures in these schools, such as individualized instruction, pupil government, and *activity method* (Theile's *entertainment* concept…additions to "book learning") Karsen undertook study trips to the U.S. and the U.S.S.R. His plans for an elaboration of his school organization to include young people aged 18 to 19 were halted by the advent of the Nazis. In 1933 Karsen left Germany, directed a school in France and settled permanently in New York, where he became professor of German at City College and professor of education at Brooklyn College. From 1946 to 1948, Karsen served as higher education specialist in the U.S. military government in Germany.

The recognition of his educational work in Germany was commemorated by the establishment of the Fritz Karsen School in Berlin. Karsen's main writings include *Die Schule der werdenden Gesellschaft* (**The School of the Nascent Society,** 1921), *Deutsche Versuchsschulen der Gegenwart und ihre Probleme* (**Present day German Experimental Schools,** 1923), and *Die neue Schulen in Deutschland* (**The New Schools in Germany,** 1924), which he edited. He obliged the government of Ecuador by accepting their request to direct a thorough reform of the educational system, but tragically died in Guayaquil in 1951, depriving the world of his skill at preparing youth for a well-rounded, democratic based education.

We observe how the exiles knew each other, organized, and worked together to return home, although most never did. The USA and other nations benefitted greatly from the "brain drain" from Germany and the contributions that those brains made to our culture in all fields of human endeavor. We can not in this study delve deeply into this, but readers may, and just to get you started and because it is so intricately related to the *Blätter*, I will tease you with just a little information of what awaits you. To name only a few of the hundreds, if not thousands in just one field, think of what Billy Wilder, Peter Lorre (those bug eyes!), Kurt Weil who worked with Bertolt Brecht ("Oh, Mackie Messer….") or Marlene Dietrich (that voice and those legsl) did for the American cinema industry.

Chances are good that readers did not associate the above names with the refugee group. A towering figure among them all in a far different field is Albert Einstein, and let us not forget Edward Teller, an atomic bomb builder. Perhaps the guy next door who became foreman at your place of work belongs to the emigrant movement.

I have informed you about some New York connections, but a high number went to California, which to most was America, period, so why settle elsewhere? With that thought in mind, we can return to the film industry for memory jarring and a little more enticement.

Hedy Lamarr (b. Hedwig Eva Maria Kiesler), a rather busty girl from

Vienna, belongs to the group as do composers (that great movie background music) Arnold Schoenberg, Frederick Kohner, Franz Waxman, Kurt Weil (mentioned above in connection with Brecht), Max Reinhardt and his incomparably talented protégé, Erich Wolfgang Korngold (a child prodigy, well on his way at age 13). Some talents arrived on American shores from Great Britain, including Christopher Isherwood and Evelyn Waugh. Some would say Ernst Lubitsch was the greatest of the directors while others would opt for Billy Wilder, although Fred Zinnemann might not agree. It would be very easy to believe that he considered his own directing to be the finest, and equally easy to agree with him.

Zinnemann directed what has come to be recognized by so many in the world of cinema as the all-time best western film, *High Noon*. I was fifteen when it hit Ogden, Utah, in 1952. Oh, my, it was something. Did not all young men want to become Marshal Will Kane (Gary Cooper) and safeguard Hadleyville? I hear the music now: "Oh don't forsake me, O, my darlin'..."It was Tex Ridder in the movie, but I preferred Frankie Laine singing Dimitri Zinovich Tiomkin's composition. And there we have another incredibly talented musician, who was an old bar-hopping friend of Serge Prokofiev in their St. Petersburg days. He studied in France and Germany and wrote music for the whole range of movie genres, *film noir* to romance, adventure to westerns. Hitler did not get too many of this type.

And the girls? Who would want, the ultra-reserved, prissy Quaker, Amy Fowler (Grace Kelly), when the sultry, unreserved and sexy Helen Ramirez (Katy Jurado), was available? Had she not been recently rejected by Kane who quickly married Amy? Kane was anguished, if not downright afraid. The two Miller brothers were coming with two other toughs. Amy did not believe in killing, and Helen was always sort of lurking around, three problems there. Both women board the train to head for safety.

And, never, as we all know, never should a movie marshal of the Old West exhibit a morsel of fear. He kept it in check. Thank God, for it was not easy, but "the Coop" still had it in him and dispatched two of them, but gets wounded. Amy, disregards her beliefs, leaves the train and shoots another in the back, but Frank takes her hostage. She struggles giving the marshal a clear shot, and Frank is history. Kane contemptuously throws his badge in the dirt.

Then, without putting more bullets in the corpses (I had seen movies in which those mean guys miraculously suddenly rose up with a weapon) the unwise marshal, who had his mind only on Amy I suppose, drove off with the pious bride, now a murderer, looking demure, at his side on the buckboard while Ritter sang: "On this our wedding day..ay." Did not the lucious Helen, in spite of being somewhat overweight, run after them for a ways? I suspect that Helen, as did I, could perceive that the marriage was not going to pan out. Kane, of all people, should have exercised better judgment.

He should have had the wound attended to. Also I note two more screw-ups, first no extra bullets for the Miller gang, just in case, and now at age 50 embarking upon married life with Amy, about age 20. Surely, Will, at his age, had an ex-wife somewhere, but I do not remember. This could cause him more problems, but the good people of Hadleyville were safe from Frank, the personification of pure evil.

Like it or not, surely all viewers recognize the genius of Zinnemann, the emigrant director, and appreciate that the producer, Stanley Kramer, perceived how talented, even gifted, he was. It was the Zinnemann's of this world and Tiomkens that the *DB* too acknowledged and wanted to save at that time and forever. Humanism throughout the world was the objective. How did Zinnemann, child prodigy from Austria, even know how to begin a Hollywood Western, especially a top rated one? This is most intriguing. Did he read Karl May?

Some 800 persons in the movie industry alone, counting cast, crews, set makers, designers and all fled from Nazism.

The war ended in May of 1945, but the Allied Powers were now confronted with a changed *German Problem* or, as Chapter Five is entitled, *New Aspects*. Is identifying, encountering and solving new elements a never ending requirement for dealing with Germany?

Chapter V

The *German Problem*—New Aspects

With the end of World War II in sight new aspects of the *German Problem* were brought into focus. In retrospect a correct assessment of the postwar *German Problem* was made by H.A. Freund who sent from Sydney for issue three of 1946: *Das deutsche Vakuum*, which begins: *Mit der Niederwerfung Deutschlands tritt das deutsche Problem in ein neues Stadium, ohne indes an Bedeutung für die Welt zu verlieren* (**With the smashing of Germany, the German Problem enters a new phase without losing significance for the world, p. 30**). Recognizing the seriousness of these new developments for Germany and Europe the, *DB* warned in the opening editorial of the first issue of 1945 that the bange Frage, (**the alarming question**) for the year was *Wird Europa sein oder nicht sein*? (**Is Europe to be or not to be?** p. 1) The editors felt that only a just peace, which would include Germany in a *new Europe*, could answer the question mercifully, positively, practically and, of course, realistically. Germany, no matter how selfish and aggressive her history, had to be a vital part of Europe of the future.

What should be the terms of peace? How severely should Germany be punished? This country where warlords were held in high esteem could not get away scott free. Are Vansittart's proposals to be serioulsy considered? can an entire nation be guilty of causing war? How can democracy be best established and maintained? Can the world be certain that Germany will not initiate another war, but instead, eagerly become a cooperating member of a European community of nations? The periodical's handling of these and related questions are analyzed in the following pages.

Articles dealing chiefly with the interrelated issues of peace and punishment of Germany are examined first. We must bear in mind that the major fear of the teutonic beligerents held by the world at the time of the surrender was the possibility of hordes rising to great military strength once again. Today this seems rather unlikely, if not downright ridiculous. Germany alone does not have the natural resources to sustain war nor the inclination. Most importantly she has learned to live in harmony with her European neighbors. Since the end of World War II, Germany, "West Germany," first achieved unprecedented economic success and then, given no choice when the despicable WALL was destroyed, took on the sociological/ financial burden of reviving and rehabilitating her former eastern portion, designated as "East Germany."

Some forty years ago William Shirer already correctly concluded that Germany had become the world's second-largest trader, the fourth-largest industrial power and the richest and strongest member of the Common Market. She already had the most stable currency in the world.[54]

And now, as I write on September 5, 2012, Germany has it all: flush toilets, heated water, central heating, super highways, marvelous bridges, common market food and long vacations in the sunny regions of Europe. Why indeed would Germans care to exchange all of that for muddy foxholes and butchering or gassing persons from other countries, ever again? Freund, who in 1946 considered the *deutsche Frage* to be *das Kernproblem des Weltfriedens* **(to be the central issue in establishing world peace)**, expressed the thinking of the times as follows: *Ein neu erwachen des deutschen Nationalismus ähnlich dem alten Nazitum, steht als Schreckgespenst für alle Freunde des Friedens (***A newly awakened German nationalism similar to the old Nazism lingers as a specter for all proponents of peace**, 30,1946, p. 4). He advocated punishment for Germany, but not to the point of forcing it to another war. It was Freund's strong belief that only through unity of the big five nations could Germany be rehabilitated; he saw the USA and Russia as the most, important members of the five. Freund points out that Germany could come out of the occupation period a communist nation or, by following the political example of the USA, a democracy, and has his own perceptive special reminder.

A major facet of consistent German warmongering, Freund warns, is the German *Mittelstand (***middle class)**; it was the green grocer and the glove maker who became the ardent followers of the Nazis and were responsibte for bringing them to power. The disappointment of losing world war I, thirst for revenge, pining for lost territory, lowering of the standard of living in the *Reich* and the desire for respect are major factors, which provoked the average citizen to support the Nazis, and he admonishes that the *Spiessbürgertum*

---

54 William L. Shirer, "From Jesse Owens to the Summer of 1972," *Saturday Review* (March 25, 1972), p. 44.

(**Philistine social class,** *common man?)* appears as spector which could again threaten peace. Vitriolic punishment would only allow similar conditions of resentment to arise.

Also, let us not forget my comments above on the modern life style, the flush toilets and accoutrements of our day, the computers and cars. Surely the Hun has at last been appeased...the Vandals long finished with their sack of Rome (455 A.D.), and the descendants of the Goths living peaceably in Jutland with their own electronic toys, nice dwellings and Vodka for all. Bismarck is buried, Hitler turned to ash, and the children of Goebbels were poisoned by their own mother.

Rukser and Theile agreed that some kind of punishment should be administered to true Nazis; proposals for strong measures of retribution against all Germans, however, were to them, appalling. The punitive plans for postwar Germany of Gilbert Lord Vansittart found virtually no listening ears, no sympathy. All of this resulted in more fevered correspondence. Rukser wrote to the man he had known for a lifetime: *Ich höre aber, daß in England unter den heutigen Verhältnissen Vansittart großen Einfluß haben soll (***I hear that under the present conditions in England Vansittart supposedly has a lot of influence.)**[55]

Again in a short paragraph in issue five of 1943 The Britsh Lord championed permanent destruction. The *DB* happily noted strong opposition to such frightfully harsh proposals. Viscount Simon was one who stated that the British government thought otherwise; did not his fellow MP know that frightful hardship and rebuilding lay ahead?

Vansittart must have been regarded in some circles as a second Hitler or had he simply not seen the photos of the bombed out nation or visited yet? However that may be, the The *London New Chronicle* was pleased at Simon's explanation. An even more fervid anti-Vansittart reaction is *Vansittarts Irrungen und Wirrungen* (**Vansittart's Misunderstandings and Confusion,** p. 2, 1944) by Joseph Kaskell who at that time was the representative for the *Blätter* in the USA.

Rukser used the English phrase "war-minded peace" in a letter to Kaskell on September 24,1943. Again on January 10,1944, he expressed his anxiety concerning a just peace: *Ich muss bekennen, daß ich sehr bedrückt bin. Denn je länger der Krieg dauert desto weniger Hoffnung besteht für sinnvolle Massnahmen concerning peace. Jeden tag wächst der Hass ins Ungemessene und wir werden die Rufer in der Wüste sein. Aber dennoch möchte ich deswegen nicht schweigen.* (**I have to admit that I am very depressed, since the longer the war lasts, the less hope there is for sensible measures concerning peace. Every day hate**

---

55 Letter from U. Rukser to J. Kaskell, January 1, 1943

grows immeasurably, and we are becoming callers in the wilderness.**) His friend Kaskell feared that with the end of the war in sight the following hardly less frightening danger had arisen: *nämlich die, daß die Allierten an die Friedensaufgaben mit Kriegsgesinnung herangehen* (**namely that the allies are approaching peace initiatives with a war attitude**, p. 6).

Kaskell could not tolerate such militaristic punishment not only for the sake of Germany, but for the entire world, and he irrately challenged Vansittart's position, beginning with the accusation that the British Lord was exhanging sides, for Just a few years earlier he had sympathized with the position of Chamberlain and thus helped to cause the destruction for which he now was eagerly seeking to fix blame on **all** Germans. Furthermore, in saying that the retribution payments of World War I were too low, Vansittart was in direct opposition to the leading British statesman of his day with whom he had apparently formerly agreed. Due to his new prejudice he fails to mention an official note of December 11, 1932, from the British government to the government of the USA, stating that one of the causes of the Depression was war debt and reparation payments. Both Lloyd George and Sir Harold Nicolson admitted after seeing the effect of the Treaty of Versailles that the payments were too high; they threatened both the conquered and the conquerors with economic collapse. Kaskell points out that Lloyd George went so far as to advocate the end of payments. Kaskell tersely concludes: *Lord Vansittart, der von Versailles bis München an allen politischen Entscheidungen beteiligt war, die die deutsche Demokratie niederzwingen und Hitler födern sollte, zieht es vor, sich nach einem Sündenbock umzusehen.* (**Lord V., who from Versailles to Munich took part in all the political decisions which repressed German democracy and promoted Hitler, now prefers to find a scapegoat**, p. 9). Vansittart, we are told, will not admit that he and his friends were wrong in thinking that the Nazis would push aside the *sozialistische Gefahr* (**danger of socialism**) and go no further. Therefore, he must now concoct a tale of a "deal" between the German democrats and the nationalistic aggressors.

Rukser's reaction to his friend's essay was expressed in a strong letter to Kaskell on December 11, 1943:

> *Ihr Beitrag über Vansittart ist sehr gut. Vielleicht fügen wir hier und da noch eine zeile ein. Überschrift: Vansittarts Irrungen und Wirrungen. Einverstanden?? Wir hatten zuerst bedenken, ob wir überhaupt anfangen sollen, in dieser Art zu polemisieren. Denn jetzt, und als Deutsche haben wir da doch alle Odds gegen uns. Aber Sie haben den einzig möglichen Weg gewählt nicht zu*

sagen: die Deutschen sind gute Leute sondern die unrichtigkeit der Angaben des Gegners zu beleuchten. Das ist der einzige Weg, um die Unschuld aufzuzeigen. Ich gehe darauf ausführlich ein, weil dieser punkt etwas programmatisch ist. Denn man wird ja oft Vorschläge polemischer Art an sie heranbringen. Also an und für sich halten wir die allgemeine politische Polemik für zwecklos und gefährlich.

TRANSLATION: Your piece on Vansittart is very good. Maybe we could add a line here and there entitled Vansittart's mistakes and confusion. Agreed?? At first we had misgivings about whether we should even get into this kind of polemics, for now and as Germans we have all odds against us. However, you have found the only way to say not that Germans are good persons, but to expose the unfairness of the charges made by the opposition. That is the only way to show their complicity. I go into the issue deeply because the point is somewhat programmatic, for persons are going to bring polemic proposals against it. Furthermore, properly speaking, we consider general political argument to be worthless and even dangerous.

A year earlier Kaskell had written (and, we take note, in English) to Rukser about the latter's apprehension concerning Vansittart: "To get back to politics, your gloomy view that Vansittart still represents the influential group in England found some con-firmation by the disappearance of Cripps from the war cabinet. But English policy will hardly be made before the elections to come after the war which have shown the tendencies of the British nation at large. However, we do not know, which sinister situation may foster the cause of Jingoism then (December 15, 1945). By the time he authored his article Kaskell was even less optimistic.

Hubertus Friedrich prinz zu Löwenstein in issue 5, 1944 (p, 5), compares Vansittart's ideas to the Nazis and finds them similar. In agreement with Löwenstein on this issue the Federal Council of Churches of Christ in America was also opposed to the harsh measures advocated by Vansittart. The eighth issue of 1944 contains the council's resolution concerning Germany signed by such prestigious names as Harry Emerson Fosdick, William Ernst Hocking and Reinhold Niebuhr.

The council opposed revenge and reprisals and recognized the existence of *das andere Deutschland*, comprised of Germans who resisted the Nazis. Expressing the view that only a feeling of common guilt for the crisis of the times could bring about the future reconciliation with the German people, the council states that the only policy which could give hope to Europe as a whole is one which would also provide for the postwar welfare of Germany. The following evaluation of future policies is recommended: *Der Prüfstein jeder Deutschlandpolitik muss darin bestehen, ob sie in der Hauptsache darauf hinausläuft, Deutschland zum dauernden Infektionszentrum im Herzen Europas zu machen* (**The touchstone of the political situation with Germany must deal with the problem of her becoming a center of infection in the very heart of Europe,** p. 33)

The council concludes its statement with an economic argument: an impoverished Germany would be a constant threat to world peace. Therefore, weare warned that a way must be found to prevent the rearmament of Gemany without ruining her industry. These humanitarian and realistic suggestions are directly opposed to the proposals of Lord Vansittart. The council foresaw that the complete destruction of German industry would not only have brought misery to Germany but would have lowered the standard of living throughout Europe as well.

After all, harsh punishment and ruining of the economy of Germany was being recognized, or perhaps better stated "admitted" as contributing to the cause of WWII and was a welcome piece of propaganda for Hitler and henchmen. It should have been obvious to even the most obtuse that when the German mark began to fall precipitously from 75 to a dollar in 1921 to 18,000 to dollar in January of 1923, then to 160,000 and on down to a million in August, to four billion in November, then quickly to trillions, that war would be one way to help recovery and at the same time crush those who had ruined them. Adolf was most articulate on the subject. However, hatred was abundant among those who had experienced a war or two, and they were not quick to settle for a "soft peace" as we will learn in examining the following proposals.

The first of three articles on the subject of peace with Germany published in the first issue of 1945, is Fritz Meyning's (Fritz Siegel) *Die letzte Schlacht* (**The Last Battle**). Meyning patterns his proposal after Guglielmo Ferrero's book, *Reconstrucíon*, and compares the peace settlement after the Napoleonic Wars to the pending peace issues of his own day. Meyning does not want a soft peace; he expects and hopes that the terms will be hard. His main point is that the peace be just. True peace, Meyning writes, should mean the restoration of order or the construction of a new and lasting order which will have to be built on hard and fast nonpartisan rules, for without such rules chaos ensues. Unselfish cooperation and single-minded pursuit of the goal can assure establishment of the order. Selfish interests such as French insistence on the possession of the left bank of the Rhein could prevent a just and lasting peace.

Peace through economic means is the subject of *Deutsche Wirtschaftsfragen in der Übergangszeit bis zur Friedensregelung.* (**Questions concerning the economy of Germany during the transition period until peace regulations are established.**) The author, Friedrich Haussmann, opposes a "hard peace" and quotes Roosevelt "I cannot believe that God has eternally condemned any race of mankind." Haussmann proffers the thesis that through economics a "sound and durable peace" can be assured for the entirety of Europe.

He cites production figures to prove the importance of an industrialized Germany to all of Europe, rejecting the idea of a German economy based on agriculture. Haussmann explains that in 1935, an average year, one fifth of all European trade was German. It is his firm conviction that making Germany once again a part of the European economy can greatly help to insure permanent peace:

> *Die wirksamste Friedenssicherung auf lange Sicht, dies kann nicht nachdrücklich genug betont worden, ist Wiedereingliederung Deutschlands in die Umwelt, das heisst seine psychologischer politische und ökonomische Reintegration und Erneuerung*

TRANSLATION: The most effective approach in assuring peace in the long run, this can not be stressed enough, is the replacement of Germany in the world, i.e. its reintegration and renewal, psychologically, politically and economically, p. 19.

Haussmann does advocate control organizations comprised of European nations to track Germany. He believes that no future war could be started without an air force and suggests the rather drastic and hardly feasible measure of creating a *Luftfahrtpolizeitruppe* (**a troop of air travel police**) to prevent clandestine strengthening of the German air force.

The third article on the subject of peace, *Die Friedensbedingung* (**Stipulations for Peace**) presents a British view to the readers of the *DB*; it is a translation of parts of an article which appeared in the *London Times* of October 4, 1944. In an editorial note Theile and Rukser express their appreciation for the objective point of view maintained by the *Times* in spite of the havoc and destruction caused by the robot bombs on England. The journal's concern, they write, for an organic Europe gives all Europeans hope.

The *Times* article is essentially in agreement with Haussmann in calling for the rejection of plans which would reduce Germany to an agricultural state; it reasons that suchplans are not feasible long term solutions. The choice between a "hard" and a "mild" peace, is an incorrect formulation of the problem; the article correctly maintains that only a peace which can be lastingly enforced and sustained should be considered.The *Times* says that the responsibility for getting German industry back on her feet belongs to the Allied Powers, who should have two mutually dependent objectives. First, lasting security against any new German attack needs to be created. The second objective is to require, but also enable, Germany to do her part in the reconstruction of Europe as well as in the maintenance of the well-being and stability of the peoples of Europe. The *Times* asks for controls in the form of sparsely staffed military bases; industry would be watched over as well as the government and people.

Such tolerant proposals were pleasing to Rukser and Theile whose thinking was succinctly summed up in a quotation from the Archbishop of Canterbury, Dr. Temple, in issue twenty-four of 1945. The Archbishop writes that the horrible destruction suffered by the German nation is punishment enough, and that those who will follow the way of Christ should be satisfied with such punishment. Strong editorial opinions against severe reprisals were expressed in a two-part article published in issues twenty-seven and twenty-eight of 1945; both are entitled *Wiedergeburt oder Untergang des Abendlandes?* (**Rebirth or Demise of the West?**)

They begin with Churchill's observation in his *My Early Life* that those who win a war can seldom establish a good peace, while those who could establish a good peace, would never have won a war. Theile and Rukser wonder if perhaps Churchill, statement has not been proved to be all too true in the peace deconstructive or vengeful or even Their great fear is that only national advantages will be considered in the peace settlements and that the responsibility for the, *new world..* belongs solely to the Allies and conclude: *Wir sind für Gerechtigkeit* (**We stand for justice**)

Commencing on page one, this editorial analyses three measures which, as a group, they label with a new coinage, *Unerträglichkeit* (**intolerableness**) and choose reduction of the German economy as the most unbearable.i.e. unthinkable. Second in degree of dire possibilities is loss of territory and the third most insufferable of all impositions would be the expulsion of Germans from lost territories. In opposing the reduction of the economy, arguments similar to those presented by Haussmann are applied. Noting that exports from and to Germany in the year 1930 by twelve European countries are listed in Reichsmarks, led the joint editors to conclude that the German market is as important for Europe as is Europe for Germany. To face dealing with the deindustrialization of Germany became so unsettling to all discussants that it became the most important in a European sense. To give their argument force, the editors quote a line from Edward Carr's Conditions of Peace: Europe cannot maintain—much less increase—her present standard of living without German productive power (p. 7). Not, only the deindustrialization is attacked, but the plan to reduce the size of the German merchant fleet is also severly criticized. How, the piece asks, are reparation payments to come from a reduced economy?

Astonishingly, Theile and Rukser reveal a typical German bias against the Polish people, which to me is one more proof of how insidious are the influences of our personal cultures, i.e. how we from birth are what we become. Germans become Germans, not many are at all aware of the *cultural baggage* they carry. The editors claim that the Polish-speaking population of the Eastern Territories comprised only five percent of the total in 1925. They feel that the land has bloomed under German administration, but all gains would be lost under the Poles, who have never been known as good administrators. Furthermore, they argue that the Russian *Drang nach Westen* (**push to the west**) simply replaces the Nazi *Drang nach Osten*.(**east**). They find it deplorable that London accepts the idea of Russian control of the Baltic.

The ugliest of the three issues according to *Blätter think* (my term), is to expell Germans from East Germany, Bohemia, and Hungary. Readers are reminded that various folk groups have always had a right to dwell in those areas where they have tilled the soil with sweat and blood. Did Germans gain the eastern lands by force? We are asked, before receiving an immediate negative response…no time allowed to ponder this one. Indeed, we readers might take issue with the proud assertion that it was a wilderness which Germans alone changed into a *Kulturland* and that only Germans ever ruled there. Afterall, the King of Bohemian was an elector of the German Reich. For Theile and Rukser Breslau and Hirschberg are as thoroughly German as are Stettin and Danzig. We are told that Saxons and Swabians never forced their way into the Danube lands, but, rather were called there because they were needed to defend against the Turks. Then, too, since the time of the migrations, Germans and Slavs have lived and worked the land together in Bohemia.

What will happen, the reader is asked, if twelve to fourteen milion people are pressed into a smaller Germany in which one-third of the population is homeless? Today, of course, we know that the effects were injurious to an already debilitated Germany. In this editorial two basic beliefs of Rukser and Theile. were expounded first, that Germany must be allowed to become a part of a new and stronger Europe and secondly that Russia was to be feared. Although the editors hated Nazism, Communism was not regarded as a substitute nor as a panacea for political problems. Rukser and Theile feared that if these three drastic measures became reality, Russia would become the supreme master of the continent, and that the *Untergang des Abendlandes* (**Demise of the West**) would result.

The second article, under the heading *Wiedergeburt oder Untergang des Abendlandes* (See prior translation) cites opposition to the proposals of Potsdam. We read the following: *Die Gebrechlichkeit der Potsdamer-Beschlüsse, die wir in Heft 27 an zu deuten versucht haben, ist offensichtlich geworden und hat zu einer internationalen Krise ersten Ranges geführt*. (**The weaknesses of the Potsdam solutions which we singled out in issue 27 of the *DB* is now common knowledge and has led to a major international crisis**). Although the Russians accept the decisions, leading statesmen such as Churchill and responsible publications like the *Economist* the *London Times* as well as North Arnerica's foremost political columnist, Walter Lippmann, have reacted negatively to Potsdam. Rukser and Theile reiterate their opposition to the planned expulsion of Gemans from Eastern Europe. They note that the *London Daily Herald* and the Italian *Osservatore Romano* agree with them.

It is asserted that the persecution of Germans in Czechoslovakia is equal to the obliquity of the Nazis, and that the Czechs are demonstrating a great eagerness to expel Germans. These two examples of man's cruelty to his fellow-man aresubstantiated by a translation of published measures to be taken against the German-speaking population of Czechoslovakia.

We are revolted to learn that the hate measures (now, *ethnic cleansing*) were formulated by the presidium of the local National Committee for Prague XII and include writing the word *Deutscher* with a lower case *d*. Addtionally all Germans over age fourteen are to wear a swastika measuring ten by ten centimeters. Such persons are to receive a reduced allotment of ration cards. Further, those wearing the swastika will not be allowed to use sidewalks, to read newspapers and magazines nor to receive tobacco.The most shocking rule prescribes that all those who fail to obtain *swastikas* are to receive the punishment which the Nazis would have administered in a similar situation. The editorial concludes with an apprehensive question: *Glaubt man wirklich mit Deportationen, Seuchen, Hunger und Elend ein neues Europa aufbauen zu können?* (**Do some really believe that a new Europe can be built with deportations, pestilence, hunger and misery?** p. 60).

Continuing to be appalled at the forced exodus of millions of Germans from the East, the editors published an article by Karl O. Paetel entitled *Der Todesmarsch der zehn Millionen* (**Death march of ten million**, 29, 1946). In an editorial note preceding the account the editors tell us that throughout the years of publication they have inveighed against inhuman acts. Now once again a horrible injustice is being enacted and they must protest. Paetel accurately portrays the expulsion. He fears the Allies are bringing a "Hitler-Frieden." It is a fact, he writes, that more than 10,000,000 refugees are pouring into Germany from the East because the Czechs and Poles are all too eager to rid their countries of Germans. When the refugees arrive in Germany, the confusion about where they should go is compounded by the Russian practice of setting up barricades in Berlin to prevent the refugees from entering the British zone. The deaths, especially of children, therapies, and other mistreatment have been documented by many. Paetel tells us, quoting Pater Alois Stegerwald-Bern of the Caritas organization, that between the Oder and Neisse rivers all children under age two had died. The author explains further that most of the Sudeten and other Eastern Germans were forced to leave their homelands on only one hours notice. Paetel reveals other measures as harsh as those of the Nazis. In Poland any marriage could be immediately dissolved if one of the partners was German. In Czechoslovakia Germans were not allowed to use the state-operated means of transportation. A letter from an unnamed Protestant minister received by the English Bishop of Chichester describes a situation worse than the German concentration camps which the minister knew. He writes of suicides, bodies in the Elbe and Oder rivers and thousands perishing from hunger on their westward journey.

A former American soldier who saw pictures of these horrors in *Life* magazine is quoted as writing that he lost his fear of death on Guadalcanal, his best friend on Okinawa, and his leg on Iwo Jima; but that he lost his faith in American democracy only when he saw the pictures in *Life*. Another political issue studied in the *DB* is the complete and permanent disarmament of postwar Germany. The journal considered the proposal to be unnecessarily cruel punishment. After the Allies had decided to enforce complete disarmament, Rukser quoted Edmund Burke's statement that "peace implies reconciliation." Because he wholeheartedly agrees with Burke, Rukser asks if a country can live and have meaning in the world if it has no army and no weapons. I

In *Die Entwaffnung Deutschlands und ihre Folgen* (**The Disarmament of Germany and the Consequences**, 30, 1946), he feared that strong disarmament measures might leave Germany without a voice in his envisioned new, humanized Europe. However, he steadfastly looks ahead and argues that future policy in Germany needs to be oriented toward the individual rights of man and a socialistic humanism. Because Germany by itself is far too weak to aspire to such new goals, it must look to other nations for help. The editor warns: *eine ungelöste deutsche Frage, ein in Interessensphären aufgeteiltes Deutschland wird unweigerlich die Beziehungen zwischen den Mächten belasten und zu Konflikten führen; wird auch jede europäische Ordnung unmöglich machen.* (**An unsolved German problem, i.e. a divided Germany will unquestionably** burden the relationships among the allied power and lead to conflicts p, 12). If there is to be a sincere change in political thinking leading to a satisfactory solution of Germany's warmongering, the disarmed nation must have its security guaranteed.

In issue 30 of 1946 Hans Schnitzlein, who was living in Brazil, angrily considered the issue of reparations from the point of view of the emigrants who lost everything to the Nazis. Well aware that these groups and their considerable losses were generally overlooked by the Allies, Schnitzlein proposes means by which to compensate them for losses and advocates the establishment of a *Reichsamt für Entschädigung Deutscher* (**Bureau of compensation for Germans**), which would study claims, determine losses and indemnify worthy applicants. He suggests that the money for the repayment of losses come from the followers of Hitler. Other articles dealing with new aspects of the issue occasionally refer to peace and punishment but treat more specifically the topics of a new Germany and the guilt and responsibility for World War II stressing that the chance for the formation of the new Germany, must not be jeopardized.

The question of the guilt of the whole German nation is the theme of a chapter from the unprinted autobiography of Egon Ranshofen-Wertheimer and an essay by Hubertus Friedrich Prinz zu Löwenstein, as well as articles by W.F. Sollmann and Erich Kahler. Ranshofen-Wertheimer is content to let Germany share equally in the collective guilt for WWII. The world's (including Germany's) imperialism and capitalism were responsible, but not Germany alone *(Die ewige Tragödie Deutschlands,* 6,1944 **Germany's Eternal Tragedy**). Blaming France for the events which follwed the first war, he notes that a single generation witnessed in World Wars I and II a double world-wide catastrophe, which seemed to arise from the same sources and were analogous in their development.

To prevent a recurrence, Ranshofen-Wertheirner admonished that d*ie Sieger von Morgen müssen die Lehre von 1918 beherzigen. Falls sie Deutschland nicht physisch vernichten wollen, so müssen sie eine Erlössung finden in der das Schlechte im deutschen Wesen neutralisiert und das Gute angespornt wird* (**Tomorrow's victors must take to heart the lessons of 1918. If they don't wish to destroy Germany physically, they have to find a solution which will neutralize the evil in the character of modern huns and stimulate the good,** p. 16). He, like so many, is willing in spite of all the Nazi atrocities, indeed the very embodiment of evil that they have exhibited, offer them yet another chance. It seems almost like: happenings of the last twelve years be damned, for democracy must be given another chance or did the thinking settle on the question: Do we really have choice? *Der versuch hatte in sich eine Chance des Gelingens ein Versagen hätte nichts Schlimmeres bringen können, als was geschehen ist* (**The attempt has a chance of

succeeding and failing can not bring anything worse than what has already occurred, p. 16).

The publishers were not in agreement about the value of Ranshofen-wertheimer's work for the *DB*, as noted in the following exchange of letters.

Kaskell to Rukser. July 31, 1943: *In Washington sprach ich Ranshofen-Wertheimer. Sein Buch, das von europäischen Parteileuten angegriffen wird, gefällt mir sehr, wenigstens seine Darstellung Europas die vor keiner Komplexität zurückschreckt, auch nicht vor Lügen, die nicht ins populäre Schlagwortschema passen..., Er versprach mir einen Aufsatz über dessen Thema wir noch beraten wollen. Über Honorar scheint er hinwegsehen zu wollen. Er bezweifelt aber, daß wir viele gute Kräfte auf die Beine bringen, wenn wir keine Honorare zahlen. Auch ich neige mehr und mehr zu der Ansicht, daß wir bescheidene Honorare, etwa 30 dollar pro Arbeitanbieten sollten.*

TRANSLATION: I spoke with Ranshofen-Wertheimer in Washington. I very much like his book, which is being attacked by European party folks, especially his portrayal of Europe which does not shrink from examining any complexity, not even from lies which do not belong in the popular catch-word scheme...He promised me an essay on a theme, which we have yet to agree upon, and apparently he can look the other way concerning an honorarium. However, he doubts that we can attract many good persons if we do not pay an honorarium. I also lean more and more to the position that we pay modest honoraria, something like 30 dollars per submission.

Kaskell to Rukser, December 11, 1943: Sie finden anliegend einen Aufsatz von Egon Ranshofen-Wertheimer, den ich reizvoll finde. Es ist wie er mir schreibe, das einleitende Kapitel zu seiner Autobiographie, die fertig vorliegt, aber wohl kaum vor Hitlers Sturz gedrückt werden kann. Ranshofen will mich wenn ich interessiert bin, einige weitere Kapitel schicken. Auf Grund seines Buches: Victory is not Enough, halte ich Ranshofen für sehr interessant und reich an politisch internationaler Erfahrung. Ich halte es daher für möglich, daß auch die weiteren Kapitel für uns von Wert sind,—in der Biog. Einleitung zu seiner Parabel könnten

Sie auf sein Buch hinweisen, sowie darauf, daß Reinige hundert Meter von Hitlers Geburtshaus geboren wurde. Er ist jezt Professor an der School of Social Sciences and Public Affairs der American University in Washington D.C. und Special Consultant to the Division of Internat. Law of the Carnegie Endowment.

TRANSLATION: Enclosed is an essay by Egon Ranshofen-Wertheimer, which I find fascinating. It is, as he wrote, the introductory chapter to his autobiography, which is finished, but certainly can not be printed prior to the fall of Hitler. It is, as he wrote me, the introductory chapter to his autobiography, which lies there ready. It can hardly be printed until Hitler falls.

If I am interested, Ranshofen will send me a few additional chapters of a literary niveau and political background. Based on his book, Victory is not Enough, I take Ranshofen to be very interesting and well grounded in international experience. Therefore, I consider it possible that the additional chapters will be valuable for us. In the introductory biographical note to his work you could mention that R was born just a few hundred meters from Hitlers place of birth and that later, due to his anti-Nazism, Hitler stripped him of his citizenship (He was *ausgebürgert*). He is now a professor at the School of Social Sciences and Public Affairs of the American University in Washington D.C. and Special Consultant to the Division of Internat. Law of the Carnegie Endowment.

Rukser to Kaskell, January 12, 1944:...der Aufsatz von Ranshofen scheint uns nicht geeignet. So geht es keinesfalls: Wir sehen mit steigender Besorgnis, wie man in aller Welt sich die Sache vereinfacht, indem man nur immer von Hitler und seinen Gangsters spricht— als ob das zufällige persönliche Dinge wären. Während doch die wirkliche Gefahr darin liegt, daß über dämonische Tendenzen am Werke sind. Ranshofen fördert den erwähnten Irrtum durch eine ganz unangebrachte idyllische Parallele.

TRANSLATION: ...Ranshofen's essay is unsuitable for us. So, it will in any case not be published. With ever greater concern we are noting that people all over the world are simplifying this matter, i.e. they are always referring to "Hitler and his Gangsters"...as if they were coincidental personal things, while the real danger lies in the impersonal demonic tendencies that are at work. Ranshofen promotes the mentioned error through an idyllic parallel.

Kaskell to Rukser, January 17, 1944: Wegen des Ranshofen Artikels bitte ich "reconsideration", Ich glaube nicht, daß die Erzählung die Tendenz hat, den Fall Hitler in ein falsches Licht zu rücken. Was die beiden Persönlichkeiten angeht, den mittelalterlichen Bauernsohn, der ein grosser Raubritter werden wollte, und Hitler, so ist der Vergleich nicht unangebracht. Der historische und psychische Hintergrund werden in beiden Fällen kaum berührt. Ranshofen ist als Freund der DB wichtig, was natürlich nicht heisst, daß Sie ihn gegen Ihre Überzeugung drucken sollten.

TRANSLATION: I request reconsideration concerning the Ranshofen article. I do not believe that the story has the tendency to place the case of Hitler in a false light. Concerning the two personalities, the farmer's son of the mittel ages, who wanted to be a great robber knight, and Hitler, there is no comparison. The historical and physical backgrounds in each case are hardly touched. Ranshofen is important as a friend of the *DB*. This, of course, does not mean that you should print him against your conviction.

Rukser to Kaskel, February 3, 1944: Ranshofens Beitrag Und Kritik. Lieber Freund, wenn sie um reconsideration bitten, dann gibt es für uns nur eine Antwort. Wir wissen zu sehr, was Ihr urteit bedeutet, als daß wir störrisch sein wollen.Curiously Rukser criticizes some aspects of Ranshofen-Wertheimer's thinking but agrees with him that Germany alone was not responsible for the war.

TRANSLATION: Ranshofen's piece and critique. Dear friend, if you request reconsideration, there is only one answer for us: We know all too well what your judgement means for us to be obstinate.

Curiously, while Rukser criticized some aspects of Ranshofen-Wertheimer's thinking, he was in agreement that Germany alone was not responsible for the war.

Prinz zu Löwenstein took an idealistic view of Germany and asked that the world consider Germany's entire history instead of focusing only on her recent errors. In *Das eine Deutschland* (**The United Germany** 5,1944) Löwenstein defends the thesis that in the dialectical process of the history of the western world two forces are at work a universal and a national; these forces continue to reach new syntheses at higher levels. Löwenstein is convinced that there is in reality only one Germany even though tre too has used the term "das andere Deutschland." He argues that even a sick people remains whole and then cites the Germanic tribes of Tacitus's days to show that the Germanic Volk as such is to be viewed as a homogeneous unit; it may develop and change, but always remains a whole. Löwenstein links these thoughts to the teachings of Augustin and the idea of a future kingdom the Civitas Dei, a kingdom of redeemed mankind comprised of all races and nations, including Jews, are striving for this ideal kingdom above earthly kingdoms. We are told *Das Heilige Römische Reich Deutscher Nation war zwar nicht Augustins Idee, entstand aber nicht ohne die politische Interpretation seiner Idee des Gottesstaates* (**The Holy Roman Empire of the German Nation was not Augustin's idea, however, the concept did not arise without the political interpretation of his idea of the State of God**, p. 5), and therefore, conclude that the empires of Charlemagne and Odoaker were attempts at the realization of Augustin's ideas.

The prince eagerly points to just treatment of Jews by Henry IV and Odoaker and insists that historically Germany has had less anti-semitism than other European nations. For him it is understandable that the idea of a strong *Reichsgewalt*, an empire which is protected from without and preserves the rights of the people within, dominates later German history. A kind of universalism prevailed until the Napoleonic Wars with France forced the Germans to more nationalistic thinking and Bismarck,s empire, the writer explains, was the only possible solution to the German problem of the day. The reader infers that Bismarck's idea son unification harmonized with universalistic political thinking. Bismarck's empire survived reform and emerged after 1918 as the German Republic and Weimar, we are assured, did not arise in a vacuum. It was the result of centuries of development.

In summary Lowenstein states that part of Germany's greatness lies in her ability to remain a mirror image of a European community in spite of her colorful divisions into tribes, customers and life styles; he emphasizes that the nationalistic teachings of the Nazis are not representative of majority thinking because the true state of affairs reflects this variety. Where, Lichtenstein asks, does the solution lie? And anwers:

Sie liegt in einer Verständigung mit dem deutschen Volk dem ersten opfer des Nationalsozialismus. sie Liegt darin, diesem Volk in glaubwüdiger weise Frieden anzubieten sobald die Schande der Hitlerregierung und alle ihre organisation mit all ihrem antichristlichen Greuel und Rassenwahne ausgelöscht sind

TRANSLATION: It lies in an understanding with the German people, the first sacrifice of National Socialism. It lies in offering these people peace in a believable manner as soon as the destruction of the Hitler Regime and all its organizations with all their anti-christian abominations and race madness is extinguished p, 10).

His conclusion? Only a European federation of nations can free the peoples of Europe from fear and danger of suppression. The good prince confidently informs us that after being set free from the swastika, Germany as a whole (*das eine Deutschland*) cleansed and hardened by so much suffering and pain, will take up its task anew, namely to seek dignity in service to the ideals of all peoples of the western world, instead of in rule and conquest. Its youthfulness and its awareness of its Christian heritage will make Germany the natural leader of a future empire of justice, peace and freedom.

Löwenstein's vision of a European federation was shared by many intellectuals of the day, not least among them Theile and Rukser. It is doubtful that the Allies shared what at that time appeared to be merely a quixotic dream of Germany leading such a federation toward the ideals of justice, peace and freedom. Yet, they were true visionaries who predicted correctly, for today, we look back and realize that Löwenstein's hopes have been become a way of life or new way of thinking. The one time warmonger is behaving itself. The new democratic Germany has to date proved its ability to be a leader without resorting to war. The subject of a new Europe will be more fully treated in the next chapter.

W.F. solmann, who played a leading role in the Social Democratic Party in Germany after world war II, is another who advises the reader to look beyond the mistakes of recent German history. In *Deutschlands Politische Wiedergeburt* (**The Political Rebirth of Germany,** 6, 1944) he writes that because of both physical and moral destruction, the weakened Germany must temporarily be ruled by her conquerors. In the writer's words: *Der Wiederaufbau einer deutschen Demokratie unter eigener Verantwortung kann erst beginnen, wenn entschieden ist was für die Deutschen übrig bleibt (***The reconstruction of a German democracy under its own responsibility can only commence when it is decided what**

will be left for the Germans, p, 18), who as part of their preparation for self-rule must learn from the British and the Armericans that *Diskussion mehr ist als Streit, viel mehr eine Methode um aus dem Abwägen verschiedener Meinungen sich gegenseitig zu belehren und zu verständigen. Hier liegt das deutsche politische Grundübel* (p, 18).

Sollmann's principal argument is that Germany can be rehabilitated only through the cooperation of large political and economic groups. He observes that the constitution of the Weimar Republic provided for such collaboration. It recommended a system of economic counselors in addition to the political parliament. The exiled publishers were in agreement with Sollmann that, the Allies would have to be counted on to lead Germany. On November 15, 1943, Kaskell wrote Rukser:

> *Es bedeutet sehr viel für mich, daß auch Sie sich zu der Auffassung durchgerungen haben, daß die Grossmächte zu Treuhändler der künftigen Rechtsordnung bestellt werden müssen.... Wird klipp und klar anerkannt, daß die* Sieger *Grossmächte die alleingen Machtfaktoren sind, so besteht wenigstens die Hoffnung, daß sie zu einem weisen Gebrauch dieser Macht überredet und erzogen werden können. Die einzige Grossmacht, die die Kontrolle über diese Grossmächte üben kann, muss die öffentliche Meinung der Welt sein, ihre Freiheit sicherzustellen, ist eine der wichtigsten Aufgaben.*

TRANSLATION: It means a lot to me that you too have struggled in your thinking to come up with the concept that the Great Powers have to be the trustees of the future order of law. It becomes immediately obvious that the victorious Great Powers constitute the sole power factor, so at least the hope exists that they can be persuaded and taught how to use this power wisely. The only single Great Power that can exercise control over these Great Powers has to be the public opinion of the world, one of the most important tasks of which is to assure freedom.

*Die Verantwortlichkeit des deutschen Volkes (***The Responsibility of the German People,** *30, 1946)* by Erich Kahler finds both the Allies and the German people to be wrong in their assessment of the question of responsibility for World War II. Some of the allies want to blame the entire German nation for Nazism, he writes, but on the other hand too many Germans do not want to admit their responsibility. In analyzing the *German Problem* Kahler is more critical of the Germans than most who treated this issue in the *DB,* and Goethe's evaluation of his people is sobering: " I have often felt a bitter sorrow at the thought of the German people, which is so estimable in the individual and so wretched in the generality." It takes great confidence indeed to disagree with the greatest of all German humanists.

Therefore, this may be the best place to segue into the analyzes of these events of the WW II years and our little but powerful anti-Nazi magazine to give the reader some thinking points. First, remember that the Hitler group (National Socialism) accomplished a perfectly legal (if somewhat strained) takeover of the government, and secondly, to continue with reminders, consider the *Sieg Heil* **(Hail victory)** screaming millions upon millions of Germans, arms raised in a Roman salute to their *Führer,* who for most (with the help of Leni Riefenstahl) had metamorphosed into true diety). God himself stood before them shouting into the microphones those now well known words of encouragement and appreciation, false, lying words which cleverly offered something to everyone, Jews excepted. He, *Gott Hitler,* the murderous phenomenon, offered the vision, the mirage really, of a classless society in which all would be equal, Jews excepted, but, then, they were barely *pithecanthropus erectus..*

Nearly all the individuals joining voices in exhilaratative support gave him full approval for six years, beginning in 1933. Then in 1939 his massive army rolled into Poland, then the Netherlands, then on and on, and immediately support began to dwindle and continued to diminisih commensurate with the aggression for six more years. When the first wounded soldier returned home and the first casket, the exhilaration weakened and decreased in intensity with all the body parts that followed. Could their *Gott* fail the people? Best to inquire of those Berliners who could not even recognize the destroyed city in 1945 under which, somewhere, lay the burned *Führer/Gott...*No more hypnotic screaming and stiff arm salutes. Only the question remained: Why did we let him do this to us? Our Zeus shouted with consummate assurance: *Heute Deutschland—Morgen die Welt!! (***Today Germany—but tomorrow the entire world**—will be ours—is implied—and understood by the hordes).

The above question prompts me to ask, indeed who was responsible for the war if not the Germans? Certainly no other nation comes to mind. Germans are baffling. I have devoted much of my life to learning both the language and literature and studying the culture, and could be designated a Germanophile, but, please, only a positive answer is possible in evaluating the thinking and the outcomes way back then when the *Thousand Year Reich* and the war ended 988 years early. They did it to themselves, although a secondary question begs to be asked: Did Hitler do this to the *Volk* or had the German people also metamorphosed...and become for a time new-age myrmidons following their new-age Achilles into his new-age Trojan War...all too ready to pursue the maniacal dreams, creative promises and obvious lies of their new *Gott*?

Kahler admonishes all Germans that they must sincerely and seriously face and important issue: the Nazis brought something new to mankind, planned systematic atrocities which were realized with scientific help. As *die besten Deutschen* (**best Germans**) such as Jaspers, Niemöller and others have done, so should all Germans bite the bullet and admit that their nation has committed a crime.

Specific proposals for the formation of a future German government, were made by a group of German Socialists living in England. Friedrich Ballhausen was intrigued by the groups utopian political goal: each future German government was to fulfill the desires of the common man, The aims of the Socialist group had recently been outlined in a Penquin Book entitled *The Next Germany* which Ballhausen discussed in *Nachkriegsdeutschland* (**Postwar Germany, 6, 1944**). Regional authority close to the people will facilitate the accomplishment of large tasks, such as demobilization, abolishment of Nazism, and private ownership of land. They are convinced that, with the aid of a free press, realization of their plans is assured.

A future Germany within a European community is another goal of the Socialists. This can not be achieved with political deals and pacts; instead there must be a drive to "create a common loyalty and a community of progressiveoutlook. " we are told that a future peace can be assured through the principle of the community of man. Succinctly stated, the *Kennzeichen der Zukunft* is *Abhänigkeit auf allen Stufen des Lebens und Wirkens*, (p. 32).The best example of a non-German view of timely aspects of the *German Problem* is *Das Deutsche problem von England ausgesehen* (8, 1944) in which Fritz Meyning (Fritz Siegel) sketches the contents of an anonymous English book, *The Problems of Germany.*[56] In printing a foreign view the editors of the *DB* are reminding their readers that although Germans love Germany, it will be more difficult, for the victors to take a moderate approach to the German problem.

The objective book written by an English study group contains two premises (1) England can not be disinterested in the German question because the development of modern weapons technique works in favor of Germany and against England, and England can rely neither on an English-American coalition nor on the Russians or French to protect it. (2) The German danger will not disappear with the irnpending defeat of Germany. A nucleus of Germans willing to believe in the myth of a near victory for Germany in World War II

---

56 Oxford Universiity Press, June, 1943

will be eager to begin World War III Because of these two premises. England's only pragmatic choice is an active policy concerning postwar Germany.

The basic problems in postwar Germany are the questions of borders, the possible division of the Reich, inner freedom for Germany economics and disarmament. The report gives no general solution to the problem of borders, but it finds proposals for the expulsion of Germans from certain territories to be unwise. it proposes instead that the *Reich* remain whole. The report is tinged with pessimism concerning internal freedom for Germanyr but with the exception of the right to choose Nazism, it recommends freedom of choice of government. The report recognizes that deterioration of the German economy can lead to political unrest and, therefore, it would allow economic development in accordance with the Atlantic Charter, always excluding the production of weapons. Heavy industry should be periodically monitored to prevent the construction of tanks airplanes and other war machinery, and in conclusion the report advocates temporary disarmament.

The analyses of the *German Problem* in the *DB* express the passionate involvement of both editors and contributors. Getting Germany back on its feet and training the Germans in the ways of democracy were the goals proposed. Severe punishment and retribution would only lead to economic chaos for all of Europe and to future war. Germany was correctly pictured as a vital economic force at the heart of Europe. The *DB* admitted German guilt and recognized a world-wide desire for vengeance, but these leaves remained conciliatory and passionately argued that the best course for Europe and the world lay in encouraging Germany to become a cooperating member of a new, European community of nations.[57]

Readers will recall "The "Marshall Plan" of the United States vs. "The Morgenthau Plan." The first was advocated by George C. Marshal, Secretary of State, known as the European Recovery Program (ERP). The second was the Treasury Plan for the Treatment of Germany, devised by Assistant Treasury Secretary, Harry Dexter White, and championed by Henry J. Morgenthau, Treasury Secretary. It was known as the "Jewish Plan" since it appeared to be based on vengeance, while the Marshall Plan intended to give aid where needed to get Germany and Europe back on their feet.

The "Morgenthau Boys," as they were known, got their way, but in a modified plan, while the millions of dollars in loans of the Marhall Plan

---

57 Nearly two years after the war and three months after the *DB* had ceased publication, the publishers' fear of severe punishment of Germany continued. Theile and Rukser, signing their own names or simply *Deutsche Blätter*, wrote to world leaders, especially Americans, and explained their thoughts on the *"German Question."* One of these bits of correspondence is in the appendix, a letter to Herbert Hoover.

produced the *Wirtschaftswunder* (**economic miracle**). It worked extremely well, as we now know, with the assistance of the high rise cranes, which seemed to sprout up all over Europe. Once again we can refer to the bridges, etc. Certainly the extreme vengeance and monetary demands placed upon Germany after WW I led to far less favorable outcomes. Reducing Germany to an agrarian state would have achieved no productive purpose. Strange, is it not how twisted the thinking of even very intelligent persons can become?

Of course, We can also be sure that a high number of persons deserving punishment never received any, but still, the Marshall Plan was key to settling down the unruly Teutons responsible for two wars in the first half of the 20th century.

Chapter VI

New Europe and New World

A SURVEY OF the best articles, essays, and editorials on the subjects of a *new Europe* and of a revitalized postwar world, both closely related to the reveals three Categories. Some writers gave comprehensive study to the issue of a *new Europe*; others focused on one problematical facet. A third group concerned themselves with the larger issue of a new world in which Europe and especially Germany, formed a major part. The following excerpts from two of Rukser's letters to Kaskell indicate the nature of his concerns about postwar Europe. He did not want the realization of his dream jeopardized.

RUKSER TO KASKEL: August 4, 1943 *Die Dinge verlaufen Ja nun schon ziemlich gut. Die Vorgänge in Italien geben jedem von uns genug zu denken. Mir macht grossen Eindruck zu sehen, wie ahnungslos auch massgebende Italiener hinsichtlich der Weltlage zu sein scheinen. Aber in Deutschland wirds wohl schneller gehen—voraus-gesetzt, daß sich die Angelsachsen mit den Russen wirklich verständigt haben, so daß sie eine gemeinsame europäische Konzeption haben. Sonst—*

TRANSLATION: Aug. 4, 1943 Things are going pretty well. The proceedings in Italy are giving all of us enough to ponder. It impresses me greatly to see how unaware even important Italians seem to be regarding the world situation. However, in Germany it will, I presume, go a lot faster since the Anglosaxons have come to an understanding with the Russians, so that they have a common conception of Europe.

RUKSER TO KASKELL: October 11, 1943: *Mit Sorge sehen wir der allierten Konferenz mit Russland entgegen. Wird es möglich sein, sich über die wirklichen Probleme zu verständigen und nicht bloss an der Oberfläche zu bleiben?Diese Konferenz kann ja nur dann den Frieden wirklich vorbereiten, wenn nicht nur gerade die aktuellen Fragen, sondern alle ganz grossen Fragen zwischen den drei Mächten auf einander abgestimrnt werden. Das ist eine ähnliche Situation wie im Altertum die Konferenz zwischen Cäsar, Pompejus und Lepidus, wo sie sich die alte Welt aufteilten, aber da es nur obenhin geschah, brach alles zusammen. Heute muss man sich eben auch über die Zukunft der Welt im Ganzen klar sein, sonst können Teilfragen Leider auch nicht gelöst werden.... Solche Authoren wie W. Lippmann lassen wenige Hoffnung auf Frieden und wenn man der Kritik über das State Dept. glauben soll die aus USA kommt, dann ist schon gar keine Hoffnung. Dann allerdings haben wir alle umsonst gelebt.*

TRANSLATION: Oct. 11, 1943: It is with worries that we approach the conference of the allies with Russian. Will it be possible to come to an understanding of the true problems and not just stay on the surface? This conference can truly prepare for freedom, if not only the current issues but also all the larger ones are agreed upon among the three powers. It is like a similar situation in antiquity, the conference among Cäsar, Pompejus and Lepidus when they divided the old world, but because it occurred only perfunctorily, it all broke apart. Again today one must be very clear about the big picture concerning the future of the world, otherwise, unfortunately, portional issues can not be solved either... Authors such as W (Walter) Lippmann place little hope in peace and if one believes criticism of the State Deparment, there is no hope whatsoever. In that case we have lived in vain.

Not all facets of the three subjects outlined above are explored in Theile's opening essay (1, 1943). *Europa sucht sich selbst* but the tone is here set for the many articles which during the following four years expounded and elucidated these topics. Theile begins by sketching recent European history, Less than thirty years earlier, he writes, the European considered his homeland to be the center of the world. It appeared that there were no limits to the potential development of European power. Already more than one half of the world belonged to Europe, and raw materials as well as technology were controlled by Europeans with London as the new financial heart of the entire world.

Europe was preaching Christianity, but she was not practicing it; she was busy exporting her technology. German officers taught the Japanese army and the English instructed her navy. Europe was attaining new heights in world influence but was losing spiritual and intellectual cohesion. Personal friends from East Asia expressed to Theile their shock at seeing the words, *Gott mit uns*, on German belt buckles. The editor warns that, if Europe is to find itself again, it rnust confess to having adopted unchristian ways. Theile deplores the nationalism that had developed in Europe and proposes a question which in varied words is frequently asked in the *DB*: *Warum sollte nicht... aus Selbstbesinnung nach diesem Kriege eine neue Blüte unserer Kultur beschert werden?"* **(Why should not through self-reflection following this war a new bloom be granted to our culture?** p. 5). The *unserer* (**our**) here refers, of course, to Europe as a whole and not to Germany, but the editor is interested in assuring his homeland a *Mittlerrolle* in Europe.Theile looks at the Soviet Union with admiration, but cautions western Europe not to follow the example of Russia and writes: *Nicht im Kampf der Klassen und Nationen, sondern in ihrer Versöhnung und Zusammenarbeit liegt Europas Zukunft* (**It is not in the struggle of classes and nations, but rather in their reconciliation and cooperation where the future of Europe lies,** p. 6). Russian Nationalism, he warns, is Europe's poison, and Nationalism should, of course, in the editor's opinion, be overthrown everywhere. His plan is to educate all Europeans to see that the individual nation must serve the collective whole. The *DB* searched history to learn of possible plans of other ages from which, it was hoped, a workable proposal for the post World War II world could be created. In the second issue of 1943 Friedrich von Hofe Looks at the reconstruction of Europe 125 years earlier after the *Napoleonic Wars*. He hopes that some valuable lessons are to be learned for the peace settlements of the 1940's. He argues that it was only through the wisdom of Talleyrand and Alexander that in less than one and a half years the Napoleonie Era was liquidated rwithout leaving behind lasting hatred. Putting the ideas of Kant and Montesquieu into practice. Talleyrand claimed that politics must be subject to ethics. von Hofe reasons that a new Europe for his day must be built by men of the political stature of Talleyrand who have only justice for all Europe in mind and who, for example pay more attention to the Polish guestion than did the statesmen of the Vienna Congress. von Hofe's call for justice harmonizes with the spirit or rhe *DB* and with the ideas set forth by Theile in the opening essay outlined above. Justice, cooperation, equality of nations, guarantees of the rights of small countries and respect for law are some of the key concepts expounded by writers calling for a new united Europe.

Udo Rukser was even more vigorous in planning and dreaming of a harmonious Europe than was Albert Theile. He knew that it would require selfless efforts from all countries concerned; still, he strove for a paradise on earth. In 1942, before launching the *DB,* he expressed a wish that was destined to permeate the periodical:

> *Ja, die grosse Frage ist, werden die Völker aus diesem Krieg was lernen? Leider breitet sich eine schwarz-weiss Malerei in der politik und der Berichterstattung immer mehr aus: alles Gute ist nur auf der Seite zufinden, wo man selbst ist, alles Unheil, alle Bosheit auf der andern. Das kann nicht gut gehen. Sollte mann statt dessen den Leuten nicht begreiflicher machen können, daß mit einem Bruchteil der Opfer, die der Krieg fordert, die ganze Welt paradiesisch hätte organisiert werden können? Daß eine Politik des Wohlwollens viel viel weniger gekostet hätte an Menschen und Gütern als die Politik des sacro egoism, die doch alle getrieben haben? Denn sie haben eisern den Status Quo festgehalten und solange man das tut, wirds eben immer Krieg geben, weil das Leben von Zeit zu Zeit Ähderungen erfordert.[58]*

Translation: Yes, the major question is will people learn anything from this war? Unfortunately a black and white portrayal of politics and reporting is becoming increasingly widespread: Everything good can only be found on the side one supports, all mischief, all evil on the other. No good can come of that. Instead should it not be made more *understandable to the masses that with a mere fraction of the sacrifice* that the war requires, the entire world could have been organized as paradise?...that politics of wellbeing would have cost much, much less in human sacrifice and goods than the politics of *sacro egosimo,* that all sides pursued? With an iron grip they held onto the *status quo,* and as long as one does that, there will always be war because life requires change from time to time.

---

58 Letter from U. Rukser to J. Kaskell, June 6, 1942

In a piece entitled *Europäische Phantasien* (3,1943) Rukser set forth some of his proposals for a Pan-Europe. This essay formed the basis of further editorial elaboration on the subject. He begins by observing that the image of a future "united Europe" was already becoming a reality. Rukser explains that a cross sectional sampling of thinking on the subject of Pan-Europe would reveal some basic trends among all plans; one important simitarity is the hope that a unified Europe will issue from the war.

After considering differences among the peoples of Europe such as levels of economic development and variances in the national characters, Rukser forsees that a *Gesamt-Europa* will not begin suddenly with a European constitution but rather will develop fron regional groups which will in time come together in a sort of European clearinghouse. In fact, because of the reluctance of old enemies to work together in Europe, Rukser believes the Allies should force the European nations to unify, and suggests further that just as the Atlantic Charter was formulated during the war as preparation for world peace, so now a kind of statue for European unity should be proclaimed. He insists that the following six objectives be of prime consideration:

1. A principle of international jurisdiction among the countries.
2. The general abolition of standing armies.
3. Lasting demilitarization of critical zones such as the Rheinland.
4. Guarantees of human rights based on the Atlantic Charter,
5. Guarantees of rights of minorities.
6. The basis for the eventual establishment of European economic unity.

Rukser then outlines possible future political deveopments in Europe, as he foresees them, and assumes that future potitical trends will be initiated by the Anglo-Russian Alliance. Belgium, the Netherlands, Denmark and Norway will feel drawn to England, which, importantly, will affirm their support of the alliance between England and Russia. While Russian in turn because of its economic potential, gigantic size, and estimated population growth will become a leader of the Western World. Continuing his recommendations, Rukser wants the future border between Russia and Europe to be limited to the line of June 20, 1941. He would give Russia the Baltic States and the Eastern regions of Poland, and lastly, would replace the French idea of a national state with a federal autonomous administration.

A lasting solution for the German-Polish debate concerning the region between the Vistula and Oder lies in joining these territories in an autonomous state with its own administration and customs agreement with the neighboring states. For Czechoslovakia Rukser hopes for an alliance with Poland and a new constitution, disgarding the concept of the little *entente*. And now…as to his homeland…the publisher calls for decentralization and a new Germanic confederation consisting of Northwest and Southern groups respectively. This would have a conciliatory effect in a demlitarized Europe. At the end of his article he acknowledges that the question persists as to whether or not the Anglo-Russian Alliance offers a sufficiently solid basis for the solutions which he proposes.

Rukser's correspondence also substantiates that the "Polish Question" as related to a future of cooperation among European states was vital in his plans. He wrote Kaskell on February 3, 1944:

> *Ja. an der polnishchen Politik ist viel zu kritisieren, und die jetzige polnische Regierung in London macht es Russen wohl auch ziemlich leicht. Aber dennoch wird am polnischen Problem jezt deutlich, ob es eine gemeinsame allierte Politik in Europe, ob es ein künftiges Gemeinwesen einmal geben wird, oder ob Europa in Interressenzonen zerfetzt und nur noch Objekt der grossen Politik sein wird. Darum ist das Schicksal Polens heute unser Schicksal!*

> **TRANSLATION: Yes, there is much to criticize concerning Polish politics, and the present Polish government in London is making things fairly easy for the Russians. Neverthless, it is becoming certain through the Polish problem whether there will be common allied politics in Europe, whether there will be a future community, or if Europa will be shredded into zones of interest and become simply an object of the greater political situation. Therefore the fate of Poland today is our fate!**

It was clear to all involved that the victorious powers could hinder the emergence of a Pan-Europe, and Rukser was groping for solutions to some of Europe's persistent problems in order to facilitate a smooth transition to a postwar unified Europe in which each national segment would work for the good of the whole.

He makes assumtions and, and is overly optimistic, but perhaps idealism and hope were needed to encourage those who would soon begin the work of rebuilding a shattered Europe.

Edward H. Carr's *Conditions of Peace* was a favorite of the editorial team because of its conciliatory thesis and optimistic plans for a "New Europe."

In the second issue of 1943 the book was reviewed by Friedrich Ballhausen with emphasis on Carr's comprehensive suggestions for the future of Europe. Ballhausen notes that Carr wants no repetition of 1919; he suggests that all of Europe be subjected by the Allies to a "productive occupation."

From this type of work the following would slowly emerge: The European Relief Commission, The European Transport Corporation and the European Reconstruction and Public Works Corporation. All of the above would be crowned by the European Planning Authority. Carr insists that only after economic cooperation is assured can political solidarity be achieved. Ballhausen is in total agreement with Carr that to avoid war a new order is required. To reduce armaments a general convention of armaments for common ends should be formed. To eliminate commercial obstacles, plans must be made for international commerce.

A speech given by Frederick Haussmann at a meeting of "friends of the DB" in New York was published in issue eight of 1944. Haussmann proceeds to prove that a Pan-Europe is a realizeable dream, and proceeds to proposes three possible courses, all of which could lead to the goal of a unified and peaceful European community of nations. He is above all concerned that Germany be a part of such a community. The first possible course is the creation of a federation on a politically constructive basis. The second is the restoration of economic relations with the surrounding world. The third possible course is the ideological and structural accommodation within what could be termed the *Europäische Schicksalsgemeinshaft* **(European Destiny Association)**.

The writer briefly outlines the history of the concept of Pan-Europe, emphasizing that it did not originate with Richard Coudenhove, who had been trying to awaken it since 1923; he explains why plans for unification have failed to succeed in recent history. England had been a major stumbing block in the past, but the England of 1944 is friendlier to Europe.[59]

Haussmann considers it foolhardy to attempt a unification of Europe sirmply by imitating a small federation like Switzerland; Swiss cantons are not nations. He believes that a kind of inner alliance among democratic lands is the correct approach. Federation is a lengthy process; economics could effect harmony more quickly. He suggests, for example a centralizing of European air travel with the Hague as the possible seat of an Inter-European airline. It could

---

59 Richard Nikolaus Graf Coudenhove-Kalergi was President of the Paneuropean Union for nearly fifty years. As politician, geopolitician and philosopher, he was one more humanist who tried to end war, man's favorite sport, once and for all. And now? We are still at it, but Count Coudenhove would be pleased at today's unified Europe…even though the unity is threatened daily.

control future German air forces and even have an international police force. Inter-European canal projects could also aid cooperation by expediting trade.

Today there is no single European airline, and no police force watches over the German air force, but cooperation on canal projects has become a reality. Haussmann and others were correct in seeing trade and economics as one of the best means of unification. This is a variation of the old saw: if you can't beat them, join them. We could say: Invite and give opportunities for the enemy to join you. Extremely stiff reparations and all as occurred following WW I, backfired as WW II. Therefore, giving consideration to inviting the enemy in, just may be better, and in the long run, even cheaper, a direct route to world peace. After such a long war, this suggestion is nearly impossible to swallow, of course, and studying a photo of your son murdered at Rhenen further deters embracing it with enthusiasm.

From his 1944 point of view Haussmann concludes that his third proposal is the best from a real-political aspect. Slowly it could be coupled with economics and politics. Haussmann is saying that Europe must think of its own fate. The nations of which it is comprised must learn to think of themselves as belonging to Europe and not to Russia or the U.S.A. A split into East-leaning and West-leaning nations is a real threat. The concept *Europe* must form a bridge between East and West and be a third entity unto itself.

As Haussmann states it: *Schaffung einer unabhängigen, ihr Schicksal selbst in die Hand nehmenden Mitte und zugleich einer Brücke zwischen Ost und West ist der tiefste Sinn der Pan-Europa Idee* (**An independent center must be created which takes charge of its own destiny and at the same time forms a bridge between East and West. This is the deepest sense of the Pan-Europe concept**, p, 6). The author reminds those who think that plans for a Pan-Europe are utopian or simply *Phantasiegebilde* of his conviction: *aus kühnen Träumen entstehen schöperische Wirklichkeiten* (**Creative reality originates in bold dreams**).

Kaskell had made arrangements for the Haussmann article to be published, and Rukser decided to print it to please Kaskell, but he did not like it. He could not resist making Kaskell aware of his evaluation:

> *Der Aufsatz von Fried. Haussmann ist gut wenn auch noch viel zu wenig eindringlich. Auch wir haben erst lernen müssen, daß man den hiesigen Lesern die Probleme so eindringlich wie Thomas Mann im Niemöller-Aufsatz beibringen muss. Aber wir werden Ihrem Wunsch gemäss nichts ändern. Aber bitte gehen Sie doch künftig keinerlei Verpflichtung wegen der Stellung eines Aufsatzes im Hefte ein. wir haben ja viel weniger Freiheit als es den Anschein hat.*[60]

---

60   Letter from U. Rukser to J. Kaskell, January 2, 1944.

TRANSLATION: The essay by Fried. Haussmann is good but lacks depth. We too had to learn that one must present the problems to the modern reader in a style so penetrating as that of Thomas Mann in the Niemöller-article. However, in accordance with your wish we won't change anything, but, please, in the future do not make any promises concerning the placement of articles in the journal. We have much less freedom than appears.

After having been taken to the woodshed, Kaskell had to be defensive in his reply:

Haussmann wird seine Mitarbeit übrigens auch nicht auf die Dauer ohne jede Honorierung leisten können, da er auf Einküinfte angewiesen ist. Er ist von grosser Wichtigkeit für uns nicht nur wegen seines fachlichen Könnens, sondern auch wegen der vielseitigen Beziehungen, die er hier zu entwickeln im Begriffe ist. [61]

TRANSLATION: Haussmann is unable to continue submitting his work for the long term without any kind of honorarium, since he is entirely reliant on an income. He has great importance for us, not only for his expert knowledge, but also for the many sided relationships that he is developing here.

The most sweeping of all the proposals for a Pan-Europe put forth in the *DB* are those of Erich Koch-Weser, the German statesman who fled from Nazi Germany to Brazil where he died in 1944. In his excellent and thought-provoking article, *Paneuropa* (25, 1945), Koch-Weser details his views on many aspects of a desired European unification. Two of his most basic beliefs were (1) that England and Russia should be admitted to a Pan-European union and (2) such a union must not become a facade for German hegemony in Europe. Koch-Weser begins with the assertion that Europe can no longer exist without an institution which will guarantee peace and then discusses some proposed plans for such an institution. Special treaties with neighboring states have always led only to new *Schützengräben (graves)*,

the author writes; therefore, treaties are not solutions. He has observed further that past attempts of strong foreign powers to assure peace in Europe

---

61 Letter from J. Kaskell to U. Rukser, February 15, 1944.

have been accompanied by grave dangers. when should these great powers interfere? Nor has the League of Nations proved effective in helping Europe to unite; it has, Koch-weser says, consistently failed in solving major problems, and has serious organizational and structural deficiencies. A major weakness is the lack of a long-term president. Another is the Lack of agencies to handle special regional problems. There is for example no agency to deal with special European questions. The statesman advocates a *Europabund* as a much better solution, and in the last half of the article outlines his proposals for the formation of such an organization of European nations.

Recognizing that a measure of sovereignty must be relinquished by member nations, the author idealistically asserts that they will do this if they are aware of the advantages of a European union. Koch-Weser states his administrative needs succinctly: *Der Europabund bedarf einer Bundesversammlung deren Mitglieder die Bundesstaaten ernennen, und eines Bundesrats, den die Bundesversammlung wählt* (**The European alliance needs a coalition whose members are appointed by the confederacy and a council chosen by the allied group** p, 29). The *Bundesrat* (**council**) would be chosen for a period of several years. The members must be nore concerned with the general welfare of all of Europe than with matters of individual national concern. War would be forbidden under Koch-weser's plan, and all disputes solved by the members of the general council (**Bund—readers may wonder that this term in German is translated differently in various places but the basic meaning is simply a** *group*).

The professor recognizes that the council must be strong. Therefore, he would give it an army because *ohne eigenes Heer wäre der Bund machtlos und unnütz* (**Without its own army the alliance would be powerless and of no value** p. 31). However, with such an army the *Bund* could enforce its decisions. If for in-stance a situation which could threaten freedom arose in a given nation, a three-fourths vote of the organization could order the guilty nation to correct the matter. If no action were taken by the given nation, the *Bund* would have to act. Koch-Weser recognizes that members of the *Bund* must, in order to function freely and properly, be assured of free speech, freedom of religion, and other basic freedoms. He also knows that problems as divergent as immigration, trade and communicable diseases must be handled equitably. A very important matter in forming a union of nations is agreement on terms for admittance and withdrawal. Koch-Weser recognizes the wisdom of the United States government of 1861 in preventing the South from withdrawing from the Federal Union.

He would not, allow secession from the *Bund* without full agreement of all member nations. The first nations would be admitted with the establishment of peace in 1945; for nations desiring to join later a two-thirds vote of approval would be required. Whether the planned union.should take the form of a league or of a superstate is a *Gelehrtenfrage* (**intellectual question**) and Koch-Weser makes no proposal. Having presented his plan clearly and thoroughly, he ends with thefollowing expression of hope: *Ich hoffe jedenfalls, ein Ziel aufgesetzt zu haben, daß Europa Genesung und den Europäern eine neue sinnvolle Aufgabe geben kann (***I hope in any case that I have laid out a goal, which will bring healing to Europe and to Europeans a new sensible task,** p. 341)

The editors of the *DB* were not content with printing numerous general presentations of the subject, but focused upon more important facets as well. economies and strengthening the position of small nations were favorite subjects. The best article on the topic of economics was written by Hans Heymann, who was teaching at Rutgers University. In 1921 at the urging of Walter Rathenau, he prepared a plan for a *Bank der Völker*. In 1941 he authored the book, *Plan for Permanent Peace*. His article on financing and dealing with the subject of a world bank appeared in the second issue of 1944. Heymann points to the work done at the Genoa Conference in 1922 and by friends of peace such as Parker Gilbert. He notes with sadness how damaging the rejection of earlier plans for a world bank have proven to be and deplores the greed for a "pound of flesh," which followed world war I. He is convinced that "makeshift plans" such as the Dawes Plan, the Young Plan, and the Basel Bank for International Settlements only contributed to World War II.

That said, in the opinion of this respected professor, a world bank is the key to world peace, arguing that, if economic stability can be established, everything will fall into place. W*ir müssen international die Welt neu aufbauen im Geiste kameradschaftlicher zusammenarbeit und eine Bank der Völker wäre der wirkungsvollste und umfassendste Mechanismus zu solchem Ziel* (**Working together, we have to build the world up internationally in a spirit of camaraderie. A Peoples Bank would be the most effective and comprehensive mechanism for achieving such an objective,** p. 121.

Because of America's belief in equality, democracy and freedom (and perhaps also because of its wealth), Heymann is convinced that the U.S.A. should lead the way in establishing and guaranteeing a world bank. After all, Heymann writes, it is a land still eager for adventure, and he is proposing a great new adventure for it. He ends with a hortatory call to humanitarian action common to so many articles in the *Blätter: Wollen wir uns selbst treu bleiben, so müssen wir der Welt beweisen, daß der traditionelle Pionier-Wagemut Amerikas noch lebt!* (**If we are to remain true to ourselves, we have to prove to the world that the traditional American spirit of adventure still lives** p, 16). Although he writes on the subject of a world bank, i.e. one with which all nations could work, Heymann gives emphasis to a future bond between only two parts of the world, the U.S.A. and Western Europe. The existence of a World Bank today is tangible proof that some of the seemingly idealistic proposals encountered in the *DB* were realized.

The life-long friends Kaskell and Rukser had grown even closer through the hardworking years, but not to the extent that they agreed on evaluations of submissions (or perhaps better said, "worth") of pieces to the journal. Heymann's contributions are an example. Kaskell agreed with F. Haussmann who criticized Heymann while Rukser was favorably impressed by his work as is clarified in the following exchange of letters.

> ***Rukser to Kaskell,*** May 3, 1943, *Können Sie fühlung nehmen mit Prof. Hans Heymann von der Rutgers universität? Im Aprilheft von Free World hat er seine Vorschläge über die Weltbank wiederholt. Ich halte das deshalb für sehr wichtig, weil nach dern Krieg ja wirklich ganz neue Finanz-methoden kommen müssen. Man muss sich dazu entschliessen, was Perikles einmal versucht hat: die Finanzierung des Friedens, womit so manche Kriegsursache im Keim erstickt würde. Und das kann nur solch ein wirklich international interessierter organismus Leisten.*

> ***Rukser to Kaskell,*** *January 10, 1944:.. Ferner lege einen Brief an Prof. Heymann bei zur Kenntnisnahme und Weiter gabe. Wenn Sie irgend wie können, nehmen Sie mit dem Mann Verbindung auf. Es lohnt sicherlich. Denn er ist einer der wenigen die Fantasie mit können verbinden: bitte senden Sie ihm doch auch Hefte der Zeitschrift zu, damit er vollends ins Bild kommt. Er könnte sicherlich viel nützen.*

> ***Kaskell to Rukser,*** *March 24, 1944: Schrieb ich lhnen schon, daß Haussmann eindri-nglich vor Hans Heymann warnt? Haussmann empfiehlt, aus Gründen der Einheitlichkeit, daß Sie alle aufsätze von politischem oder wirtschaftspolitischem Charakter, die aus den Vereinigten Staaten kommen, durch unsre Hände gehen zu lassen, weil wir es leichter haben, über die Qualität der Authoren zu informieren.*

> ***Kaskell to Rukser,*** *April 27, 1944, bezüglich Hans Heymann kann ich Haussmann nicht unrecht geben. Wirtschaftsfragen kann man nicht im Gartenlaube Stil behandeln.*

TRANSLATION (essence): Rukser and Kaskell were in minor disagreement. Rukser requests Kaskell to make contact with Prof. Hans Heyman at Rutgers since he wrote a good piece on the need for a World Bank and the need for new finance methods. He suggest they follow Pericles who once tried to finance peace. The second letter is still asking for that meeting with Heymann and includes a letter from Rukser to introduce himself. Furthermore, he wants him to receive some copies of the *Leaves* so that he may become fully informed.

In the March 24 letter Kaskell reminds that **Haussmann has urgently warned about Heymann. Haussmann suggests that all submissions on political or economic issues from the USA go through Kaskell and Haussmann because it is easier for them to judge the quality of the authors. (I imagine that did not sit well!)** In the final little note Kaskell says **Haussmann is correct, economic questions can not be handled in a sentimental** trashy—*Gardenlaube* style—**garden arbor**—refers to a junky style of writing.

Repeatedly the DB warns that the rights of small nations must be respected and their sovereignty guaranteed. Rukser had long been preoccupied with this matter. On July 27, 1942, he wrote Kaskell: *Sehen Sie die Wucht der Tatsachen ist doch derart, daß Mittel- und Kleinstaaten in der ganzen Welt gar keine Möglichkei mehr haben sich der Übermacht der Grossen zu erwehren* **(You see the impact of the facts is of such a nature that middle size and small size states throughout the world absolutely no longer have the super strength of the large ones with which to defend themselves).**

One article on the subject of small nations, *Nachkriegseuropa slawisch gesehen (***Postwar Europa from a Slavic Point of View**, 3, 1944) will suffice as a sampling of the treatment of this problem. It discusses the matter of a *New Europa* from the prospect of the Slavic Nations. In essence the author, Rudolf Bicantisch, recommends that the Slavic countries resolve their own petty disputes and unite to become a part of the *New Europe*. He cautions, however, that Pan-Slavism be avoided because it could be equal in malevolence to Pan-Germanism. The *DB* was anxious to warn of this danger; similar sentiments were expressed in other articles on the subject.

Many articles deal with a *New Europe*, but the ideas presented are repetitious. The best have been analyzed. In the following pages some pieces which broaden their scope to include the world and world peace organizations will be reviewed. In the majority of such articles Europe is the primary concern of the writers even though they are elaborating on the subject of a world organization. We have already encountered similar treatment of broader world-wide thinking in F. Heymann's ideas for the establishment of a World Bank, and it was noted that he too was primarity concerned with Europe. Furthermore, it must be observed that whether contributors are writing chiefly on a European union or on an international organization, the place and role of Germany within the whole is of major conceren. However, as we will see next, it was wise of the journal's publishers to present the outlook of another part of the world, unburdened with the "cultural baggage" of Germany and Europe and focusing on international cooperation and peace.

The first article to be examined is by Alejandro Alvarez, a Chilean professor of international law. His essay *La Futura Organización Internacional* appeared in Spanish with a German translation in issue twenty-three of 1945. In a short preface to the essay the editors avow their great respect for Alvarez and also assert the need for internationally minded political thinking in the postwar world. Nationalism was necessary in the last century, they write, in order to break the power of feudal lords, but in 1945 mankind needs to break through to a higher order, internationalism.

Dr. Alvarez begins his insightful essay with a caustic criticism of earlier studies concerning a future international organization. Since the beginning of the war such studies were freely made by many, but after the Conference of Dumbarton Oaks further work was based on the decisions made there by the U.S.A., England and Russia who were later joined by China. It was from the discussions conducted at this estate in the District of Columbia that the decisions were made and principles established upon which the United Nations was founded.

The Chilean professor argues that any author of a plan dating after Dumbarton Oaks was careful not to misplease those powers. The preliminary principles formulated at the conference which have come to be considered permanent are the following:

1. The big powers must have a dominant influence in the new organization.

2. The organization must be chiefly concerned with the maintenance of peace.

3. Peace is defined as the avoidance of war.

4. Because future war can come only from Germany and other conquered lands, measures for defense have to begin with this assumption (principle 3).

5. War must be suppressed by joint action of all countries against the aggressor.

6. Therefore, the new organization has to be a kind of alliance against the attacker. For this reason only those countries which truly love peace may participate.

7. The organization must rest on a single pact which has definitive character.

8. In the new organization continentalism, especially American, must receive partial recognition. The Latin American nations, therefore propose three stipulations:

   A. Equality under the law for both large and small countries.
   B. Preservation of sovereignty.
   C. Non-interference, especially military, in affairs outside of the continent.

Alvarez asserts that all of the above points are either incorrect or invite studied comment, and then logically begins his critique with point one by agreeing that the big powers should be assigned the primary responsibility for maintaining peace. However, they should not be empowered to interfere in the internal affairs of weaker nations or dominate in other matters. Secondly the professor believes that a future international organization must also eliminate the causes of social misunderstanding, which can also endanger peace. Thirdly, he does not share the definition that peace is simply the avoidance of war, but rather calls for a broader designation in agreement with the "new cooperative life" of all nations. Considering point four he states the obvious, any future wars could well be initiated by one of the victorious powers instead of former enemies.

Dr. Alvarez reminds us in considering principle five that in World War II certain nations which had pledged to assist an attacked country did not honor their commitment, while others, the USA included, had made no pledges, but helped anyway, and exactly how is a "peace loving nation" of principle six defined? All nations, he suggests, should be required to participate in an international organization whose foremost *raison d'être* would be word peace.

Alvarez objects to the seventh point, believing that the new organization can not rest on one comprehensive pact, since several are necessary.

Dumbarton Oaks did not sufficiently recognize American Continentalism in the professor's view; therefore, principle eight is his final objection. However, he agrees wholeheartedly with the proposal of the Latin American lands that they not intervene in European affairs unless world peace is threatened. Having stated his objections, professor Alvarez considers the theoretical bases for a future international organization, and, clearly, he is very focused on his personal definition of "proper functioning." He warns, as did so many in the pages of the *DB* that peace treaties must contain stipulations which will make such a future international organization possible rather than preparing the way for another war.

Alvarez broadens the scope of future plans. He does not limit himself to a *German Problem* nor to considerations for a united, cooperative and peace-loving Europe, foreseeing that only through international concern can peace be achieved in the technologically advanced twentieth century. His proposals were so totally agreeable to Rukser and Theile that in the following issue of the *DB* (24, 1945) they published a second article by the Chilean. *La Conferencia de Mexico* with a German translation is a continuation of his thoughts on internationalism. In his second article Alvarez gives increased attention to reorganization of the Pan-American Union and advocates a closer federation of American nations.

In a series of articles written in 1943, Rukser also enlarged his view of the future to include the entire world. Beginning with issue eight of 1943, the section formerly entitled *Im Schatten von Morgen* was renamed *Neue Methoden!* In that issue and in three others of that year the editor presented his thoughts on ways to establish a stable world order. His first essay under the new section heading was *Souveränität und Weltordnung.*

In the essay Rukser concerns himself primarily with the sovereignty of small nations. Their independence and rights should be guaranteed. He is writing of small nations throughout the world, not just in Europe. Rukser reiterates his thesis: States, both large and small, will have to be willing to give up part of their sovereignty to an international system. In *Weltordnung erfordert Weltinformation* **(World order requires World Information, 9, 1943)**. Rukser presented the unique idea that a stable international order could be more easily maintained if the entire world were better informed.

Rukser advises that world information is something other than news concerning day to day events, and he distrusts reports by diplomats because they may be slanted, He calls for unbiased information from all the world, a summary of news concerning political, military, economic and social happenings. Such information, given biannually, would facilitate accurate judgments about the state of each country. Rukser cautions that such information can be useful in preventing wars only if it is general, regular, and completely free of bias. It could also have other positive effects such as helping to solve economic and social problems throughout the world. In a defining summary he writes:

> *International Information Service besteht darin, daß er der öffentlichen Meinung der Welt die Grundlage für eine Stellungnahme zu gewissen Fragen liefern würde. Er würde also erst die Möglichkeit schaffen für eine unparteiische und gut unterrichtete öffentliche Meinung. Für solches Ziel müssen aber alle erdenklichen Opfer gebracht werden, weil nur eine gut fundierte öffentliche Meinung der Welt die moralische Kraft hat, den widerstrebenden Völkern und auch den Grossmächten das Gesetz der internationalen Solidarität aufzuerlegen!* (p. 12).

TRANSLATION: An International Information Service would offer the public opinion of the world the basis for taking a position on certain issues. It would in the first place create the possibility for impartial and well-informed public opinion. To achieve such an objective, however, all conceivable sacrifices must be made because only a well-founded public world opinion has the moral power to impose international solidarity on the resisting public and also the Great Powers.

We will assume that all compassionate human beings would agree with Rukser that the abolition of war should be a prime goal of mankind and worthy of the most strenuous efforts.

In an article in the next issue (10, 1943) Rukser discusses agricultural reform as a means of assuring world peace. He felt that modern man with his technology and industry had forgotten that the destiny of man lies in his relationship to the earth. Of course, Rukser himself had been farming for a number of years in Germany and Chile. Quoting the North American, Murray Butler, Rukser agrees that history teaches us that nothing contributes more to social stability and the general welfare than the broadest possible distribution of the land. The soil was and remains the basis for our existence, and it should be made available to all people.

In the last issue of 1943 Rukser gave his opinions on the role of basic freedoms in maintaining world order. He observes that it is foolish to equate democracy with peace and poses a questions: Have not so-called democractic states also caused war? A chief evil of totalitarian governments is that they lose no time in abolishing basic freedoms such as freedom of the press and of speech. Therefore, Rukser decideds that nations which uphold basic freedoms are more likely to support world peace. An international society should assure the right to these freedoms throughout the world.

Rukser's articles on the preservation of international law and order welcome any plan that could possibly effect the unification of Europe and international cooperation. Other contributors to the *DB* shared Rukser's hopes. No less a figure than our now familiar, Thomas Mann, is quoted on the subject of international unification (2, 1944): *Was am Ausgange dieses Krieges stehen muss und wird, ist klar. Es ist der Beginn einer Weltvereinigung.... die Völker sind reif für eine solche Neuordnung der Welt* (**It is clear that at the end of this war a new world organization must, and will exist...the people are ready for such a new order of the world,** p. 2). Mann prophesied the creation of a new balance of freedom and equality and the preservation of individuality vithin the framework of the collective whole. His most, utopian prophecy foresaw the establishment of a society of free but socially responsible peoples having equal rights and duties; Mann thought Europe was ripe for this development.

It is especially interesting to note the mixed reaction of the *DB* to the establishment of the United Nations. *Der neue Völkerbund* is the title of an editorial which appeared in the July/August issue of 1945, welcoming the new organization as a step in the right direction with these words: *Es besteht kein Zweifel, daß der neue Völkerbund für den Weltfrieden von höchster Bedeutung ist* (**Without doubt the new United Nations has the highest significance for world peace,** p. 52). However, it is observed that the organization is powerless to enforce peace, especially with regard to powerful nations. *Darum steht ausser Zweifel, daß der neue Weltbund versagen wird und versagen muss, wenn etwa ein Angriff von einer Grossmacht ausgeht oder von ihr gedeckt wird (***Therefore, the new federation will fail [and fail it must] if one of the great powers initiates an attack or hides one,** p. 52).

However, the self-expatriated duo displayed their usual optimism about the future in expressing hope that weaknesses would be corrected to such a degree that the UN would become an effective enforcer of world peace. Here, we might again let the reader decide, perhaps *blog* about this matter. Would our editors have enjoyed *blogging*? Think about it, for now we continue.

Rukser expressed some thoughts on a replacement for the League of Nations in a letter to Kaskel on January 1, 1943:

Ich halte es für sehr wichtig sich klar zu machen was es bedeutet, daß sich jedes volk durch Geburt und Tod, durch Erfindungen und arbeit ständig verändert, Diesem ewigen Wechsel entspricht die innerstaatliche organisation durch Anpassung der Gesetze oder durch Revolution. Aber im internationalen Leben war bisher meist der Krieg das entsprechende Ventil. Bis zum Völkerbund hat das Konzert der Grossmächte diese Frage der Anpassung an neue Verhältnisse gar nicht sclecht gelöst. Aber der Völkerbund hat gerade da so vollständig versagt, weil niemand opfer bringen wollte am wenigsten Herr Benesch, Herr Sikorski usw, einschl. der Franzose. Die künftige international Ordnung steht und fällt mit der Lösung dieses Problems. Ich glaube, daß es viel besser wäre sich erst mal zu machen, aus welchen Fehlern die heutige Lage entstanden ist und dann auf der Basis des Genfer Völkerbundes weiter zu bauen.

TRANSLATION: I find it to be of great importance to make clear what it means that all peoples through birth and death, through experience and work are contantly changing. This eternal change corresponds to the organization within states of applying laws or through revolution. However, in the international world to date war has been the corresponding outlet. Up to the time of the United Nations the concerted effort of the great powers in solving this issue of adjusting to new relationships has not been bad at all. But the League of Nations failed so miserably because no one would make a sacrifice, especially Mr. Benesch, Mr. Sikorski, etc., including the French. The future international order will stand or fall with the solution of this problem. I think that it would be much better first to make clear what the mistakes were which led to the present situation and then rebuild on the basis of the Geneva organization.

To a great extent the dreams of a *New Europe* as envisioned in the *DB* have today been realized. While world peace has yet to be achieved, there is cooperation among Western European nations and rapprochment between Eastern and Western Europe. The U.S.A. has fulfilled the periodical's hopes by becoming a leading force for international, peace, but the UN has remained frustratingly ineffective as an enforcer of peace; small nations are still oppressed. Although all the suggestions for world improvement have not been implemented the *DB* must be credited for its far-sighted leadership in advocating sincere world-wide brotherhood.

Chapter VII
Nazism, Socialism, Communism

THE THREE POLITICAL movements on which the *DB* concentrated in its coverage of political thinking of the day were National Socialism, Communism and Socialism. Obviously, National Socialism was odious to the *DB* because it disregarded basic human rights; it tried to pattern the thinking of human beings for vile purposes instead of encouraging free development, in accordance with humanistic principles. Furthermore, Dr. Rukser saw National Socialism as an impediment to Germany's natural tendency to world citizenship. He was possessed with *One Worldism* and argues in *Nationalismus? Patriotismus?* (8, 1944) that Germany did not have a natural bent for fanatic nationalism; the Nazi government was repressing Germany's enlightened leadership of Europe.

Some arguments tend to be somewhat irrealistic and lead nowhere. The best rational evaluation of National Socialism in the periodical is Rukser's *Recht ist, was dem Volke nützt* (**Right is that which serves the People**, 2, 1943). In this essay Rukser refrains from denouncing, Nazis pointing to atrocities or exposing the depravity of Hitler. Logically and tersely, as though presenting a court case against National Socialism, Rukser, the lawyer, analyzes the legal basis of one of its well-known premises, *Recht ist was dem Volke nützt*. He knows that certain Nazi slogans, especially this one he is examining, appear at first glance to reveal *gesunden Menschenverstand* (**sound understanding**). The average man or woman upon reading this slogan about serving the people accepts the idea. So it is, Rukser says, that people fall into the Nazi trap.

Does this slogan form the basis for a new system of law as the Nazis assert? In order to judge this objectively, the editor writes, one must determine its general validity. If it is a basic principle of law, then stealing and murder are justified when committed for the advantage of the *Volk*. Using similar examples, Rukser proceeds to argue that the Nazi claim is ludicrous; in order to apply the principle equitably one would have to determine objectively whether or not the people are served if X murders Y. A principle of law can not properly be judged by its **utility** (*Nützlichkeit*). Rukser lucidly clarifies:

> *Wenn man daraufhin den Begriff des Nützens prüft, so stellt sich rasch heraus, daß Nützlichkeit ja immer nur in Beziehung auf irgend ein Ziel besteht, daß Nützlichkeit an und für sich notwendig relativ ist und somit gar kein allgemeines Criterium abgeben kann, sondern von der Verschiedenheit der Zwecke wie von den Umständen des Falles abhängt (p. 7).*

TRANSLATION: If one consequently tests the concept of need, it quickly becomes obvious that need is always determined in relationship with an objective. Need on its own is notably relative and, therefore, can not present a general criterium, but rather is dependent on the different purposes and circumstances of the situation.

Rukser proves that even the Nazis have found it impossible to erect a new legislative order based on the principles of utilitarianism and have been forced to modify the concept several times, which has led to their modified definition based on race: *Recht ist was die arischen Menschen dafür halten (***Right is what the Aryan people hold it to be)**. Becoming ever more simplistic they have now, inevitably, regressed to the most unobjective of all their slogans: *Der Wille des Führers ist Recht* **(The will of the Führer is right)**. Yes, indeed! There we have it, plain and simple. How many years did it take to get there? Hitler had completely metamorphosed into a deity. This Jesus? God? Zeus? or whatever kind of savior, from Lenz, Austria, who in spite of speaking funny German and rolling his R's with his tongue, was superior to mortals. Why not now add that he was born in a manger?

Maybe, like the Inca of Peru, he was sent directly from on high. We know that many people will believe anything, at least for awhile. Then too every soul in the Incan Empire knew well that the will of the Inca was right, was law. One did exactly what was laid out for one to do, and virtually every aspect of a person's life was contolled, even to the point of choosing whom one should marry and when one should get drunk on the native *chicha*. It was Yet another, though earlier, unmitigated despotism on the planet. Perhaps Hitler learned from the Incas and **The** Inca (ruler)as well. One could never be certain about what he had read or learned and retained.

Rukser was disheartened, indeed. Germans were not the 16th century Natives to which I made a connection or had they really developed only that far? His fellow countrymen should be long past acceptance of a leader with magical powers sent down from the heavens with his sister as wife. How could *das Volk* possibly worship this paradoy of an emperor? It is a pity that I can not share with the frustrated lawyer my comparison to this ancient dictatorship. In all truth it is not that different in basic ways to what Rukser observed.

In the thinking of Dr. Rukser, the lawyer, society must be based on sound principles of law and order and in despair reminds readers of the insidious and illegal dangers inherent in the Nazi slogan: *Der Wille eines Einzeln is kein Ordnungsprinzip, er ist nackte Willkür. Der Versuch, das Rechtssystem auf Nützlichkeit zu gründen führt notwendig ins chaos. In den Abgrund des Nihilismus* (**The will of an individual is not a regulation; it is naked will. The attempt to found a system of law upon need [utility] leads inevitably to chaos,** *p.8).*

In order to transfer the meaning of National Socialism from the abstract to the concrete and personal, early issues of the *DB* publicized instances of Nazi cruelty to individuals. Frequently the cold logic of Rukser's article summarized above was replaced by a highly emotional appeal.The life and good acts of Kaj Munk, the benevolent poet, Protestant minister and Danish patriot, are related in some detail in *Vom Martyrium Europasl Kaj Munk, ein dänischer Patriot* (**Danish patriot**) by A.H. Winsnes (5, 1944), The purpose of the *DB* in publishing this account is explained in a fervent editorial introduction:

> *Am 3. Januar 1944 erschienen im Pfarrhaus der kleinen westjütländischen Stadt Vederö vier Burschen, die sich als Beamte der GESTAPO ausgaben. Kaj Munk der seit zwanzig Jahren in diesem Pfarrhaus wirkte, telefonierte gerade mit einem Freunde. "Die Deutschen holen mich." Dann hing Kaj Munk ein. Vor fünf Monaten hatten sie ihn zum ersten Male geholt. Seit langem stund Kaj Munk auf der Liste der Gestapo. Von diesem stillen Pfarrhaus ging vom ersten Tag der Besetzung Dänemarks durch die Nazis der leidenschaftlichste und zugleich geistigste Wiederstand aus: Wir Dänen hätten kämpfen müssen, predigte Kaj Munk; kämpfen wie unsere Brüder und Schwestern in Norwegen. Für das, was dir teuer, kämpf und stirb! Dieses alte Lied hatte man wohl gesungen, die Botschaft nachzuleben vergessen... Elise Marie Munk stand mit ihren fünf Kindern dabei als die Büttel der GESTAPO ihren Mann ins Auto stiessen und fortführen.*

Am nächsten Morgen fand ein Bauer in den Wäldern um Silkeborg ein halbes hundert Kilometeer entfernt die Leiche. Die Nazis leugneten den Mord, behaupteten, jene Bürschen wären keine Gestapobeamte gewesen. Niemand schenkte ihnen Glauben; Überall verbreitete sich das Entsetzen über den Mord. Wir alle kennen die rastlose Brutalität der Nazi Methoden. Hier hatten sie das Leben eines grossen und edlen Mann ausgelöscht (p, l).

TRANSLATION: On January 3, 1944, four punks appeared at the parrish house of the small Jutland town of Vederö. They claimed to represent the GESTAPO. Kaj Munk, who had labored in this parrish house for twenty years immediately telephoned his friend: "The Germans have come for me." He then hung up. Five months earlier they had picked him up for the first time. For a long time his name had been assigned to the GESTAPO list. Since the first day of the occupation of Denmark by the Nazis a passionate and at the same time moral resistance had emanated from this quiet house. We Danes should have fought, Kaj preached; fought as did our brothers and sisters in Norway. For that which is dear to you, fight and die! This old song was sung, but we forgot to live up to its message…Elise Marie Munk stood next to him with her five children as the leader of the GESTAPO pushed her husband into the car and drove off. The next morning, in the forest surrounding Silkeborg, fifty kilometers away a farmer found Kaj Munk's body. The Nazis denied the murder, claiming that those punks were not representative of the GESTAPO. No one believed them. Anger over the murder spread everywhere. All of us understood the never ceasing brutality of the Nazi methods. This time they had rubbed out the life of a great and noble man.

In *Carl von Ossietzky zum Gedenk*en (**In Memory of Carl…9/10, 1944**) Alfred Kantorowicz gives a personal, sympathetic account of the editor of the *Weltbühne* (**World Stage**), and winner in November, 1936 of the Nobel Peace Prize. Nazi barbarity appears particularly horrible when directed against this benign human being, small of stature and shy. Kantorowicz relates how he and some friends accompanied the Nobel Laureate to Tegel prison near Berlin where, accused of writing about the illegal rearmament of Germany in the *Weltbühne* (**world stage**)he was sentenced to serve eighteen months for the crime of high treason. After suffering numerous physical and mental tortures at the hands of the Nazis, this expositor of peace died on May 4, 1938, only fifty years of age. It has been reported that Ossietzky's demonstration of unforgettable valor and nobility was one of the gravest moral defeats suffered by Hitler. Kantorowicz continues to remember not only his deceased friend, he also memorializes those others who accompanied Ossietzky to Tegel to be murdered.

The *DB* taught that it was not only well-known persons who were victimized by National Socialism. *Morgen werde ich erschossen* (**Tomorrow I'll be Shot,** 7, 1943) gives one of the best pictures of Nazi disregard for the common man and contempt for human life. It is a letter composed by a twenty-five-year-old Frenchman for his wife, daughter and mother shortly before he was executed in Paris, even though Germany had signed the *Haager Landkriegs-Ordnung* **(Hague Convention)** forbidding murder of hostages. The last lines of the Letter read: *Einen Gruss noch an alle Freunde. Ich hoffe, daß sie mich nie vergessen. Bewahrt diesen Brief als ein Andenken. Einen Kuss für mein Kleines* (**A final greeting to all friends. I hope that you will never forget me. Save this letter as a memorial. A kiss for my little one** *p.1*). Suppose he was shot through the head? What happens to people? Of course orders are orders, but sometimes the executioners were drunk. Bullets flew everywhere. Did any of these *Schergen* **(hangmans' assistants, i.e. doers of the dirty work)** also have a little daughter back home?

The *DB* remained unrelenting in disclosing the depravity of far too many Germans. Thomas Mann had termed Hitler an unmitigated Swine, but did the label apply to all Nazis?... Perhaps so. The murder of the young French father and his tender expression of love for his family induced frustration, tears and outrage as mournful readers pondered the inhuman horror of this deed. Surely, we can assume that all who read of the incident form a mental picture of the savagery. In further issues the journal recounts several execrable deeds committed against political opponents, Jews and citizens of Nazi occupied lands; reprisals for the twentieth of June attempt on Hitler's life and other examples of revenge were also reported. Repugnant as some of the accounts may be, a realistic picture of the evils of National Socialism emerges, deemed necessary in order to arouse the indignation of readers.

Could even worse acts and forms of genocide occur, perpetrated even on the most innocent of persons, who had neither committed nor revenged brutality they had received? You already know my positive response: of course. This was the time when generally the word *German* became a symbol of everything humanity condemns as brutal, despicable and inhuman. Indeed, Hitler did not win the war, but he succeeded very well at instilling deep wretching fear in millions. Of that he was exceedingly proud.

National Socialism was also attacked in articles which revealed the personality and thinking of Adolf Hitler, a rather novel touch linked to the question of how the war was caused. In *Der Führer* (3, 1944) Karl Paetel gave a documented account of Hitler's treachery and false promises in dealing with foreign nations. Paetel treated Hitler in another article with the same title (8, 1944) in which he calls Hitler, *eine der grossen negativen Figuren der Weltgeschichte* (**one of the greatest negative figures of world history** p. 18).

Ernst Wilhelm Meyer, who in protest against Hitler, gave up his post with the German Foreign service, outlined for readers an inside look at what a Nazi victory would mean for Germany and the world in **Hitler's Sieg, eine Tragödie für Deutschland** (2, 1944). In Dr. Myer's opinion the war is being fought against Hitler not against the German people, but because of Hitler they will suffer. Then, too, he notes that chances for the realization of a European community may have been damaged for many years because of the malevolent ideas of one psychopath. He asks Germans to see Hitler for what he really is, not the savior of Germany but a destructive egomaniac.

The *DB* allowed Hitler to reveal himself in issue three of 1944. The entire speech given by the beloved leader (Deity) to his staff on August 22, 1939, is reprinted; it had been recorded by the Associated Press correspondent, Louis Lochner as he listened to it. Hitler explains that he is going to invade Poland without regard for world opinion. His derogatory comments on world leaders, his insistence on *Lebensraum* (**living space**—viewed by the Nazis as an entitlement) and his contempt for human life clearly reveal his character. Readers of the *DB* needed no explanations.

Eduard Sinn in *Führerprinzip* (The Leader Principle, 4, 1943) exposes the true meaning of the concept. He writes that the idea is not new in history. At times in the past the affairs of a country have become chaotic. A *Führer* has then restored order. this has seemed good for a while Sinn reminds us, but, what it really means is, in his words, *Autorität nach unten—Verantwortung nach oben* (p. 4). He explains what this means in the case of Hitler.

> *Auf Nazistisch heisst vielmehr, Autorität nach unten, unbedingter willkürliche Befehlsgewalt: Verantwortung nach oben heisst, wie wir oft genug zu hören bekommen haben: blinder Gehorsam—ohne Rücksicht auf Staat, Gesetz, Moral, Menschlichkeit und Vernunft. Der Untergebene hat jede ihm erteilte Anordnung ohne—jedwede eigene Prüfung der Legalität blindlings auszuführen. Das ist*

nichts anderes als das Prinzip des Terrors im totalen Staat, dessen Furchtbarkeit wir jetzt täglich erleben (p. 4).

TRANSLATION: [beginning with *Autoriteit* in the case of Hitler] It really means in referring to Hitler or *in Nazi-speak [auf Nazistisch]* **a lot more, authority down, unlimited arbitrary power of command: Responsibility toward the top means, as we frequently enough have had to hear, blind obedience—without consideration of the state, law, morality, humanity and good sense. The underling must blindly carry out every request issued to him without any kind of proof of legality. This is nothing more than the principle of terror in a totalitarian state, the horribleness of which we are experiencing daily.**

Needless to say, the *Deutsche Blätter* uncovered no positive values in National Socialism. The periodical was only interested in exposing it both through accounts of its methods and examination of its principles. It has been emphasized that the *DB* did not represent any one political party. in answer to criticism by Hans Richter and others Rukser wrote Richter on January 5, 1944, reiterating the independence of the magazine: *Freilich Parteistandpunkte wird man bei uns nicht finden. und wer will mag uns deshalb unklar nennen. Das schadet gar nichts. Denn man kann es ja nicht allen recht machen* **(To be sure, party positions will not be found with us, and whoever will, may, therefore, label us as unclear. That doesn't bother us for one can not make it right with every body.)**

Nevertheless, in spite of its striving to remain neutral, certain sympathies naturally emerged. In keeping with the journal's emphasis on humanitarian goals, a leaning to socialism is discernible. The periodical's views on communism however are usually associated with its analysis of the Soviet Union; Russia and its communism are feared and approached with caution. In issue seven of 1943 Udo Rukser pointed out in *Bolschewismus als Schreckgespenst* **(Bolshevism as a Nightmare)** that many Germans were being duped by the following argument: *Hitler hat unzweifelhaft sehr viel Übles getan, aber wenn es ihm gelingt mit dem Bolschewismus fertig zu werden dann ist er gerechtfertigt…*(**Hitler has doubltless carried out a good deal of evil, but if he is successful in finishing off Bolshevism, then he is justified**, p. 14).

Rukser portrays Bolshevism as being chiefly an agrarian reform for the betterment of the desperate condition of the farmers of Czarist Russia. The editor does not recommend Bolshevism as a panacea for social problem, but he deplores Nazi exploitation of German fear of the Russian movement as an evil system, which will engulf Germany with its terror. He expresses this as follows: *Der Nazismus hat natürlich alles Interesse daran, Terror und Bolschevismus gleich zu setzen, jener politischen Bewegung alle erdenklichen Greuel anzukreiden, um so die sachliche Stellungnahme zu vermeiden, ja unmöglich zu machen* (**Nazism, of course, has great interest in making Bolshevism and terror equal, to mark that political movement with all possible atrocities in order to avoid an objective position, indeed, make it impossible,** p. 16).

The editor finds no difference between Bolshevist terror and Nazi terror. Both are political systems which replace true religion with a godless secular religion and justify any means which achieve their ends.The Russians, Rukser states, wish to identify themselves with world Communism, but they have hurt the international movement by participating in the Spanish Civil War, practicing *Volksfront-Politik* and making a pact with the Nazis. The Russian Bolshevist movement is for Rukser indicative that beterment of social conditions is needed through out the world, but Bolshevism is not, he says, the best solution. Rather, He suggests that the best way to combat it is by offering more attractive solutions to social problems, and in *Das neue Weltbild* (3, 1944) Rukser explains how *ein gewaltiger Szenerwechsel auf der Weltbühne* (**a powerful change of scenery on the world stage**) has taken place since the end of the First World War.

Europe has by no means been the acknowledged center of the world; it has lost the position of power that it, once enjoyed. The great powers of the day, and even more so of the future are the U.S.A. and Russia. The editor is especially intrigued with the phenomenal growth of Russia and the ever increasing strength of its position as a world power. His admiration and wonder are apparent in the following statement: *Wenn wir bedenkenl was Russland alles in den letzten 25 Jahren erlebt hat, und Russlands unerklärlichen wie phänomenalen Aufstieg betrachten, dann können wir das nur als eines der grossen historischen Ereignisse bezeichnen (***When we consider all Russia has experienced in the last 25 years, and observe Russia's inexplicable and phenomenal rise, we can describe it only as a great historic occurrence,** *p, 6).* Then he admonishes that we stay alert to this giant among nations because nobody can say what outcomes will emerge.

As in the first article discussed above Dr. Rukser faces political realities, while while again admitting that Russia is a power to reckon with. The editor seems in fact fascinated with the phenomenon, what will the future of Russia be? what is its next step? How will it fit into a new Europe? Rukser can only speculate about possible answers.

Albert Theile admired the Russian army without having great admiration for Bolshevism. His article *Die unbekante Armee* (**The Unknown Army**, 8, 1943) begins with a revelation of Russian military strength. *Zu den den grössten Überraschungen (nicht nur für die Nazis) gehört in diesem Kriege die Schlagkraft. der sowjetrussischen Armee. Die Nazis haben zugeben müssen, daß ihnen die Rote Armee als Militärmacht* überlegen ist (**One of the biggest surprises [(not only for the Nazis] coming out of this war is the striking power of the Soviet Russian Army,** p. 20). Theile sketches the history of the Russian army and explains reasons for its strength. He praises it for stopping Hitler, but is not convinced that the brilliant accomplishments of the army indicate a strength of the soviet system.

The publisher opines that the fervent defense of the homeland is solely due to a great love of Russia; he is not willing to admit the possibility that the Russian soldiers approved of the communist government.

Issue nine of 1943 presented a negative view of Karl Marx in *Begegnung mit Karl Marx* (**meeting with…**) which was excerpted from Karl schurz's account of his meeting with Marx. Schurz, who found the thirty-year-old Marx to be most arrogant, writes that Marx manifested contempt for fellow human beings.

However, he also seemed pleased at having learned from this experience, primarily that, *Wer ein Führer oder ein Lehrer des Volkes sein will, muss seine Zuhörer mit Achtung behandeln.* Schurz was at least to some extent a slow learner if he was only coming to this obvious knowledge that **he who aspires to be a leader or teacher of the masses must treat his followers with respect.**

Russia was not simply a country with an experimental form of government called communism which one should try to understand, but also a country whose armies were invading Germany bringing in one hand freedom from Nazism, but in the other terrible revenge (*furchtbare Vergeltung)*. The edtorial asks questions to which we now well know the answers. *Wird also Russland die edlere Rolle des Befreiers whälen, der die Hindernisse weg räumt, welche einer gedeihlichen Entwicklung Europas entgegenstehen? Wird es den Deutschen, wenn nicht heute und morgen, so doch später die Möglichkeit geben, eine soziale Demokratie von innen her zu entwickeln?* (**Will Russian take the more noble role of liberator which would push aside obstacles blocking a successful development of Europe? Will the Germans, if not today and tomorrow, get the opportunity later to develop a social democracy from within?** p, 1).

some of Rukser's correspondence also shows concern with Russia and its Communism. On January 10, 1944, Rukser wrote to Kaskell:

Inzwischen hat sich die russische Politik ja wieder etwas mehr dekouvriert und unsere Befürchtungen vor einem russischen

Militarismus sind keinesfalls geringer geworden. Leider sieht man, daß in Teheran keine politische Einigung erzielt worden ist: was von den Abstimmungen zuhalten ist, die die Russen für Osteuropa vorschlagen, wissen wir. Ob es andere auch wissen? Das sind nähmlich Abstimrnungen nach Hitlers Rezept: Leider. Lassen sie sich also da nicht dumm machen!

TRANSLATION: In the meantime the Russian political situation has revealed itself a little more, and our fears of Russian militarism have not been lessened. Unfortunately one perceives that in Teheran there is no intention to achieve political agreement: we know what to think of the voting that Russian is proposing for Eastern Europe. Do others also know? Those are votes of the Hitler pattern

On February 19, 1944, Rukser again poured his heart out to his life-long friend. Neither liked current developments in Europe *(Die Entwicklung in Europa)*. It *macht uns die grösste Sorge. Was geschieht, wenn die Russen vor den Allierten in Deutschland sind? Am Beispiel Polen kann mans sich klar* machen *(***It causes us the greatest concern. What will happen if if the Russians get to Germany ahead of the Allies? The example of Poland clarifies what will happen)**. Clearly these two friends held mixed feelings about Russia and its Communism, but socialism is unequivocally favored in Several articles ranging from portraits of individual socialist leaders to analyses of socialistic plans for society.

Carl Zuckmayer was sympathetic to the solcialist, Carlo Mierendorff,and the *DB* agreed by printing his *Carlo Mierendorff, Porträt eines deutschen Sozialisten (6, 1944)* in which he outlined the history of his personal friendship with Mierendorff and emphasized the well-known socialist's humanitarianism. Mierendorff emerges as the type of human being the *DB* most admires.

Zuckmayer describes him as *beglückend und ansteckend lebensvoll. gesund, stark und heiter* **(a bringer of good cheer and evidencing an infectious abundance of life. Healthy, strong and upbeat.)**He was *fähig, wie ein Dramatiker,das Wesen der anderen Seite zu sehen und ihren Standort zu begreifen, auch wenn er ihn bekämpfte (***like an actor he had the capacity to see the essence of the other side and to comprehend their position, even when they strongly opposed him, p.3)** . Zuckmayer explains that Mierendorff's *entscheidene Eigenschaften waren einfacher und mannhafter Art: Mut, Offenheit, Treue* **(Mierendorff's defining characteristics were simple and manly: courage, honesty and reliability, p, 4)**. The socialist Leader was an idealist who unfailingly stood up for his principles. He refused to flee Germany in 1933, posing the question: *Was sollen denn unsere Arbeiter denken, wenn wir sie da allein lassen? Sie können doch nicht alle an die Riviera ziehen!* (**What will then out workers think if we leave them here alone? They can't all move to the Riviera,** p. 10). Even throughout the horrors of life in concentration camps Mierendorff remained committed to his beliefs, Just as a negative description of Karl Marx sheds unfavorable light on communism, Zuckmayer's eulogy of Mierendorff implies a positive evaluation of socialism.

Short appreciations of the lives and political activities of Hans vogel. (28, 1945) and Kurt schmidt (30, 1946) further add to the general picture of socialist leaders as humanitarians. We learn from Vogel's own letters that he passionately desired a democratic Germany after the war. Schmidt is praised for remaining true to his socialistic views throughout seven years of imprisonment by the Nazis. An editorial-note on Schmidt is indicative of the magazine's sympathy for socialist causes, especially for betterment of the lot, of the worker. *Vieler Jahrzehnten Lasten, Hunger und Qual hat der deutsche Arbeiter. getragen. Kriegs- und FriedensLasten, aber niemals hat er eine schwerere Last getragen als in diesen zwölf Jahren. Niemals auch eine ehrenvollere und keine Hand einer dunklen oder hellen Zukunft soll diesen unvergänglichen Glanz von seiner Stirne wischen!* (**Throughout many centuries the German worker suffered with burdens, hunger and suffering, but never has he experienced such a heavy burden as in the last twelve years. Nor a period filled with more honor, and no hand from a darker or brighter future shall wipe this everlasting lustre from his brow,** p, 53)

In issue twelve, 1943, Theile and Rukser praised England's Beveridge Plan as a great step forward in socialistic progress. They correctly state that until the interruption of world war II Germany was the leader in establishing socialistic laws. Now this position must be conceded to Great Britain. The publishers find it astounding that England could take such a step in the middle of the war and praise the action as being not a law, but a *Denkschrift für die Gesetzgeber* (**memorial to the law makers,** p. 31). The highlights of the plan are then outlined for readers.

The periodical approves of family subsidies from the government for children under fifteen and welcomes the forthcoming assistance for schooling and free medical care. It seems that everything has been provided for in the plan: costs of illnesses, old age assistance, education and employment comprise the most beneficial. The editors of the *DB* agree with the objectives of Lord Beveridge that the plan is an attempt at mutual support by all members of the English nation. It is an effort to assure the basic needs of life to all. The proposals are proof that the first concern of a government must be the welfare of its common citizens.

We read that *es ist die schönste Sozialversicherung der Welt, die Beveridge an seinem Schreibtisch entworfen hat, gewiss die vollständigste und die übersichtlichste,* **(It is the finest social insurance in the world, conceptualized by Beveridge at his desk. Certainly it is the most complete and clear,** *p. 33).* Does the world never change? Do the same problems, along with new ones, never go away? The foregoing reads like minutes from a USA senate meeting of today. In the USA, taking best care possible of the citizens does not appear to be an objective of government.

Another excellent piece, *Internationale Politik deutscher Sozialisten (4, 1944)* presented the views of the *Union deutscher sozialistischer Organisationen in Grossbritanien.* The periodical promised to publish opinions of other socialist groups in subsequent issues, but the promise was only partially kept.

The first proposal of the German socialists living in England was most appealing to our *DB* friends. It reads: *Als internationale Sozialisten erstreben wir eine internationale Ordnung, die die Ursachen kriegerischer Konflikte beseitigt* **(As international socialists we strive for international order, which eliminates the causes of militant conflicts,** p. 37). The second proposal on the same page was completely in keeping with one of the most favored of *DB objectives: Wir setzen uns ein für eine Föderation aller europäischen Völker da die volle nationalstaatliche Souveränität nicht länger mit den wirtschaftlichen und politischen Existenz-Bedingungen in Europa vereinbar ist* **(We champion a federation of all the people of Europe in as much as full national state souvereignty is no longer connected with the business and political requirements of existence in Europe.)**

The group was understandably against any further alliance between the German military and industrialists. It is obvious that many, if not all of the objectives of the exiled socialsts, were shared by the *DB*. The points made briefly in this article were treated at length in several other pieces throughout the four years of publication. Briefly, to end this chapter I will allow myself one further example to drive home my point of great sympathy for the goals of the socialists, Kurt Schumacher's *Aufruf der S.P.D. für ein neues, besseres Deutschland* **(call by the SPD for a new and better Germany,** 1946).

Schumacher was faced with the difficult task of rebuilding the Social Democratic Party in Germany after the war. The editors of the *Blätter* pronounced Schumacher's *Aufruf* **(The call)** to be *ein Dokument politischer Einsicht, von höchstem Rang* **(ein document offering political insight of the highest level,** p. 59). One infers that the publishes of the *DB* are in complete agreement with Schumacher's following assertion; *Die sozialdemokratische Partei* *steht in dern Bewusstsein, die einzige Partei in Deutschland zu sein deren Potitik der Demokratie und des Friedens die probe vor dem Richterstuhl der Geschichte bestanden hat, jetzt vor ihrer grössten Aufgabe aus den Trümmern Deutschlands ein neues, besseres Reich aufzubauen* (**The social democratic party exists in our awareness as the only party in Germany whose politics of democracy and peace withstood the test of the judgement bench of history, and now stands ready for its greatest task, to form a new and better** *Reich* **from the ruins of Germany,** p. 59).

There is no statement denying editorial concurrence with schumacher's views. His further comments on the besmirching of Germany's good name by the Nazis, his denunciation of the political influence of *Grosskapital*, and his hope for cooperation among European nations are principle concerns of the journal. The socialist leader admonishes readers as does the *DB*: *Kämpft mit uns für Frieden, Freiheit und Sozialismus*. To fight for **Peace, Freedom and Socialism** could have been the motto of the journal.

Chapter VIII
Religion

So, we have arrived at the chapter on religion, a topic which I, perhaps, should not cover at all, since my mind is already set with the notion that religion is one of the elements that causes rather than prevents wars, and all religions throughout the world encourage belief in hocus-pocus and general nonsense. The Middle Ages in the German lands and elsewhere were formed and permeated by religious forces which assured a degree of cohesion among disparate elements of existence through the acceptance by the people of a precise scale of values, viewed as a "hierarchy of being" or *scala naturae*.

God, the Prime Mover, sits atop the "Great Chain of Being" which descends from that highest point of the *scala* down to the bottom where the minerals are placed. Elements may be pure spirit in form or mortal flesh. Earthly flesh is mutable, fallible and ever-changing. Spirit, however, is permanent. Man is special since he is both. The ongoing struggle between spirit and flesh is a moral one. Correctly, most readers will assume this medieval thinking had political implications. Not only did the *scala* concept provide a rationale for the authority of rulers, who were assigned or assumed higher places in the hierarchy, but it also reinforced their authority by providing a source or basis for it.

I ponder what daily existence was like under the pressure of such shared thinking and to what extent the chain was still evident in the 1900's and through the years of the two big wars in which the entire world was involved, including the publishers, workers and writers of the *Blätter*.

German and European ideals and values moved on, but is it any wonder that much Renaissance literature is focused on the character of a ruler? Think of that famous *Prince* of Machiavelli or Shakespears's *Henry V.* Humanism came to prevail as an intellectual movement and, in my view, made a hugh leap forward and, obviously, a lasting contribution to western civilization. Hitler promised above all hatred and revanchism. He missed the lesson while our devotees to the *Leaves,* as we know, held completely opposites views which they promulgated.

To learn the convictions of our exiled publishers, however, we must study and evaluate, then report the findings. We will begin with Dr. Rukser's letter of May 10, 1944, to Kaskell, who seemed to influence him more than did Theile: *Das Problem Protestantismus und Katholizismus in den verschiedenen sozialen Auswirkungen zu beleuchten halten wir für sehr wichtig* (**We consider it very important to elucidate the problem of the various societal consequences of Protestantism and Catholicism.)**

With the erosion of spiritual values in Germany, it is understandable that the *DB* posed and sought answers to many questions concerning Christianity and the churches. Evil had permeated a government that was waging war for world dominance and destroying Germany's humanistic traditions, which should have been recognized by the religionists early on. Brazenly, I pose a challenge with questions I share with the *DB.*

Were the religious institutions not alarmed at the ever increasing influence of satanic forces? How diligently did Protestant and Catholic churches in Germany oppose this progress of Hitlerian evil? To what degree did the churches have a duty to be involved in affairs of state? what should be the future role of the churches? If religion is really a force for good, to what extent does it influence human behavior?

There, we have listed the four most pertinent questions that articles in the *Blätter* posed, staying in line with the basic editorial position of looking to the supposed guardians and teachers of humanitarian objectives, the churches, to never abandon their duty and, indeed, their *raison d' être.* For plausible answers the two directors looked to theologians, churchmen and statesmen.

Thomas Mann's essay on the prominent theologian, Martin Niemöller, has been referred to as underpinning editorial positions on religion. This essay has further utilitarian value for its revelation of the pastor as a leading (***THE*** leading, some believe) example of Protestant resistance. However, In a translated article by Karl Barth, written for *Foreign Affairs* in 1943, the intensity of Protestant commitment is analyzed in greater depth and the results evaluated. Were the outcomes of resistance sufficiently positive to warrant the punishments, reprisals, destruction of material goods, imprisonments and murders? Such questions received at least partial responses.

Barth inquires: *Was haben die* Protestantischen *Kirchen Europas in der*

Weltkrisis gelernt, gelitten und vollbracht? Was kann von ihnen künftig erwartet werden? (**In the world crisis what have the protestant churches of Europe learned, suffered and accomplished? What can be expected of them in the future?** (7, 1943, p. 29).

He observes that there must be a confrontation *auf Leben und Tod* (**mortal—life and death struggle**) between National Socialism and Protestantism because of the anti-spiritual nihilism of the former, but he laments that the churches were too little prepared for this fight when Nazism arose. Barth, and perhaps readers of the DB, took comfort in the rationalization that French, English and American Protestants were as ill-prepared for the fight as were German Protestants. Barth makes two points, first German Protestantism did speak out against Hitler and second, European Protestantism now unitedly and firmly recognizes that an absolute antithesis exists between Protestantism and Nazism. This positive appraisal of Protestantism by a famous theologian must have been accepted as a welcome reassurance by readers living in exile with their doubts and questions. However, not until issue twenty-nine of 1945 were Barth's claims to be substantiated in *Die unterirdische Opposition in Deutschland während des Krieges* (**The Underground opposition in Germany during the war.**) Religion was not completely avoided until then, however.

The tenth issue (1943) of the DB carried the first article examining answers to a question posed by Rukser and Theile, *Was ist von der Religion zu erwarten* (**What is to be expected from Religion)?** Dissatisfaction with the influence of religion on human behavior and doubts as to the rebirth of true religious feelings are the subject of a short preface to the article:

> *Dieser Krieg hat mit seiner so entsetzlichen Unmenschlichkeit etwas enthüllt, was man wohl ahnte, aber in dem Masse doch nicht für möglich gehalten hat: die Einflußlosigkeit der Religion auf das Verhalten der Menschen. Was müssen wir daraus schliessen? was haben wir auf praktisch religiösem Gebiet zu erwarten? völligen Verfall oder Wiederbelebung des religiösen Gefühls?*

TRANSLATION: Due to its appaling inhumanity this war has revealed something which was suspected but not believed to be possible to such an extent, namely the complete lack of influence of religion on human behavior. What should we conclude from that? What should we anticipate in the area of practical religion?...complete decline or a revival of religious feelings p. 6)?

This introduction by the two editors, both Catholic, sets the stage for the perceptive criticism of the role of the Catholic Church in matters of state authored by the Spanish statesman, Angel Ossorio y Gallardo.

The Spaniard hits fast and hard in outlining vigorous criticism and admonishing immediate reform of the church he loves, but he readily admits that inherently it has within its basic culture some of the greatest impediments to the founding of the new world order which they all so much wanted to establish. The *katholischen Kirche steht mit an erster Stelle* (**stands in first place with problems.** p. 6)

Considering its many editorial statements on a humanizing of the state, civil equality, and freedom of thought, the *DB* indubitably agreed. The serious question for the statesman is whether the Vatican is soley a moral or also a wordly power. He is profoundly disappointed that historically the church has meddled in many governments, while, he believes it should be concerned only with mankind's spiritual needs. Yet, he will not abandon his Catholic heritage and teachings.

That Ossorio y Gallardo remains devoted to the church is clear in his enthusiastic commendation of the Church's defense of Jews; he is advocating reform, not overthrow, insisting that religion is a private matter. The concept, "Church," must remain separate from the concept, "State," and now, with the end of the long struggle against Hitler approaching, he applied his thoughts on this vital separation to future peace proposals.

Clear in his enthusiastic commendation of the church's defense of Jews, he is advocating reform, not overthrow, insisting that religion is a private matter. Church must remain separate from state. With the end of the long struggle approaching he concentrated his thinking less on separation and applied more time to future peace proposals. The church, he argues, should only be involved in an unofficial capacity as an advocate of peace. Ossorio y Gallardo's conclusion could stand as the prototype of an opinion that was to be expresssed more than once in the *DB*:

> *Mit einem Wort die Kirche muss in Zukunft die grösste geistige Macht sein und soII ihre Lehren in der ganzen Welt verbreiten, ohne viel zu unterscheiden zwischen Gläubigen und Nichtgläubigen, den die Moral Christi ist so mächtig, daß sie sogar diejenigen bestätigen, die sie verleugnen. Und sie soll sich entschieden weigern, am Weltlichen teil zunehmen, denn das ist das Erbteil der Menschen und denen soll sie es überlassen zur vollen Verantwortung (p. 8).*

TRANSLATION: In a word, the church must in the future

be the greatest moral force and should spread its teachings throughout the world without differentiating much between believers and nonbelievers, for the moral of Christ is so powerful that it even acknowledges those who deny it. And it should categorically refuse to take part in worldly aspects, for that is the inheritance of mankind to whom it should be entrusted with full responsibility.

After such strong criticism of the church, it was only fair to print a reply by Bishop Guido Beck de Ramberga of Chile, even though, for the most part, it simply rationalized a defensive position. The reply entitled *Die katholische Kirche in Kampf* (**The Catholic Church in a Battle**, 4, 1944), lacks the vigor of Ossorio y Gallardo's criticism. It admits widespread dissatisfaction with the Church, but seems to imply cowardice in those who would desert and berate her in a time of need.

Bishop Beck begins his defense by listing names of churchmen who openly opposed fascism, including Archbishop Göber and Cardinal Faulhaber and makes an emotional appeal: There have always been unscrupulous churchmen among the many good, he writes. Then abruptly, as though cornered and groping for a rationalization, Beck leads the reader away from the topic of church responsibility and denounces German philosophers for having enticed Germans away from the true path of faith. His concluding statement frees the church of responsibility:

> *Die entsetzlichen Unmenschlichkeiten des Krieges sind nicht nach meiner festen Auffassung dem versagen des Christentums aufs Schuldkonto zu setzen, sondern den Elementen, die beständig und systematisch mit Wort und Schrift den Gottesglauben im deutschen Volk zu untergraben suchten, dort, müssen wir anklagen (p. 11).*

TRANSLATION: It is my firm view that the horrid barbarities of the war can not be blamed on the church, but rather on those elements which persistently and systematically with both spoken and written word sought to undermine the belief in God of the German people. It is to them that we must complain.

A laconic disclaimer by the editors implies their assessment of Beck's defense of the church. *Es versteht sich von selbst, daß die Äusserungen zu solchen Themen die persönliche Stellungnahme der verfasser sind und nicht eine solche der*

Zeitschrift (**It is obvious that the expression of such themes are the personal position of the creator and not that of the magazine,** p. 8)...and to us, the readers of today, it is apparent that the *DB* was more closely allied with Ossorio y Gallardo's general thinking and his specific suggestions for reform. In fact the opinions of the Spanish statesman were so highly regarded that he was allowed additional space in the last issue of 1944 to augment his thoughts on *Zweierlei Katholizismus* in which he warns of a fascist threat in North and South America.

In the second article accusations are even more damning than in the first. *Der spanische Bürgerkrieg ist in den Kirchen vorbereitet und geschürt worden* (**The Spanish Civil War,** he writes, **was instigated and incited in the churches**) and names churchmen who supported Franco. Ossorio y Gallardo carefully substantiates charges that representatives of the church approved of Hitler's and Mussolini's anti-semitism and of their destruction of Free Masonry.

Two kinds of Catholicism exist; one leads to God the other to Fascism. In a final note of warning directed at the American nations, the statesman is explicit in calling for a fight against the second kind of Catholicism and a strengthening of the first.

> *Es gibt also wie ich anfangs sagte, zwei Arten von Katholizismus, den der uns zum Gebet zu Gott erhebt, und jenen, der es sich zum Ziel gesetzt hat, die Völker für die Politik Hitlers, Mussolinis und Francos zu gewinnen. Der Erstere sei geeignet; den anderen wollen wir bekämpfen. Lasst uns nicht Unsere Augen versehliessen vor so deutlichen Anzeichen dieses Angriffs auf die Freiheit der Menschen und Völker,* (p. 26)

TRANSLATION: As I said at the beginning, there are two kinds of Catholicism; one which lifts us to prayer and to God and the other which has taken as its objective to win the people over to the politics of Hitler, Mussolini and Franco. The first are ok; however, we'll take a stand against the others. Let's not close our eyes to such obvious signs of these attacks on the freedom of the people.

Ossorio y Gallardo's exposition was welcomed by the editors who explain the reasons for their appraisal in an introductory commentary. First, they are anxious to teach the world that a good portion of Europe fell prey to "totalitarian poison" before Nazism came to Germany; secondly, they fear that the nations of the world, especially in the Americas are so preoccupied with fear of the swastika that they may fail to recognize totalitarianism represented by icons. Thirdly, although this is not explicitly stated by Theile and Rukser, it is logical to assume that they, too, wished to warn of the second kind of Catholicism.

The editors admitted in the September/October issue of 1945 that there had been strong reaction to Ossorio y Gallardo's second article. They did not refer specifically, however, to vicious criticism by Bishop Beck nor to Rukser's answer to the Bishop. In an undated letter to the churchman Rukser defended Ossorio:

> *Mit Erstaunen und Befremden haben wir gelesen was Sie anlässlich des Aufsatzes von Ossorio* **Zweierlei Katholizismus** *veröffentlicht haben. Sie ergreifen das Wort als Bischof, weil man versucht habe „das Kleid meiner Mutter, der katholischen Kirche in böser und ungerechter Weise zu beschmutzen." Der Zweck Ihrer Zeilen „ist ein rein ideeller und religiöser." In der Folge machen Sie Ausführungen derart, als sei in dem Artikel die katholische Kirche in schmählicher Weise angegriffen unter Entstellung des Sachverhalts. Alles das muss den Leser Ihres Aufsatzes zu der Meinung bringen als habe Ossorio etwa die kath. Kirche als solche angegriffen und als hiesse der Aufsatz „Einerlei Katholizismus". Der Aufsatz betitelt sich aber* **Zweierlei Katholizismus,** *Monseñor!.. Sein klar ausgesprochenes ziel ist also die politische Haltung gewisser katholischer Kreise zu kritisieren, keineswegs aber wie man nach Ihren Zeilen glauben muss, den religiösen Katholizismus anzugreifen. Warum antworten Sie, Monseñor auf ausgesprochen politische Darlegungen, mit Zeilen, deren zweck rein ideeller und religiöser sein soll? Sie unterstellen also Ossorio im klaren Gegensatz zu seinen deutlichen ausgesprochen Absichten religiöse Polemic. Halten Sie das für zuläsig?*

> *Sie nehmen sich nicht die Mühe, Monseñor, auf die von Ossorio angeführten Tatsachen einzugehen, sondern berufen sich staat dessen einmal auf gewisse kirchliche Kundgebungen, die niemand in Zweifel gezogen hat. Sie rennen damit also offene Türen ein und könnten sich mit demselben Recht gegen Ossorio darauf berufen, daß die Kirche das Gebot der Nächstenliebe predige. Aber um die Tatsachen, die zum Himmel schreien gerade weil sie zum Teil von katholischen Priestern begangen oder gefördert sind, dazu schweigen Sie. Muss das nicht so verstanden werden, daß Sie alles das decken wollen, was Ossorio anführt? Wir glauben zu wissen, daß dies*

nicht Ihren Überzeugungen entspricht, aber Ihre Darlegungen enthalten kein Word des Tadels für jene Schandtaten. [62]

TRANSLATION: It is with shock and wonder that we recently read what you wrote regarding Ossorio's essay, *Zweierlei Katholizismus*. You seize the authoritative word as Bishop because people tried to sully the dress of *my mother, the Catholic Church*, in a nasty and unjustified manner. The objective of your writing is "pure, ideal and religious." As you continue, you make accusations of a sort which make it seem that in the article the Catholic Church is attacked in a slanderous manner through misrepresentation of the contents. All of that must bring readers of your essay to the conclusion that Ossorio attacked the Catholic Church as such and as though the essay were titled "One kind of Catholicism." The essay, however, Monseignor, is titled "Two kinds of Catholicism!"…The clearly announced objective is to criticize the political attitude of certain Catholic circles. But, if one must believe according to your words, in no way to attack the religious Catholicism. Why, Monseignor, do you answer obvious political analyses with words whose purpose is "pure idealism" and religious"? You place Ossorio in obvious opposition to his clearly announced objectives of religious polemics. Do you consider that permissible? You do not take the trouble, Monseignor, to bring up Ossorio's facts, but instead convoke certain church pronouncements which no one doubts. You run therefore through open doors with these accusations and could, with the same justification against Ossorio, charge that the church preaches the order of "love thy neighbor." However, regarding the facts that scream to the heavens,

---

62 In a letter to Kaskell of January 1, 1943, Rukser expressed disappointment with the leaders of the church: "Die politik des Vatikans wird gerade von wahren Katholiken tief bedauert. Aber auch hier gibt es katholischen Nazis! Auch unter den Chilean! Sie glauben nicht, was man zu hören kriegt. Und das wird sich kaum ändern, solange im Vatikan der italienische und spanische Klerus vorherrscht." On November 17, 1943, he added the following thoughts on the church: "Man kann eine Organisation ausdenken, so schön wie möglich, aber wenn dieser der Geist der Humanität abhanden kommt, dann gehts schief!" **The central point here is that true Catholics are most disappointed with the church. Known Catholic Nazis exist even in Chile, and that will continue as long as Italian and Spanish clergy are ruling. The church has gone off course because it has lost the spirit of humanity.**

> exactly because they are in part executed by Catholic priests or propogated by them, you are silent. Shouldn't that be so understood, namely, that you want to hide all what Ossorio brings up? We believe that this does not correspond to your convictions, but your clarifications contain not one word of censor for this disgrace.

The above letter leaves little doubt where the sympathies of Rukser lay! Partially because of reader criticism of Gallardo's attack especially Beck's, but perhaps even more because of deep editorial anxiety concerning Catholicism, another article on the subject, authored by the brilliant thirty-five year old Chilean professor and statesman, Manuel Garreton Walker, was published. The title of the article was *Katholizismus und Gegenwart* (**Catholicism Today**).

Garreton's more moderate statements on church and state rnust have been preferable to Catholic readers of the *DB*; nevertheless criticisms are implied.

He begins by quoting both Pope Leo XIII and Pius XII on the strict separation of the church and political parties. No political party, he claims, can represent the Catholic Church because politics parties and the Church are separate realms. Like Ossorio y Gallardo he is not afraid to point to the tragedy that, resulted in Spain from the union of the Church and a political party. For Garreton:

Der Fall Spaniens ist der Musterfall. Er steht da als tragische Warnung, daß wir uns nicht von solchen Bewegungen fortreissen lassen die als christliche Kreuzüge beginnen und als furchtbare Prüfungen der Menschheit enden (**The case of Spain is the model case. It stands there as a tragic warning that we do let ourselves be torn away from such movements which begin as Christian crusades and end as a horrible testing of humanity,** p, 22l).

Garreton raises the question of Communism, an issue on which both Bishop Beck and Ossorio had been silent. He perceives that Communism has cleverly formulated solutions to social problems. Time favors the Communists, since it will now take even better solutions to successfully replace those already in place.

A chief goal of the modern Catholic Church should lie in alleviating social problems, he states: the Church must do this free of any connections to political parties. Garreton was granted the final word on Catholicism and its relationship to the state, Perhaps the editors of the *DB* were satisfied that the subject had been sufficiently aired. It was left to the readers to effect change.

The problem of church and state was faced for the last time in the summer issue of 1945, but from the protestant (protestant**S?**) point of view. Paula Herty in *Die Stellung zum Staat im kontinentalen und anglo-anmerikanischen*

Protestantismus (**The Position of the State in continental and anglo-american Protestantism**) does not advocate the union of church and state, but at the same time she warns of the loose watch on the state that the German Protestants were keeping as Hitler rose to power. The Church was so powerless against the state, we read that the *Kirche allein mit allem was das einschloss, nicht genug war,* when the time came, *um einen ausschlaggebenden, tatsächlichen Einfluss auf den in Korruption verfallenen Staat auszuüben (***In summary: The church had insuffient power and influence over the corrupted state,** *p. 12)*.

The author explains that although in Germany the administration, organization, and financing of the church had been a function of the state, there was a strong tradition of noninterference by the church into affairs of state. Herty finds the system in America and England preferable; church and state are strictly separate, but churches are involved in politics and government. The author approves of this and proposes that it must be imitated by Prostestantism everywhere.

In the USA today we could debate this either way, but we would have to be mindful of the strong religious traditions of many churches and cults. The Mormons of Utah come to mind where daily life is church dictated existence, along with all fundamentalist religious organizations, Jehovah's Witness congregations, the strong Baptist divisions and several others.

Mrs. Herty's article was composed after the church conference of Treisa, held under the leadership of Wurm, Niemöller and Azmann, at which serious faults of the Lutheran Church in Germany were recognized and proposals for necessary changes advanced. The editors of the *DB* urgently wished to makes these advances for improvement from within the church known, and they looked to Herty's article for assistance. *Das Verständnis dieser bedeutsamen Entwicklung hoffen wir durch nachfolgenden Aufsatz zu fördern* (**We hope to convey an understanding of this meaningful development through the following essay),** they explain.

Freedom of religion is an issue in many of the articles on religion in the *DB*, but it was the specific subject of only one, Edouard Laboulaye's *Über Religionsfreiheit* (24,1945 p. 35). Written in the last century, Laboulaye's thoughts will always be timely; the *DB* put them to good use in 1945 by reaffirming what might be termed "the principle of noninterference." It was a respected concept, generally embraced, that the state must in no way interfere with the practice of any religion. Laboulaye's opening words are:

> *Religionsfreiheit bedeutet zweierlei. Im weistesten Sinne gleichbedeutend mit Gewissensfreiheit, bezeichnet sie das Recht, die religiöse Wahrheit zu suchen, ein Recht, das jedem Menschenwesen*

zukommt, sobald es fühlt, was es mit Seinem Schöpfer verbindet. Im engeren sinne drückt dieses Wort die politische Unabhänigkeit der religiösen Gemeinschaften aus, die Trennung von Staat und Kirche. Es sind zwei Freiheiten, die sich entsprechen, zwei natürliche Rechte, welche die Gesellschaft anerkannt, aber nicht schafft (p. 35).

TRANSLATION: "Religious freedom" has a double meaning. In the broadest sense it has the same significance as freedom of conscience, i.e. the right to seek religious truth, a right that is granted to every human being as soon as it feels what binds it with its creator. In the narrower sense this term expresses the political independence of the religious community, the separation of church and state. These two freedoms are in accord, two natural rights which society recognizes, but does not create.

Organized religion had completely failed to prevent world war II and to keep the world sane. Was there another system of thought, ethical-social principles, that would more effectively keep man moral and peace-loving? This possibllity was addressed only twice in the *DB*, and both articles concluded that religion could not be replaced.

As early as December, 1943, *Die künftige Rolle des Christentums* (**The Future Role of Christianity**) reports that the British leftist periodical the *New Statesman and Nation* was advancing the conviction that the world could be saved without religion. Human being would simply have to learn to become altruistic, creating a better society which would then result in the creation of a happier world. *Let man have his dreams,* seems to be a universal concept. The unsigned article argues that most people who lose their religious faith turn to another *ism* such as fascism. It is futile to propose that man discipline himself to live morally, for experience shows he needs religion.

I highly, respect our anonymous scribe, but I for one do not see a "need," but perhaps for now we should just stop writing, since we do not have to concur either way, and simply ponder this concept. I ask readers, however, to also think of replacements for religious teachings. Can we not be *good* without the interference of extraneous deity? As asserted above and grabbing a song title from Elvis, *The Man in the Sky* has not had great success in stopping wars. Our good *DB* included thoughts on the subject.

In issue four of 1944 Katharina Möller-Rosenthal examined the idea of a replacement for religion in *Religion als Grundlage der Gesellschaft,* (**Religion as** the Basis for Society, p. 23). *Die Frage* (**The question**), she begins…*ob wir bei einer Neuordnung der Gesellschaft auf die Religion als Grundlage verzichten können, ist heute wichtiger geworden denn je* (**The question is today more important than ever. Can we reject religion as the basis for a new order of society?**)

The increasing influence in the world of Russian Communism with its rejection of religion caused her to reflect on the matter. Möller-Rosenthal finds, however, that it would be most difficult to find a replacement and is compelled to define and defend her interpretation of Christianity:

> *In der Idee des Christentums ist sicher das Reinste und Höchste enthalten, was die Beziehungen der Menschen untereinander gestalten kann, und die Stellung des Menschen zu sich selbst, zu seinem Innern klärt und vertieft*

TRANSLATION: Unquestionably, the idea of Christianity embodies the very highest that the relationships of human beings among themselves can create as well as clarifying and deepening the comfort of man with himself, p.23).

Does she not simplify? Her intensity tells me that Christians need not seek elsewhere for a system of ethics by which to live; they have only to follow diligently the Christian principles they already know.

We may agree, but, of course, to *know* the principles is not to *live* them or even to "believe" them, let alone to promulgate the inclusive but broader *evangel* through which we may be saved (or at least not start wars).

The *DB's* discussions of religion in this chapter produced some answers to questions it raised. Articles affirm that religion had failed to stop the rise of National Socialism and the war, and that throughout history church and state too frequently had spoken as one. However, it is stressed that there were always churchmen who exemplified rectitude, and that the principles of religion as a guideline for life are indispensable. Man needs religion, we are told. but reform and change are also needed within the churches; they must move with the times and seek more determinedly for solutions to social problems. However, suggestions for overthrow of the churches are rejected; instead, organized religion must be revitalized for the task of improving mankind. The periodical's position on the churches is another key part of its general concern for man with the message to keep that which is beneficial.

My own response to the above is for the most part approbation, but, since I am unable to find need for a need, i.e. "Man *needs* religion," I ask, Why?--to cause more wars and other forms of human suffering?

This topic needs more books to scrutinize the issue, and then?—still more books perhaps. For now I can not resist sharing the observation of the Evangelist, Billy Graham, when he visited Europe way back in 1959 and remarked on very low church attendance in Europe; he labeled the Netherlands "Godless."

I have observed for many years that the pattern of church attendance in Europe and South America has been that women attend church with children or mothers or sisters. Men do not. Busloads of tourists are dropped at famous cathedrals, but that doesn't count for helping reform. The most devout are those impecunious, withered and very old appearing ladies who mop the floors and clean, while a few others are crossing themselves or lying prostrate in front of an altar. The committed fanatics even walk or crawl long distances to prove their devotion. As to church leaders changing things or being better prepared to stifle war and violence than they were in 1939, it appears that little progress has been made or is desired.

Since some readers will be of the opinion that this statement does not reflect the true situation, I will be quick to laud any churchmen who hold the views and demonstrate devotion to the cause of Dietrich Bonhoeffer, the Protestant theologian, or Karl Bart or Thomas Merton. Barth was aggressively anti-Nazi and even as a student dismayed at witnessing his teachers' support of the war policy of Kaiser Wilhelm. He spoke out against Hitler's seeking to impose Nazi ideology on the Protestant churches in Germany, believing it to be a heathen profanation of God's message. Merton, a Roman Catholic monk, heroically championed the cause of the oppressed and poor while living a life of contemplation, different from Bart but each, as did Bonhoeffer, brought to the world a message of love that was ardently Christian and in the view of each worth struggling to proclaim. They, like Kaj Munk, could have sacrificed their lives to fight Nazism. Still, contemplating the actions of the religious majority and to stick with the truth, I will have to accept my own observations. Attacking one's presumed enemies provides fun without end for the world; war is a welcome activity.

Consider the constant condition of war, somewhere on earth, and attacks on individual "heretics," defined quite simply as those who have arrived at a different belief than you. It has always been so. We are taught, for example about Peter Abelard, the theologian, poet and teacher who in 12th century France fell so madly in love with Heloise. He was 37 and she 17. They had a child, then married, but she was forced by her uncle, fellow canon of poor old Abelard, to leave him. Next thing you know he was waylaid by a group of jolly fellows and emasculated. She went to a nunnery and commenced writing those famous love letters. He lived in the French-Burgundian monastery of

Cluny where, in the tenth century an ecclesiastical reform movement had been initiated. It became so austere in spirit as to make binding the rule of celibacy on all priests. The rule was imposed on all clergy in their entirety. Widespread opposition and stubborn resistance came from many priests, especially the Germans.

Perhaps they did not recognize positive changes being initiated as well. And what of Abelard? He had little choice. This brilliant man continued to write until he died at age sixty-four. Logic should rule human thinking, not authority, he taught. Sure! But, keep it quiet. Nine hundred years ago that was, and *Tristan und Isolde*, even earlier, and since then…how many?

My question: Were those thugs hired by St. Bernard and the Church council that had condemned Abelard as a heretic? He was obstensibly condemned for writing his *Sic et Non* (**Yes and No**) exposing contradictory teachings of the Church through his "new" dedication to learning and exposition of a wholly unacceptable critical method of research.

To continue hammering my point vigorously, I recommend reading Franz Werfel's, *The Forty Days of Musa Dagh*, which Werfel said was conceived in March of 1929 when he was visiting Damascus. The plot treats the truly incomprehensible destiny of the Armenian nation. The ruthless Turks for months engaged in terrorizing the Armenians through hanging, looting, raping as well as the time tested tactic of plain old murder. Then, in 1915, these butchers embarked on a concentrated campaign of complete extermination. Sound familiar? Hitler knew details of the Turkish genocide, and he and applauded it.

He even assembled his *Wehrmacht* generals at Berchtesgaden to explain this admired model of the greatest ethnic cleansing to date:

> *Unsere Stärke ist unsere Schnelligkeit und unsere Brutalität. Dschingis Khan hat Millionen Frauen und Kinder in den Tod gejagt, bewußt und fröhlichen Herzens… und ich lasse jeden füsilieren, der auch nur ein Wort der Kritik äußert. Das Kriegsziel besteht in der physischen Vernichtung des Gegners. So habe ich, einstweilen nur im Osten, meine Totenkopfverbände bereitgestellt mit dem Befehl, unbarmherzig und mitleidslos Mann, Weib und Kind polnischer Abstammung und Sprache in den Tod zu schicken. Nur so gewinnen wir den Lebensraum, den wir brauchen. Wer redet heute noch von der Vernichtung der Armenier?*

TRANSLATION: Our strength lies in our speed and in our brutality. On purpose and with a happy heart

Genghis Khan drove millions of women and children to their deaths…I have issued the command, and anybody who utters a single word of criticism will go before a firing squad…Our objective is the physical destruction of the enemy. Accordingly, I have placed my death-head formation in readiness, for the present only in the East…with orders to send to death mercilessly and without compassion, men, women, and children of Polish derivation and language. Only thus shall we gain the Lebensraum **(living space) which we need. Who, after all, speaks to-day of the annihilation of the Armenians?**

Two more of the thousands of personal stories. The editors of the *DB* obtained from Louis P. Lochner a copy of the entire speech from which the above passage is excerpted. And, what was the role of religion? My thoughts return to the *Grebbeberg*. *"Das ist Krieg"*.

Chapter IX

Literature

THE FINE REPUTATION of the *Deutsche Blätter* may be better substantiated by its treatment of Literature than the more numerous articles on political issues. Although it was primarily politically oriented, famous men of letters, mostly German and South American, were also represented along with lesser known writers. Some were exiles living in South America including Paul Zech, José Antonio Benton and Gustav Regler. Others have no presence in the *DB*, perhaps due to ideological differences with the editors. Selections include poems, short stories, essays on literature and writers as well as reviews of books, magazines and newspapers.

One quickly perceives that literary selections were chosen to serve definite goals. Many short quotations used as fillers gave support to humanitarian themes of the *DB*, including world peace; educating mankind for nonviolence, justice; social equality; and the brotherhood of all men. A statement by Goethe or a reference to Kant and other great Germans functions as evidence that the Nazi is the exception, and not the rule in the history of Germany and affirms the journal's goal of keeping German culture alive. Other material in the magazine was printed solely for its *belletristic* value. Its aesthetic beauty softens the frequent hard denunciations and admonishments of the *DB* and brightens the general tone of the magazine.

Udo Rukser intended that it function as *ein gewisses Gegenwicht gegen die vielen betrachtenden Beiträge*[63] **(a kind of counter weight compared to the numerous pieces of greater intellectuality)**. Making South American

---

63 Letter from Rukser to Kaskell, May 10, 1944.

literature better known to the German speaking world emerged as a notable objective of the editors with the fifth issue. The twosome later explained the rationale for the inclusion of Latin American literature in an editorial note preceding Borges's *Im Traumkreis der Ruinen* (**In the Dream Sphere of the Ruins**, 8, 1944):

> *Mit der Veröffentlichung der folgenden Erzählung des argentinischen Dichters Jorge Luis Borges wollen wir den Aufgabenkreis der DB erweitern. Wir wollen versuchen unseren Lesern die südamerikanische Literatur durch sie kennzeichnende Proben nahezubringen und damit geistig auch die Umwelt in der wir leben. Die südamerikanischen Schriftsteller sind längst über die Zeit reiner Nachahmung zu Selbstbeständigkeit und oft reizvoller Eigenart gereift; an dieser Entwicklung haben neben spanischen auch deutsche Dichter starken Anteil gehabt* (P. 221).

TRANSLATION: Commencing with the publication of the following story by the Argentine writer, Borges, we intend to broaden the offerings of the *DB*. We will try to better familiarize our readers with Southamerican literature by bringing them outstanding examples as well as a deeper understanding of the intellectual environment in which we live. South American writers have matured far beyond a period of imitation to independence and frequently even a delightful uniqueness in which both Spanish and German men/women of letters have been involved.

The first issue of the *DB* gave little indication of preoccupation with literature that was later to emerge; however, the use of literature to support *DB* political positions was already evident. A few sentences by Jean Paul (Jean Paul Friedrich Richter) on the horrors of war and Adalbert Stifter's pithy assertion that governments should educate man for humanitarian purposes put the two well-known German writers on the side of the anti-Hitler journal. The following quote by Friedrich Hölderlin is used to substantiate belief in resistance within Germany: *Wo aber Gefahr ist, wächst das Rettende auch* (**Wherever danger exists that which saves also flourishes**, p. 21). Even the single book review (of a nonliterary work) was a subtle anti-Nazi statement. It examined Hermann Rauschning's *Die konservative Revolution* which sought reasons for the Nazi rise to power. Subsequent issues of the first few months continued to review only factual books. No creative, imaginative examples of fiction were analyzed until later, but the practice of calling upon great German authors of the past to lend credence to the *DB*'s conviction that the principles and ideals which it espoused were in fact historically deeply rooted in German thought, set a trend to be followed throughout the years of publication.

Further anti-war support was offered in Hermann Hesse's poem, *Der Jüngling im Krieg* (**The Boy in War**). The reader is depressed by the naiveté of this lad, who says that he and others like him will die for a future peaceful world.

Even more touching is Gerrit Engelke's *An die Soldaten des grossen Krieges* (**To the Soldiers of the Great War**, 4, 1943) since the poet himself, just twenty-three years old, fell in 1918, only three days before the armistice. His call to dead soldiers in *Gräbern, Lehmhölen, Betonkeller, Steinbrüchen, and Schlamm* (**graves, clay foxholes, cement cellars and mud**) promises a better world. The poet expressed his sentiments in superlatives: *O, unser allerhöchste Glück heist: Leben* (**Oh, our highest possible happiness is called: Life**). The editors, it seems, considered the emotional appeal of poetry in making their point. An intellectual treatise may even be overkill in trying to make a point as compared with a simple rhyme that immediately evokes an emotion.

In the December issue of 1943 Georg Heym's *Krieg* denounced war and Erwin Bock's *Herr was haben sie aus Dir gemacht* (**Lord, What have they made of Thee**) heightened the longing for peace. Paul Zech's lyrical but utilitarian poetry strengthened editorial positions. His *Sonnette auf das Jahr 1944* (1,1944), consisting of one sonnet dedicated to each month are reminiscent of some writings of the Romanticists and the literary movement termed *Junges Deutschland* (**Young Germans***)* of a hundred years earlier. One may recall the poety of Heinrich Heine to list one. Zech paints a picture of a humiliated Germany under the swastika and calls for peace and freedom. In his November sonnet the poet cries:

> *Revolution: Noch einmal die Fanfare,*
> *Aus tiefer Brust heraus das Kampfgeschrei,*
> *Das uns befreit von all der Tyrannei*
> *Ohnmächtig hingelebter Wanderjahre* (p. 29).

TRANSLATION: Revolution: Once again
The fanfare from deep within the breast the
Battlecry that frees us from all tyranny
Helpless, spent journeyman years

With WW II ended, Gert Conitzer's *Auf ein von Bombensplittern getötetes*

Kind (*To a child killed by bomb fragments*, issue 32) reminds the reader in 1946 once again of the war's wanton horrors and mindless destruction.

The *Leaves* looked back to German classicism in the struggle against despotism to give German support to the desire for peace. Schiller raises his voice against tyranny in a passage from *Wilhelm Tell* in the second issue of 1943. The idealistic poet appears to sympathize with the action of three Norwegian bus drivers who steered their busloads of Nazi soldiers into a fjord, and in several short quotations Goethe stood as a staunch supporter of peace and humanitarianism. Several essays on German writers recall altruistic Intelectuals in the field of literature. The opening sentences of Julius Bab's essay on Lessing cogently proclaims:

> *Wenn wir in einer Epoche die Deutschlands Namen mit blutiger Gewalt und moralischer Feigheit befleckt hat, eine Gestalt suchen, die vor der Welt und vor allem vor uns selbst die Ehre deutschLands rettet so erscheint mir vor allen anderen Gotthold Ephraim Lessing* (7, 1944, p. 14).

TRANSLATION: In an epoch that has sullied Germany's name with violence and moral cowardice when we seek a person of stature, who has saved the honor of Germany for the world and especially for us, it seems to me that Lessing stands out among all others,

This writer's personal first remembrance of Lessing is the introductory seven word phrase commonly used to describe the child prodigy, who came to be known as Germany's Voltaire: *ein Pferd das dobbeltes Futter haben muß* (**a horse that needs double fodder**), which refers to the extremely bright youngster who read voraciously and studied with unequaled zeal and, indeed, who was supplied with double portions of academic and intellectual fodder by his teachers.

Bab treats Lessing as a paradoxicarly modest and proud man. Lessing, he says, was the first German writer to support himself solely by his pen, but the value of the essay to the editors af the *DB* was Bab's portrayal of Lessing as a champion of freedom:

> *Kein anderer Deutscher hat die totale Freiheit des Denkens und Fühlens Handelns und Lebens so rein verköpert... Es ist diese Fähigkeit zur Freiheit vor aIlem, an der man mit dem Blick auf das heutige Deutschland verzweifeln möchte und um derentwillen*

mir Lessing der grosse deutsche Trost dieser Tage zu sein scheint (p. 14).

TRANSLATION: ...no other German has so embodied the total freedom of thoughts, feelings, actions and living... It is above all this capacity for freedom which one may doubt in looking at today's Germany and for whose sake Lessing is for me the greatest German solace of these days.

Albert Schweitzer belongs to a most exclusive and extremely limited number of us *homo sapiens* who have progressed ever higher intelectualy and through loving goodness toward a higher state, be it self-realization, nirvana or simply selflessness. His thinking had to be included in the *Blätter*, and for the state of the world, the Nazi oppression, the demoralization, the doubts, hopes, guesses, proposals, and on and on and...one of his best pieces was published. It gave food for thought to all who were fortunate enough to read (no... rather to *experience)* it.

Schweitzer's now well known address delivered at the centennial celebration of Goethe's death in Frankfurt, March 22, 1932, was printed almost in its entirety in the last issue of 1943. The insights on Goethe are extensive, but for the purposes of the *DB* the most valuable passages are those which praise Goethe as educator, humanitarian and intellectual giant. The fundamental characteristics of Goethe's personality, Schweitzer enlightens, were honesty and sincerity; lying, hypocrisy, intrigue, vanity, envy and ingratitude were all alien to him. He continues with additional compliments, writing that Germany's great man of letters (tritely referred to by some professors of English as the *Shakespeare of Germany*—This writer has never heard the description reversed.) was by nature affectionate, sympathetic, and generous, the very antithesis of Nazism, admittedly even very difficult for most of us.

Dr. Schweitzer, the Alsatian missionary, writer, physician, musician and the greatest of humanitarians, explains that in Goethe's philosophy the first cause of the world was at the same time the first cause of love. This love emerging from the eternal has a concern for us and wishes to find expression in us. For Goethe true self-realization could be achieved only after true loving goodness was reached. (Isn't this all sounding very oriental?) In a few sentences Schweitzer summarizes Goethe's message to the world of his day, indeed, the same message being promulgated by the Germanic *DB* publishers from their new home in Chile.

Alles Denken, in dem ein Mensch sich nicht an die Gesellschaft, einer Zeit sondern an den Menschen als solchen und als einzelnen wendet—und dies ist bei Goethe der Fall, wie bei kaum einem andern—hat etwas über jede Zeit Erhabenes an sich. Die Gesellschaft ist etwas zeitlich Veränderliches; der Mensch aber ist immer der Mensch. So ist die Botschaft Goethes an den heutigen Menschen dieselbe wie an den damaligen und an den Menschen aller Zeiten: "Strebe nach wahrem Menschentum! Werde du selbst als ein sich verinnerlichender Mensch, der in einer seiner Natur entsprechender Weise Tatmensch ist (p.7).

TRANSLATION: All thinking, in which a person does not address the society of his day, but rather directs it to the people as such and as individuals—and this is more so the case with Goethe than hardly any other—has something lofty about it with each incident. Society is something that changes with time; mankind is, however, simply mankind. So Goethe's message to modern man today is the same as it was to those of his own day and for mankind of all time: Strive for true humanity! You, yourself, become an introspective human being who in one of the states related to your nature is a TATMENSCH (active person, a doer).

Dr. Schweitzer himself was destined to receive the Nobel Prize in 1952, and he was for the *DB* another pillar of German moral decency and intellectual achievement. Stefan Zweig in *Begegnung zweier Europäer* (**Meeting of two Europeans**, 5, 1943) evaluates the gifted and giving Alsatian *as eine einzige und einmalige, eine unwiederholbar gebundene Vielfalt* (This is a fun translation: **a singular and unique, a solo and unreptitive combined multiplication**, p. 19). Zweig's List of Schweitzer's achievements furnished the *DB* with a weighty counter argument to assertions of innate German depravity, and others could be found to help the cause and prove the point, Thomas Mann among them.

The periodical focused on Mann as a modern day champion of humanitarianism and a symbol of all that is commendable in the German cultural tradition. Essays and statenents about Mann and some of his own essays strengthen this view. One could designate issue twenty-five of 1945 the *Thomas Mann issue*. The first few pages are devoted soley to expressions of homage to Mann in Spanish, German and English by thirteen intellectuals, many of whom were Latin Americans. Hermann Broch contributed a poem, *An die Phantasie (für Thomas Mann)*. Following this *Huldigung/Homenaje (***homage***) a Thomas Mann* is an article entitled *Thomas Manns künstlerische Sendung* (**The

Artistic Mission of Thomas Mann) by Hans Fischer who was living in La Paz, Bolivia. Another essay, *Thomas Mann und Goethe* was mailed by Berthold Bierman from New York.

So...here they came!...manuscripts from all over the world to form a single new country or place to belong, *DB land*, if you will, or we could perhaps refer to *Exile Land* even coin *Emigrantlandia*. More appealing might be *United states of Conviction*, for the single common place of residence existed only in the mind; physically, thousands were represented by hundreds (and even fewer had a chance to give expression in the germanic *DB* of Chile*)*, but as a single new nation the expatriates struggled against the National Socialist enemy in their homeland, and from the USA, Mexico, Brazil, Chile and all points of the globe longed to return, to reconstruct, to practice their professions, simply, to be *good* and to live a life of freedom. It was up to the Messieurs Rukser and Theile to determine what kind of writing would be offered and how (in today's jargon) it would be packaged and marketed.

An introductory editorial appraisal (marketing?) of Germany's dean of the *literati* praises the gentleman writer from Lübeck as a *Verkünder der Humanität* (**proclaimer of humanity**). The very title reveals his inestimable value as a depository of what Germans and Germany should be, and the article is one of the most laudatory.

> *Er bezeugt uns die Existenz des geistigen Deutschlands und seiner gestaltenden Kräfte. Keiner unter den heutigen Deutschen repräsentiert so wie Thomas Mann alles Universelle der deutschen Kultur—Dichtung, Musik und Philosophie zu einem erhabenen, allumfassenden Horizont gestaltend. In seinem Schaffen gipfelt das klassische Deutschland, aber auch das der Romantik; das Deutschland Lessings und Goethes, aber auch das des Novalis, Beethovens und Wagners; das Kants und Schopenhauers, aber auch Nietzches. Er ist Sohn und Vollender dieser übernationalen, humanitären Kultur.... Daß aus seinem Munde, daß in deutscher Sprache immer wieder das Bekenntnis und die Mahnung zur Humanität erklang, als nur Blut und Schweiss und Tränen verheissen wurden, dafür sind alle Menschen, vor allem aber wir Deutsche, ihm Unendliches schuldig geworden. Wieviele hat er zur Besinnung gebracht, aufgerichtet und im Glauben an menschliche Werte neu gestärkt! (p, 3)*

TRANSLATION: He is living testimony of the intellectual/spiritual Germany and her creative powers. Nobody among

> the present-day Germans represents as well as Thomas Mann all the universal aspects of German culture, which in writing, music and philosophy stretch to a lofty all-inclusive horizon. The classical period of German literature reaches a high point in his work, but romantic Germany does so as well along with the Germany of Lessing and Goethe, but also that of Novalis, Beethoven and Wagner, of Kant, Schopenhauer even Niezsche. He is both the son and the finisher of this humanitarian culture which rises above nationalities...While only blood, sweat and tears were promised, his voice repeatedly rang out in German a testimony of humanitarianism and his admmonisment to embrace it. Because of this all people, but above all we Germans are eternally in his debt. How many has he consoled, brought to their senses and strengthened in a renewed belief in the worth of all human kind.

The selection of essays reinforced this editorial evaluation, and, as presumed, the collaborators remained fervently devoted to the *Verkünder* (**proclaimer**) of the humanities to the extent that throughout 1945 they consulted Mann on his thoughts about their establishing a German language publishing house in Santiago. From his letters of June and October we conclude that he was willing to name manuscripts with which to begin, but was not displeased when the two awakened from their reverie and aborted the project. Germany could now publish in German, after all. Mann was of the hook and could easily assure that a publishing house in Chile would have his *volle moralische Unterstützung* (**full moral support**). Moral support being not quite the same things as monetary support.

Although the editors themselves never made a negative comment about their prestigious moral benefactor in print, we should, for the sake of honest research and accounting at least refer to some negativism in the last issue of 1945 where Walter von Molo's open letter appeared and in which von Molo criticizes this representative of *good Germany* for having failed in his responsibility to his homeland. In strong language he urges Mann to abandon his comfortable Californian exile and return to Germany.

Why? We ask, and so did Mann, who stayed where he was, earning our eternal gratitude as he penned more against the Nazis and encouraged Germans and all mankind to achieve their highest potential.

Mann's essays , *Niemöller* and *Joseph und seine Brüder* were gratefullyy accepted for publication in the *DB*. *Niemöller*, (10, 1943), written in 1941, praises the highly respected Lutheran pastor as an anti-Nazi symbol of resistance. The pastor had been acquitted of treason by a People's Tribunal but was re-arrested by personal order of Hitler at the back door of the court room and sent to a concentration camp where he was still being held when Mann wrote the essay in which he chastized the people of the Western World for not following the example of Niemöller and asserts that their apathy is partly responsible for the theologian's imprisonment. It was, according to Mann only due to a *hirnlose gesittete Welt a (***brainless polite world***)* that National Socialism grew. *Sie begriff nicht, daß Untaten, wie die an Niemöller begangene der Vorbereitung dessen dienten, was nun über sie gekommen ist* (**Society did not believe that crimes such as the one committed on Niemöller were preparation for what it has now experienced,** p. 21). This blaming of the sleeping Western nations instead of Germany alone for the rise of Nazism conform to editorial thinking. Mann's concluding paragraph expresses both hope and doubt in the power of the civilized world to free itself; philosophically Theile und Rukser agreed that:

> *Der Kerker dieses Märtyrers ist nur ein Symbol. Wird, da nun alles gekommen, wie es durch unser aller Stumpfheit kommen musste und da es ums Letzte geht, wird, was sich die gesittete, die christliche Welt nannte die physische und vor allem die moralische Kraft besitzen den Kerker zu sprengen? (p. 5).*

TRANSLATION: The jail of this martyr is only a symbol. Had everything come about the way it had to happen due to our stupidity, and we were dealing with the last moment would the civilized, the Christian world possess what it calls the physical and above all the moral power to break into the jail?

Mann's famous *Joseph und seine Brüder* (24, 1945) is a confession of faith in the artist and an elaboration of Mann's personal creed. The author explains how he conceived the work which occupied so many years of his Life and how he expanded a few verses of the *Biblical Book of Genesis* into a tetralogy. Mann comments on each of the four novels, refers to his use of irony, and explains influences from *Tristam Shandy* and *Faust*. This information alone was interesting and enlightening for readers and justified the appearance of the essay, but greater value for the *DB* lay in Mann's thoughts on humanity and religion as related to the 1930's and 1940's when the novels were being written. The author explains his definition of religion as follows: *Sollte ich bestimmen was ich persönlich unter Religiosität verstehe so würde ich sagen sie is Aufmerksamkeit und Gehorsam* (**Were I to designate what I personally understand by religion I would say attentiveness and obedience**). He then explains what he means:

> *Aufmerksamkeit auf innere Veränderungen der Welt, auf den Wechsel im Bilde der Wahrheit und des Rechten; gehorsam, der nicht säumt, Leben und Wirklichkeit diesen Veränderungen, diesem Wechsel anzupassen und so dem Geiste gerecht zu warden (p. 11).*

TRANSLATION: attentiveness to inner changes in the world, to change in the image of truth and of what is right, obedience that does not tarry in applying this change to life and reality and thereby become reconciled with the spirit.

For Mann living in sin means being *unaufmerksam* and *ungehorsam*, clinging to the antiquated, failing to move with the times. This master of penetrating, analytical novels (Consider *Buddenbrooks* [1901] and *The Magic Mountain [1924]*) who wrote of the greatness and concomitant deterioration and loss of vitality of Western civilization prior to the First World War, now elucidates the troubled times of the second great war by applying his definition of religion, and herein lay the greatest worth of the essay for the *DB*:

> *Europa, die Welt waren voll von Überständigkeiten, von Offenkundigen und schon frevelhaften Obsoletheiten und Anachronismen, über die der Weltwille klar hinaus war, und die wir, im ungehorsam gegen ihn, stumpfen Sinnes bestehen Liessen. Daß immer der Geist, der Wirklichkeit voran is, daß die Materie ihm nur schwerfällig folgt, das versteht sich. Aber eine so krankhafte so unverkennbar gefahrdrohende Spannung im politischen, sozialen und ökonomischen Leben der Völker zwischen Wahrheit und Wirklichkeit zwischen der im Geiste längst Erreichten und Vollzogenen und dem was sich immer noch Wirklichkeit zu nennen erlaubt hatte es vielleicht nie zuvor gegeben, und in dem närrischen Ungehorsam gegen den Geist, oder religiös ausgedrückt, gegen Gottes Willen, haben wir gewiss die eigentliche Ursache der Wetterentladung zu suchen, die uns betäut* (p. 13).

TRANSLATON: Europe, the world were full of things which had outlived their usefullness, of over familiar and well-known wanton obsolescences and anachronisms

which the will of the world had clearly left behind, and which we in our disobedience against it stupidly let exist. It is understood that the spirit of reality moves ahead, that substance follows only with difficulty, but such sick unknown tension threatening danger between truth and reality in the political, social and economic lives of the people, between what already is long achieved and completed in spirit and that which allowed itself to be termed reality has probably never existed before, and in the foolish disobedience against the spirit, or expressed in a religious way, against the will of God, we certainly have to seek the actual source of the burst of weather which soaks us.

As an interesting aside, be advised that the above is a most difficult translation. The good Thomas was known for his very long and complicated sentences. Does not *The Magic Mountain* sport a sentence of four pages or so? Yes, ONE sentence.

Those readers of the *DB* who could interpret it (and then thinking that perhaps the man should have gone to war) were left on their own to react to Mann's erudite diagnosis of the times; no editorial commentary was provided. Who would do it? We can try it now that the competitors of the *DB* years have moved on. Did they progress ever higher and higher? We can with documented conviction assert that the patrician from Lübeck was intrigued by human beings whose cultural refinement has resulted from physical decay. Recall poor old Aschenbach, who was destined to progressively degenerate to the point of putrefecation of his spirit and face ultimate death in Venice (*Tod in Venedig [1913]*). Decadence was, indeed, on Tom's mind. Let us be reminded that he had also studied history and politics. His *Friedrich der Grosse und die Grosse Koalition (1914)* is primarily a eulogy of Frederick, the Prussian King, whose intelligence and achievements, such as the **great coalition** would understandably appeal to Mann.

There was only one T. Mann, so to speak, but certainly Germany had produced other great thinkers and good Germans. Two, Karl Kraus and Hermann Hesse, were singled out as ardent pacifists. Explaining Kraus's character, Kurt Hiller writes: *Er zog an, kann man sagen, durch Abstossung. Er stiess mit einer Wucht heiligen Hasses gegen würdevolle Dummheit und polierte Halbbarbarei (***He advanced against repulsion. He pushed with a force of righteous hate against worthy stupidity and polished half barbarity.** In *Memoriam Karl Kraus*, 33, 1946, p. 53) Hiller exclaims: O, *Wie Fehlt Uns Karl*

Kraus! (**Oh, How We Miss Karl Kraus,** p. 55). Were he alive, his satirical pen could be put to good use in the 1940's in opposing war and helping to bring Germans and Austrians to their senses. For Hiller Kraus was *der erlauchteste deutsche Literat* (**the most illustrious man of letters**) of the first third of the twentieth century. *Sein stern funkelt über der zukunft (***His star twinkles over the future)** as an inspiration to advocates of peace.

In the real world the expatriate creators of the *German Leaves* and Hermann Hesse, the *hippie guru and pide piper* of the drug culture, were distant, but as fellow laborers in *belletristic,* also used to oppose the Nazi government, they were in total agreement

An Hermann Hesse zum Nobelpreis (34, 1940) jointly composed by the Rukser/Theile team lauds Hesse for his early pacifism. 1915, they write, *hat Hermann Hesse zum zeichen des protests gegen die Politiker die Deutschland in den ersten Weltkrieg und später zum Nazismus geführt hat, sich freiwillig in die Schweiz verbannt* (p. 57). Other German writers and intellectuals supported their homeland in World War I. Nevertheless Hesse's individualism and foresight, his devotion to peace throughout his life are commended.

Ernst Toller, regarged as the leading Communist among the expressionistic dramatists, was sympathetically pictured by Kurt Hiller as a writer whose suicide was partially due to the depressing times in which he lived and to his disappointment with Germany (*Nachruf für Ernst Toller,* 9/10, 1944). He was, according to Hiller, a humanitarian activist who worked tirelessly for the cause of freedom. However, his suicide was a *klare Kapitulation* to the times, for it was common knowledge that he viewed his struggle as ultimately futile.

In *Ernst und Friedrich Georg Jüngers politische Wandlung* (10, 1943) Karl Paetel argues that Ernst Jünger, the former Prussian anarchist, has changed. Both Jünger brothers, he says, arefirmly on the side of anti-Hitler forces. In order to document the existence of good Germans were the editors implying that even a militarist like E.Jünger could have a change of heart? Jünger hardly ranks with Lessing, schiller, Kant and Thomas Man as a supporter and defender of *DB* objectives. Joseph Kaskell liked Paetel's essay but he doubted the sincereity of E. Jüngers conversion to the journal's ideals. In a letter to Dr. Rukser he explained:

> *Sein Jünger Aufsatz ist ausgezeichnet. Mein einziges Bedenken ist, daß Paetel sowohl wie Jünger vielleicht doch noch zu sehr in den Gedankengängen nationalistisch-konservativer Art gefangen sind, die unseren Ideen von Frieden und Fortschritt nicht conform sind. Paetel sagt von Jünger, daß er sich sehr geändert habe. Ich kann mir aber noch nicht recht vorstellen, daß Männer dieses Schlages*

auch sich damit einverstanden erklären, daß der Begriff "Nation" auf das kulturelle Gebiet beschränkt wird, mit anderen Worten, daß Begriffe wie Europa und Menschheit verstandesmässig und emotional zu einem erheblichen Teil an die Stelle des Begriffes Vaterland treten.[64]

TRANSLATION: His Jünger essay is outstanding. My single concern is that Paetel as well as Jünger are perhaps so tightly caught up in nationalistic-conservative thinking patterns that our ideas of freedom and progress are not compatible. Paetel says of Jünger that he has greatly changed. I can not imagine that men of his type can declare themselves to be in agreement that the term *Nation* be limited to the cultural sphere, in other words that concepts like *Europa* and *humanity* understandably and emotionally to a greater degree be raised to replace the concept *Vaterland*.

With the possible exception of the Jünger essay, these compositions must have been effective in reminding the world of German advocates of peace and humanitarianism. Cleverly, the publishing twosome sought confirmation outside of Germany as well. Who could be a better choice than Thomas Wolfe, the American friend of Germany from North Carolina, a writer who belongs among the very best?

In *You Can't Go Home Again*, Wolfe, who both loved and disliked Germany, revealed his keen insights on the land of his ancestors and their current passion for Nazism. The editors of the *DB* published a German translation of the passage from this thick tome that best served their purposes, for Wolfe observes that *Hitlerei* equaled the *Barbarei* of days gone by, but as if with the *DB* in mind, he adds that the spirit which supported Hitler's madness *war nicht auf Deutschland beschränkt. Er gehörte keiner Rasse zu* (**The madness did not belong to any single ethnic group,** 9, 1943, p. 8).

Wolfe's protagonist, George (Wolfe), recognizes Germany's enlightened past and proposes that salvation is possible only through truth. So, from our American man of letters yet, another explanation.

Maybe we need to simply admit that Germans had no money; Hitler appealed. He offered everything to everybody. Far too many Germans accepted and believed the screwball from Lenz, Austria, because they wanted to. Too many already did not like Jews, making it less difficult to go along with killing them first and foremost and subjugating or killing everybody else, hoping all

---

64   Letter from J. Kaskell to U. Rukser, November 15, 1943.

the while to finally secure those flush toilets, operable telephones, tunnels through the mountainous areas, bridges across the watery regions and everyday quality *Kuchen und kaffee*—No more *Ersatz Kaffee!* Is the above rather silly? Consider it along with what George had to say in the 1930's:

Denn das klare durchdringende Licht der Wahrheit, daß hier in Deutschland bis zur Erlöschung verdunkelt war, das war das Heilmittel, das einzige, das die leidende Menschenseele reinigen und heilen könnte (**For the clear penetrating light of truth that was darkened here in Germany to the point of extinction, that was the cure, the only one that could purify and heal the suffering human souls.**) Indeed, the above quotation evidences that at least one famous American writer was supportive of the *DB's* views.

Another utilitarian use of literature is the picture of the German exile that emerges from some writing, especially from several poems. The second issue contained three *Deutsche Oden,* one by Ludwig uhland and two by Max Barth in which exile is the topic. Uhland writes that Germany's best have had to flee *An des Fremden Herd* (**to the stranger's hearth**) and Barth laments, *Wir haben das bittere Brot des Exils gegessen und sind wie Bettler fern vom Tische* (**We have eaten the bitter bread of exile and are like beggars far from the table**). Max Barth's *Ragnarok* is *die deutsche Stimme* of issue eleven, 1943.[65] The poem describes the deteriorating Germany of the day and twice observes: *Dies ist der letzte Winter im Exil* (**This is last winter in exile**). The alienation, longing, and frustralion that come from being uprooted from one's homeland emanates from Werner Bock's *Gesänge aus Frankreich* (**Songs from France,** 8, 1944) Julius Lips's *Exotische Gedichte* (26, 1945), Karl Wolfskehl's *Sänge aus dem Exil* and Ernst Waldinger's three poems, *Zwischen Hudson und Donau, Stimme der Heimat* and *Geburt aus der Muttersprache* (**Between the Hudson and the Danube, Voices from the Homeland** and **Birth from the Mother Tongue,** 2, 1944).[66]

Little comfort can be found in the article entitled *Verpflanzte Schriftsteller* (**Transplanted Writers,** 2, 1943) which observes that the greatest of all exiled

---

65   Rukser expressed the following opinions on Barth in a letter to Kaskell, September 24, 1943: "**Barth**—besten dank. Treffen Sie sich mit ihm. Es lohnt, weil er ein Dichter ist. Freilich seine Aufsätze sind bisher für uns nicht recht brauchbar weil sie in einer Art polemisch sind, die zu sehr auf den Alltag und zu wenig auf das Bleibende geht. Wir glauben, daß Sie durch etliche Aussprache ihn beeinflussen könnten." (**Essence: Go meet with him because he is a writer it will be worthwhile. Of course to date his essays have not contained the most usable content for us because they are polemical in a way that is too heavy on the banal and too light on permanency. We think that through a few conversations you could influence him.**")

66   Kaskell would like to have seen more work by Waldinger in the magazine. On April 27, 1944, he wrote to Rukser: "Waldingers Gedichte sind interessant und gut" (**Waldinger's poems are interesting and good**).

men of letters was Dante Alighieri, and that could well be. However, Dante was long gone and could not make the situation of the war years any better through commiseration. The point may be that if Mr. Alighieri got through it, so can you. The article adds a concept worth pondering in observing that *es gibt aber—leider—keinen grösseren schöpferischen Impuls als Leiden* (**sadly, no creative impulse is greater than suffering**, p. 25). Has anyone followed up on that concept? Any studies been done?

The exile situation affects individual families differently in its disruption of normal every day life, but worst of all are the differences in thinking which may result (the *Weltanschauung)* where parents and children, due to Nazi propaganda, are politically far apart. Nowhere is the separation of father and son caused by ideological differences more poignantly expressed than in Gustav Regler's *Zehn Briefe an meinen Sohn (***Ten Letters to my Son**, 26, 1945).

This was highly useful material for the collaborative publishers, for the loneliness of the exile emerges from the letters, and Regler's heartache at the estrangement from his beloved son can be blamed on the young man's subcoming to the allure of Nazi teachings. Each year for ten of his twelve years in exile Regler penned a letter to his son who he knew was serving the new *Reich* in Hitler's army. The author, who fought fascism in the Spanish Civil War, sketches his many years of exile experiences and thoughts on National Socialism in the letters, and although Regler admonishes and teaches his son in a firm fatherly manner, his loneliness and suffering are evident in spite of the didactic tone.

Much literature in the *DB* was published primarily for its aesthetic appeal, even though a secondary utilitarian value was evident; the publishers may have hoped for subtle influences favoring their convictions. This was especially true of the final year and a half of the journal's life when the excoriations of Hitler and Nazism had subsided. Again, I stress that any piece of quality literature authored by a German could stand as an example of German achievement and *goodness*. This was obvious although the given selection did not directly support an editorial point of view. Rather, from many, a moral lesson could be drawn.

Short stories, poems and essays comprise this belletristic group of both German and foreign writings; some of the best were penned by Latin Americans. The co-publishers virtually exuberated their belief that *ein Volk lebt in seinen Dichtern, nicht in seinen Politikern. Der Dichter ist es, der unsere wahren Erlebnisse, unsre tiefste Qual wie die höchste Freude ausspricht, durch ihn erst lernen wir uns selbst und unsre Mitmenschen kennen (***A nation lives in her writers, not in her politicians. The writer is the one who defines our deepest** suffering and highest joy, through him we first learn to known ourselves and our fellowman, 6. 1943, p. 11).

A poem by Paul Verlaine was accepted in a German translation by Paul Zech in issue four of 1944; one finds no overt political propaganda value in the poem, but an introductory word on Verlaine by Stefan Zweig calls Verlaine the only French poet who can empathize with German understanding of a poem. This may be construed as a favorable sidelight on German-French relations. It has never been a salient characteristic of the people of either country to highly care for the other. Zweig is encouraging in expressing the hope that a kind of spiritual relationship between poets can achieve what politicians have been unable to do, namely bring Germans and Frenchmen closer because in this time of war they truly needed each other.

Dr. Rukser and Theile looked for uplifting, fine literature everywhere, and in issue nine of 1943 shared with readers Hermann Bahr's *Der Botschafter Amerikas, Walt Whitman* (**America's Ambassador Whitman**). This exemplary proof of their interest in world literature, evaluates Whitman's important breakthrough to free verse and his influence througout the Western World, but just as important for Bahr, and certainly for the *DB*, was Whitman's praise of democracy and his empathy for fellow human beings.

The purely aesthetical in the *DB* is sometimes difficult to separate from the utilitarian; in some pieces the two overlapped. For example a story by Johann Peter Hebel, written 125 years earlier, contained a moral lesson applicable to the current times. *Der Husar in Neisse* (23, 1945) is a tightly written and entertaining short story that offers pedagogical value. It tells of a soldier who stole from a French family at the beginning of the French Revolution when Prussia was fighting France. Some years later, in 1806, the son of the robbed French family recognizes the former Prussian sergeant when the tables are turned and the young Frenchman is quartered with other French soldiers in Neisse. He is not ruthless as was the Prussian.

The same theme of kindness is also artfully and tenderly illustrated by Ernst wiechert in *Der Kinderkreuzzug* (**Childrens Crusade,** 12, 1943) in which,at the risk of losing his job, a shepherd gives food and shelter to starving children.[67] These four selections are representative of literature and essays on literature that had a muted but nevertheless obvious influence as propaganda supporting editorial didactic aims. These pieces were not published soley in support of editorial objectives, but neither were aesthetic qualities the only

---

67 Wiechert was confined in a concentration camp during the summer of 1938, and the *DB* editors thought he was dead. On June 11, 1943, Rukser wrote to Kaskell about Wiechert's assumed death. Miraculously, although for some time very close to death, he lived through the ordeal and wrote of what he experienced in *Der Totenwald* (**The Forest of Death**).

consideration. In contrast the group of writings to be considered next is almost completely free from moralizing or even sublte support of *DB* views.

LITERATURE AS UPLIFTING FINE ART

José Antonio Benton's *Die Onça* (**jaguar,** 29, 1946) and his *Brasilianische Legenden* (33, 1946) are delightfully entertaining. The first is a short story about a Brasilian *onca* which outwits a hunter and regains the cubs the latter has stolen. The hunter learns to respect her. *Die Flohjagd* (**Catching Flies**) and *Die wunder des Heiligen Cosmos* (**The Miracles of Saint Cosmos**) are the legends related by Benton.

The first tells of an old woman who complained of her lot. one day Jesus comes to her hut and teaches her how to catch flies. With her new purpose in life, fly catching, she is happy for the rest of her days.

The two miracles of Saint Cosmos have to do with skin color. For natives of Brazil light skin is preferable to dark, but in both legends skin color means nothing to the saint who knows no prejudice. Benton is one of the exiled writers who contributed to the *DB*. He was born in Strassburg in 1894 and moved to Sao Paulo in 1936 where he taught Latin and Greek and diligently studied Brazilian literature. His profound understanding of both the people and literature of Brazil is evident in the selections. Benton is among those few expatriats who were able to assimilate the culture of their host countries.

Paul Zech, whom we normally find energetically excoriating Nazis or championing freedom in his *DB* publications, contributed his sensuous short story *Der Nebelregen von Ouro Muemo* (**The Drizzle of Ouro Muero**) to the seventh issue of 1943. Zech's description of a rain forest is perceptively and artistically executed in a manner reminiscent of Max Dauthendey's *Exotische Novellen* (**Exotic Novelas**). No moralizing or admonishing is even implied; the impressinistic selection appealed to the editors of the *DB* solely for its aesthetic worth. This was also true of Zech's *Indianische Tänze* (23, 1945) and other short stories as well as several poems by various authors.

Nonpropagandistic treatment of a writer is exemplified in comments on Theodor Fontane who is honored in issue 9/10, 1944, in remembrance of his 125th birthday. We read that Fontane remained a happy individual in spite of problems and hardships in his life. Readers may well find Fontane's tenacity worthy of imitation, but there is no special emphasis on Fontane as a fighter for favorite causes. He is not presented as were Lessing Goethe, or even Walt Whitman. Several excerpts from his letters reveal Fontane the man, the husband, the writer. Essays on Kafka, Rilke in England, and Georg Kaiser, as well as essays on French literature also do not represent *littérature engangé* favoring editorial positions. Each is solely a reflective criticism restricted to its topic.

The Latin American selections were seldom used to support causes except for the subtle kind of assistance which could come from the work of a writer who sympathized with such issues as peace or human equality. Theile and Rukser unquestionable hoped for such influence from some of the pieces although ostensibly their purpose was to familiarize readers with literature of the South American countries. Some of the very best writing was sampled; in retrospect some readers may wish that the *Blätter* had published more Latin American literature and placed less emphasis on politics, dialectics and speculation about the future.

Latin American Literature made its debut in the journal with the appearance of Pablo Neruda's *Cuatro Poemas de Amor* (5, 1943), with masterful German translations by Totila Albert, the German-Chilean sculptor. In recognizing Neruda's poetic genius Theile and Rukser were thirty years ahead of their time. Neruda had to wait until 1972 to receive international recognition as the recipient of the Nobel Prize for Literature. However, recognition did come from a source unwelcome to many.

During the war he was well known in communist circles and worked with the *Alemania Libre (Freies Deutschland* or **Free Germany***)* movement in Mexico.[68] His anti-Nazi activities earned him the enmity of German Nazis living in Mexico whose animosity grew until on December 28, 1945, a group of Nazis attacked and stabbed the poet, leaving him for dead. To them his very existence was a symbol of resistance. Fortunately Neruda, a *nom de plume* whose real name was Neftalí Ricardo Reyes, lived to create more enobling, inspiring and informative poetry. Today, critics of Hispanic literature regard his body of work as the very pinnacle of contemporary achievement, i.e. the culmination of the evolution of modern poetry which for so long was not regarded as equal to Spanish and European literature. The inspiring Chilean is regarded as equal to such respected *literati* of the old country as Juan Ramón Jimenéz or even Federico García Lorca.

The editors of the *DB*, who deserve kudos for sharing their appreciation of Neruda and recognizing his genius, made little use of the attack. In all liklehood they did not wish to emphasize his support of communism, They introduce him as a rejuvenator of the Spanish language and creator of new philosophical metaphors. His *Cuatro Poemas* are love poems free of political implications

One of Jorge Borges's Kafkaesque stories appeared in issue eight of 1944.

---

68   *Alemania Libre* was a communist group very active in Mexico.

Im Traumkreis der Ruinen (**In the Dream Circle of Ruins**) gave most German readers of the *DB* a first acquaintance with the brilliant Argentinian who when he was aged and blind began to receive the world-wide recognition he had so diligently earned and rightly deserved. Any lingering doubt concerning the intellectual maturity and depth of artistic sensitivity and ability of Spanish American writers should have dissipated when Borges came on the scene.

Living in South America, in fact very near to Neruda and across the mountain from Borges, Rukser and Theile had unique opportunity to acquaint both themselves and their readers with such masterpieces as Borges's short story. They are to be commended for bringing to the attention of their readers the great body of work (poetry, essays, short stories) of one of the finest literary minds that Argentina (or the world for that matter) has produced. Few of Borges's prolific works have been translated into other languages until the last few years; Paul Zech aided by Herta Landshoff, was once again of service to the *DB* in producing a German translation.

Though the plot of the story is simple, it's conception is most unique: a human being creates another man by dreaming him. Because of Borges's surrealistic plots many critics discern the influence of Franz Kafka in his work. That may well be, but Borges did not need to be influenced. His own mind was indeed sufficient. He is difficult to classify (which critics and professors love to do since it justifies their labors). However, this grand old gentleman's style and topics were personal, intellectual and unique. For a time he was the leader of the so-called *Ultraistas*, but later said he was sorry to have joined the group.

It seems that writers in the Hispanic world love their.. .*ismos*. They have ascribed to so many: *futurismo, vanguardismo, cubismo, creacionismo, naturalismo, superealismo*. They go on and on. *Ultraísmo* originated in Spain and became an …ismo more sureal than *surealismo*, Therefore, the new name for a movement which wanted to go even farther (*ir más allá*) in the renovation of aesthetics, even carry it to what they termed its ultimate consequences. It seems Borges had good reason to depart the group, for who could predict these consequences?

In issue twenty-seven of 1945 Borges as essayist is represented by his *Gaucho-Literatur in Argentinien und Uruguay*. This is an appropriate subject for this writer who was fascinated by the *Gaucho* and the stories of their physical prowess and equestrian skills claimed to be *nonpareil*, possibly a slight exaggeration, but once well-established such tales continue. Doubtlessly, the horsemen of the *pampas* are, if not the very best anywhere, they are at the least, among the best.

Borges observes that *Gaucho* literature has been the topic of many essays, and one recalls the *Gaucho* stories in *El Aleph*. Because all the critics writing them have been city dwellers, however, Borges finds that they share the common mistake of mythicizing. Finally, does the uncommon absence of editorial comment on the essay tell us that the editors agreed none was needed?

After all, the essay itself is a perceptive evaluation of the subject and a succinct but enlightening introduction to this literature which contains universal values projected through the culture of Argentina. The reader should be able to discern that the human condition consists of the same elements everywhere. Poverty, wealth, crime, illness, stupidity, jealousy, kindess and other aspects of life are common to all.

The essay ends with an introduction to *Der Schwache Punkt*, a story by Enrique Amorín who, Borges observes, draws his plots frorn the Uruguayan pampas, the raw land of the North. The story is as bizarre as Borges's own. A story teller (*cuentero*) of the pampas is apparently killed by his own fear. This fear is the *Punkt* repeatedly referred to by the mentally retarded Candidor who speaks no words except, *der schwache Punkt*.

Jorge Icaza was chosen to represent Equador in the *DB*. His *Gewitter in den Bergen* (**Mountain Storm**, 9/10, 1944) is a translation by Paul Zech of a few pages of the novel, *Hausipungo*. The passage seems at first to be only an eloquent description of a mountain storm, The entire novel, however, is a sociological study depicting the cruel exploitation of the Indians of Equador by the Catholic Church and land owners. The editors tell their readers in a note that Icaza was awarded a literary prize by his government for this novel, but two years later *Hausipungo* was forbidden in Ecuador by this same government. Bringing another fine example of South American literature to their readers was the chief concern of the editors, but because Icaza was a paladin fighting for improvement of conditions among the native inhabitants, he was also grist to the DB's political mill. Icaza, like exiled German writers, had experienced repression of truth by a government that could not tolerate criticism.

The two Germanic editors were pleased to congratulate the Chilean poetess, Gabriela Mistral, on being awarded the Nobel Prize for Literature (1, 1946). Mistral's poems in the *DB* have great value as expressions of the emotions of a great heart and as beautiful poetry, her one page descriptiontion of a Mexican Indian woman *Die Silhouette der mexikanischen Indianerin* (**Silhouette of a Mexican woman,** 23, 1945, is lyrical in its description of the colorful and stately native women of Mexico, whom Mistral observed when she was helping to improve education in that country. Her portrayal is sympathetic, perceptive. and impressionistic. An introductory note to this first appearance of Mistral's poetry observes: *Ihre Seele ist voll aufgeschlossen wenn sie mit Christus ringt um die Rettung der verdorbenen Menschheit, wenn sie das Schicksal des jüdischen Volkes bedauert oder wenn ihr Mitleid der unverheirateten Mutter gilt oder dem verlorenen Kind* (**She pours out her heart when she struggles with Christ to save sinful** humanity, when she pities the Jewish people or when she empathizes with the prodigal child, p. 40).

The original Spanish versions of her poems are given in each issue with German translations because her admirers recognized and admonished that the linguistic, phonetic and emotive gualities of Mistral's work were best understood in Spanish: *um die Dichtung Gabriela Mistrals zu würdigen muss man nicht nur der spanischen Sprache mächtig sein, sonder auch tief in ihre vielfältigen Verzweigungen in Südamerica eingedrungen sein* (**To truly appreciate Mistral's writing one must not only master Spanish, but also be deeply conversant with its multiple South American variations** 29, 1946, p. 67). Readers are encouraged to read more of Mistral's work in the original Spanish.

Eduardo Mallea, the prolific writer of the Argentine, contributed two pieces to the German journal. The first, *Einsame, zeitgemässe Aufzeichnungen* (**Unique, Timely Sketches**), was an original work written specifically for the *DB*; it is comprised of several short Proustian and Joycean flashes of memory with titles including *Paula, Das Schwalbenbuch, Gespräche and Orangen*.

Two of these thirteen *Aufzeichnungen* strongly express the author's horror at the war he hears of in Europe. *Vor mir brandet die furchtbare europäische Erschütterung, gleichwie gegen Abend der ozean vor dem Spaziergänger an der Küste. Aufruhr, Finsternis, Was wird auf Erden geschehen?* (**Before me the horrible European destruction is burning just as toward evening the ocean in front of the walker on the coast. Turmoil, darkness, what is happening on earth,** p. 55?). Although most of these short memories are not related to war, Mallea through their messages doubtlessly became one more intellectua ally of the *DB* in expressing horror at the holocaust in Europe.

In his second contribution to the *DB* the Argentinean deals soley with his own country. *Das unsichtbare Land* (**The Invisible Land**) examines the vast differences between the inhabitants of the back country and the city dwellers. It gave the reader of the *DB* an inside view of Argentina penetrating far beyond the travel book descriptions, for Mallea analyzes here the very minds and souls of his countrymen. Through examples of South America's best literature, readers could learn to better understand the various cultures thriving south of the border and gain insight into their psychological, ethnic and sociological problems.

The brilliant Mexican essayist, Alfonso Reyes, generally known in his country as the *Hombre de letras*, belongs to the so-called *Generacion del Centenario (1910)*, one of the most fruitful intellectual advancements of Mexico, translated as the **generation of the decade.** He served in the diplomatic corp of his country and founded the department of philosophy and letters at the *Universidad Nacional*. Reyes received the title of **Doctor Honoris Causa** from several prestigious universities inluding the U of Mexico, U of California, Harvard and Princeton. Schopenhauer, Nietzsche, Kant, and Burckhardt are among the subjects of his erudite essays. His *Goethe und Amerika* was a wise choice to bring to readers of the *DB* (32,1946) because it links Germany with the Americas.

In the essay Reyes notes that America is mentioned twice in *Stella*, a play of Goethe's youth then expands:

> *Aber später als diese harmonische Natur in dem neutralen Boden Weimars Wurzel gefasst hat, Öffnen sich die Horizonte und man kann ohne Übertreibung sagen, daß der sesshafte Goethe ohne den Juno Saal zu verlassen mehr gereist ist als der stürmische, der Werthersche Goethe, der ersten Epoche.* (p. 32).

TRANSLATION: But later when this harmonic nature had established roots in the neutral soil of Weimar, the horizon opened, and one can say without exaggeration that without leaving the hall of Juno the sedentary Goethe traveled more than the stormy, Werther-like Goethe of his first epoch.

The hall of Juno?...well...Reyes was waxing a little exuberant, He did indeed worship the great man. We may agree when we learn that Goethe truly was a universal genius with enough interests to overwhelm most. Furthermore, he excelled in each, including painter, actor statesman, scientist with interests in geology, botany, anatomy. He was and still is Germany's greatest poet and man of letters. He read, even lectured in several languages. At a loss for words Napoleon said of him simply: *Voilà un homme!*

Reyes notes that Goethe translated two songs by Brazilian cannibals for the *Tiefurter Journal* of 1783, no. 38. Goethe broadened his knowledge of the American lands through conversations with many travelers to the new world. The most important of these was Alexander von Humboldt. Goethe, we read was interested in everything about America; its geography and its colonies of Blacks established by the British were equally fascinating, *Was hätte Goethe von America gedacht?* (**What did Goethe think of America?**) Reyes asks, then answers, *Immer war Amerika eine Utopie, die Hoffnung auf eine bessere Republik, der man nachzuleben hat... Dieser Anziehungskraft Amerikas konnte sich Goethe nicht entziehen* (**America was always a utopia, the hope for a better republic that one had to lived up to. Goethe could not escape its appeal,** pp. 35-36).

Referring to Goethes *Wilhelm Meister*, one of the great apprenticeship novels in German and world literature, from Goethe's classical period. Reyes penned a memorable sentence worthy of Thomas Mann or Goethe himself, *Vorne im Kahn stehend, kreuzt Wilhelm Meister—Goethe—die Arme und blickt voll Vertrauen auf Amerika in die Zukunft* (**Standing forward in the barge, Meister—Goethe—crosses his arms and looks with full trust toward America in the future,** p. 36). German readers of the *Blätter* must have been pleased to learn that the gifted Mexican intellectual was so familiar with Goethe, and we may rest assured that Theile and Rukser were advocating *soto voce* (or maybe *forte*) that subscribers should familiarize themselves with the writings of Reyes and all his gifted Latin American peers. The message was discernible.

The above sampling of the *DB* presentation of Latin American literature indicates that the collaborating German publishers held it in high esteem. They generally let the pieces speak for themselves, calculating that the quality of the selections would stimulate readers to seek more. Due to the circumspection and innate ability of the duo, many gifted Latin American writers were lifted from obscurity, but the workload increased, for now in addition to the many poems, short stories and essays came books, magazine and newspapers from around the world, a service as noted by Robert Cazden,"which was widely appreciated." [69]

Most reviews were printed in the *Bücher* section of the magazine; occasionally a book was the subject of an entire article. The reviews in the first months of publication dealt exclusively with political subjects including National Socialism, the history defyingrise of Hitler and that ubiquitous subject the *German Problem*. Issue one reviewed only Hermann Rauschning's *Die konservative Revolution*. The second issue of the journal devoted a half page to Thomas Mann's radio broadcasts to Germany, *Deutsche Hörer!* (**German listeners!**) While Joseph Kaskell in a longer review reported on *Economic Peace Aims* by Oswald Dutch

In an attempt to hasten the conversion of readers to their personal *Weltanschauung* (**ideology, worldview**), the joint editors presumptuously planted a reading list in the second and tenth issues of their magazine. Some selected titles hint at the contents: Rohan D. Butler's *The Roots of National Socialism 1783-1933*, Paul Hagen's *Will Germany Crack?*, Benedetto Groce's *History as the Story of Liberty*, Victor Gollancz's *Shall our Children Live or Die? A Reply to Lord Vansittart on the German Problem*, Richard M. Brickner's *Is Germany Incurable?* and many more with the same or related subjects. Quotations by intellectuals of various countries confirm editorial faith in the power of books. The following words by Archibald MacLeish are typical:

---

69 Robert Cazden, *German Exile Literature in America 1933-1950* (American Library Association, 1970), p. 59.

Die Nazis verübte ihre schmutzigen und gehässigen Handlungen, weil sie wussten... daß Bücher Waffen sind, solche Bücher wie sie nur freie Menschen mit dem Stolz freier Menschen schreiben können. Waffen so scharf und von solchem Gewicht und solcher Gewalt, daß jene die die Freiheit in der Welt zerstören wollen, erst einmal die Bücher zerstören müssen, mit denen die Freiheit kämpft (10, 1943, p. 30).

TRANSLATION: The Nazis carried out their filthy and loathsome acts because they well knew that books are weapons, those books, which only free persons bearing their freedom with pride, can create—Weapons so sharp, so heavy and of such force (or here perhaps *authority*) that those who wish to disrupt the freedom of the world have to first destroy the <u>books which are its weapons.</u>

After the first few months the book review section included fictional works and nonpolitical titles. For example, art was the subject of the *Bücher* section of issue nine which reviewed Jan Tschichold's *Der Holzschneider* (**The Woodcutter**) und *Bild-drucker Hu Cheng-Yen* (**Image Printer...**) and Rudolf Bernoulli's *Mein Weg zu Klee* (**My Way to Klee**). The *Literarische Kurznotizen* (**Short Literary Notes**) in this issue ranged from books on China to Robert Frost and Brazilian and Mexican poets. Though political works were always included in *DB* book reviews, creative literature became increasingly more prominent. Principal reviewers were Theile, Rukser and Karl Paetel who were assisted by Joseph Kaskell, Fritz Meyning (Fritz Siegel), Friedrich Ballhausen, Anna Steuerwald-Landmann, and occasionally others.

Reviews of magazine and newspaper articles began with subjects similar to those of the early *Bücher* section. At first only such articles which treated Hitler, the Nazi Party, peace and the like were reviewed. The *German Problem* drew primary attention. Everyone wanted to get into the act, it seems, for the *krauts, Huns, Germanic hordes* or whatever they were termed had to be stopped... forever.

Before long, in periodicals from around the world our favorite anti-Nazi journal was seeking support for its philosophy through creating the *Zeitschriftenschau*, born with the fifth issue. It reviewed the Chilean sister publication of *Free World, Mundo Libre*, in addition to *Foreign Affairs*, the Mexican magazine, *Cuadernos Americanos* and *Free World*. Understandably, articles receiving greatest interest had titles such as *Post-war Problems of Refugees* and *Plans for the Future*. A comparison of early issues with the March/April issue of 1946 indicates the expanded coverage of both topics and number of magazines. However, unlike the book reviews, magazine reviews remained primarily politically oriented.

The contents of nine magazines were reviewed in this issue. The *Deutsche Blätter sind erfreut, we are told, einen Kampfgenossen begrüssen zu können in Die neue Rundschau (**DB is pleased to be able to greet a fellow fighter in the appearance of the new R** ...Rundschau means literally review, view, look around).* The other eight magazines were from England and the United States. The *Zeitschriften-Zeitungsschau* (**A Look at Newspapers and Magazines**) a feature of nearly every issue, consistently presented varied and thorough coverage favoring publications in agreement with the given editorial position espoused by the *Leaves,* among which was the question of how devasting would be the longterm effect of the Nazi corruption of German and consideration of semantics.

Our native language is an integral part of our natural heritage, a personal possession as much our own as the geography of our place of birth. Man and language are inseparable, and life without language is nonhuman. It is probably true to assert that from the second year of life on, with little variation, everybody speaks a language. With the exception of those who study and teach languages, we give little thought to the possibility that any given language is "corruptible," but all are.

It was never an area of study in which I concentrated, but the science of linguistic development and changes in language, the study of meaning, has intrigued me throughout my career as a student and teacher of languages. My interest is due not only to observations as a language teacher, but also to the work of Dr. S.I. Hayakawa, professor, President of the University of San Francisco, US. Senator and a true "character,"now deceased.

"A piece of work" may be the best term to apply to him today, although I hasten to add that this accomplished gentleman would ask: "What does that mean?" I would be forced to say: "I can not define it, but the phrase applies." The "meaning of meaning" is very seriously addressed by some academics, but the phrase also lends itself to a bit of humor. "What does it mean?" requires an enigmatically complex answer, believe it or not, because it involves psychology, literal and figurative meanings, subtle indications and other sciences. Furthermore, it is disagreeable, frustrating or possibly welcome to observe that one's communal language does not remain fixed. The scholars, who tackle these linguistic mysteries, speak even of the meaning of meaning. They are a unique group of intelligencia. We are fortunate to benefit from their learning and teaching.

The phenomenon of linguistic change is doubtlessly related to the employment of the reservoir of the language common to all members of a language community as they speak and listen. Of course, establishing the power of the word is the very subject of this study. Therefore, semantics and Nazi degradation of the mother tongue requires closer scrutiny, which will not be lengthy, but, hopefully, will be sufficiently informative for our present purposes and in examining the speech and behavior of modern and future despots as they come along.

I know that humans sometimes act without thinking, but it should seem obvious to all that how we act is, with very few exceptions, determined by how we think. Arguably, even on those occasions when we appear to behave without thinking, we follow our solidly established patterns of thought which emerge from utterances ("talk"). Yes, we talk to ourselves in our minds, frequently. We form what semanticists term an entire complex of "language habits." How we talk as well as our attitudes toward our remarks, are perhaps open-minded or maybe rigid. This obviates the notion that when we "accept" any language (our native tongue as infants), we do not realize what tremendous power the structure of an habitual language has. In summary, how we think and evaluate is inextricably bound up with how we talk. Meanings, then, and keep this in mind as we study more of the *DB's* articles on German, are 1. semantic reactions that take place in human beings, and 2. language to be language must have meaning. Somehow, it seems to me that persons such as Hitler and his primary bootlicker, Goebbels, tapped into the "accepted" language habits and meaings of their countrymen held deep within their collective psyche. Maybe that is simply corny, but give it some thought because the larger question keeps arising: Why were Germans so enthusiastically accepting and ready?

The use and misuse of German is the subject of a group of four articles in the *Blätter,* of which three were published in 1945, and the fourth in 1946. The long title of the first indicates both humor and disgust at Nazi degradation of German literature: *Neue deutsche Reimstandarte, Behördlich anerkannte Poesien von Muster-Poeten des dritten Reiches für die Nachwelt aufbewahrt und an den Tag gegeben von Tim Borah (***New German rhyme standards, poetry of outstanding poets of the Third Reich, officially recognized, brought to light and filed for posterity** by Tim Borah, 24,*1945, p.42).* Indeed,Tim Borah collected poems by the Nazi poets, Ernst Bertram, Richard Billinger, Rudolf T. Binding, Hans Johst and Joseph Weinheber. For the sake of objectivity it must be clarified that these poets exhibited different degrees of allegiance to Nazism; not all were party fanatics. Borah, however does not differentiate. Understandably his repugnance was too strong. The titles of Bertram's and Johst's poems indicate the tenor of Borah's article *Nordische Mannen* (**Nordic Men**) and *Dem*

Fünfzigjährigen im Tausendjährigen (**To the fifty-year-old in the Thousand Year (Reich)**)

The *Führer*, dying for the *Vaterland*, and praise of Germany's greatness are typical subjects of this *Blut und Boden* (**Blut and Soil**) poetry, which today is regarded only as a ludicrous anomaly in the history of German literature. The German readers of the *Blätter*, however, must have despaired at these perverted creations in their mother tongue, which raised the humble farmer to new heights above the urbanite. **Blood** and **soil** reflected an anti-urban animus, for it was through the workers and rural handcraftsmen sharing the same blood and soil (some newly and brutally conquered) that the new, Nazi socialism was to be created. The new motive of common B and B brought together worker motif and the farmer motif.

Werner Bock writing from Argentina for the fall issue of 1945, had strong sentiments about the corruption by Nazis of German literature and language.[70] For Bock *eine dichterische Neugeburt aus gereinigtem Geist und Herzen* (**a complete poetic rebirth of language from the very soul and heart**) would have to be an important facet of any effective anti-Nazi program. He makes an emotional appeal for an immediate rebirth because he sees no hope from the writings of Germans in South America and harshly cries: *Werfen wir einen Blick auf die literarischen Neuerscheinungen deutscher Sprache in südamerikanischen Ländern, überkommt uns Hoffnungslosigkeit* (**Hopelessness overcomes us when we cast a glance at the new literature written in German appearing in the South American countries** p. 55). Theile and Rukser did not comment on Bock's negative pronouncement. Should the reader assume their silence implies endorsement of his concerns?

Verfall und Erneuerung der deutschen Sprache (**The Decay and Renewal of the German Language,** 28,1945) by Arthur Salz is the most perspicacious of the articles on Nazi abuse of the German language. Dr. Salz, former professor at Heidelberg, was teaching at the University of Ohio when he wrote this article diagnosing the illness of his native tongue. He seems to be personally injured when he writes:

> *In dem letzten Jahrzehnt und länger ist diese unsere Muttersprache missbraucht worden und verwildert. Es ist auf Deutsch gelogen,*

---

70 Karl Paetel co-authored *Nazi-Deutsch—A Glossary of Contemporary German Usage*. Rukser was most interested in it. However, it was no best seller. Dear Dr. (Paetel…he at least received an honorary Dr. title) struggled on, poor and ill, to his last day on earth in that tiny apartment in Forest Hills, N.Y. surrounded by stack upon stack of newspapers and periodicals, tinder dry, and chain smoking (unbelievable)!! I thoroughly enjoyed hearing so many of his experiences, but was greatly relieved upon leaving his small fire trap. Thank God he had his Elizabeth! Even in their poverty she would brew a good cup of *Kaffee*.

gelästert, verleumdet und auf Deutsch beredt geschwiegen worden so sehr, daß Deutsch und Unwahr gleichbedeutend geworden sind

TRANSLATION: For more than a decade our mother tongue has been misused and perverted. German has been employed to lie, blaspheme, and slander, yet also been eloquently silent to the extent that *German* has become synonymous with falsehood, p.16).

The last line says it all about one kind of abuse. German became completely lacking in probity, at least as used by those who were knowingly churning out the stream of prefabrications. Salz believes that German is (or "was") both a work of art and a means of communication; it reflects the spirit, the culture, the character of its speakers. and now the German tongue, having progressed through the cleansing and polishing of Martin Luther and others to modern times must be purified if it is correctly to reflect what is good in German culture and trigger for readers of today remembrances of the language of Goethe, Schiller, Lessing, Fontane and Thomas Mann. However, the professor has no faith in a *Sprachreinigungsverein* (**a language cleansing organization***)* imposed from without. Instead, it his opinion that:

Nichts *anderes ist nötig als der feste Wille, der Grundsatz, daß ein jeder ehrlich Deutsch redet, reines Deutsch schreibe, das Beste lese und daß wir eine gereinigte Sprache unseren Nachkomm als wertvolles Erbteil überliefern—ein Vermächtnis des alten Deutschland und das Neue der zukunft.*

TRANSLATION: Nothing more is needed than the unshakable will, the basic position that everyone speak unadulterated German, write pure German and read only the best, and that we leave to our progeny as a worthwhile inheritance a cleansed language—a legacy of the Germany of old as well of the future, *(p. 17).*

What, however, should an author do when he lives in exile far removed from his native tongue? should he write in the language of his host country or rely on translations? Johannes Urzidil poses these guestions in *Die sprache im Exil* (32, 1946). Basing much of his essay on the experience of Julian Green, the author born to American parents in Paris, Urzidil observes that languages interpret the world in different ways, making it impossible to produce really true translations. He continues writing, however, as he questions any author's ability to create a quality work in a foreign language. We must resort to translations, but skill in translating can be improved by accepting the task Urzidil assigns:

> *Die Aufgabe des Autors ist, es innerhalb der eigenen Sprache jenes Geheimidom der Allgemeinmenschlichkeit aufzudecken das eine ebensolche Entsprechung in der Tiefe aller fremden Sprachen findet. In diesem idiom, so sehr wie möglich muss er dichten. Dies ist die am weitesten übersetzbare Sprache. Was immer auch durch Übersetzungen noch verloren gehe, zertrümmert werde oder sich selbst auflöse etwas wird bleiben, das alle verstehen, auf das alle sich einigen können, durch das alle besser werden,* (p. 27).

TRANSLATION: The task of the author is to uncover within his own language that particular corresponding secret idiom of universal humanity which is found in the depths of all foreign languages. It is in this idiom, to the extent it is possible that he must write, for this language is the most widely translatable. No matter whatever is lost in translation, is garbled or dissolves itself, something will remain that everyone understands and can agree upon and through which all improve.

The expats must have found it difficult indeed to find the *Geheimidiom* (**secret language**) proposed by Urzidil. Do we detect influence of Ludwig Wittgenstein here? He and fellow philosophers were espousing the definition of aesthetics as an examination of the ways in which language is used.

The whole question of language usage is far too vexing for simplistic magic suggestions such as searching for a *Geheimidiom*! The very livelihood of the authors living abroad depended on competence and highly skillful manipulation of their native tongue, which they had been forced to at least partially abandon. Do not all authors of high repute strive to communicate in the clearest language possible something of importance to mankind? Afterall, we often are reminded in various media that man is the "talking animal," no doubt that Hitler was a voluminous talker. Language is one of the most pervasive elements in human existence. Perhaps we should look back to our remote ancestors and deliberate the possibility of language having magic properties.

All the literary aspects of the *DB* analyzed above attest to its cultural merit, and It speaks well of the editorial policy of Rukser and Theile that aesthetics could be so highly regarded when many other exile periodicals published soley political articles, which ranted on and on. These writings of some of Germany's finest authors helped to keep German culture alive, and unquestionably the objective of introducing German readers to Latin American Literature was at least partially achieved. Be reminded of Archibald McLeish's conviction that books (the written word) are the weapons of freedom.

Chapter X
Travel, Philosophy, Music, Art

THE *Deutsche Blätter* never emphasized the subjects of travel, music, art and philosophy, but the few pieces that appeared were perceptive and informative and held to the same high standards. Although a few articles on exotic parts of the world were printed in early issues, it was not until the crushing of Hitler was assured that the editors turned more to these subjects perhaps in an attempt to broaden the scope of the periodical and to enhance its attractiveness to readers.

The new sentiment seemed to say: enough of the ceaseless hortatory lest we become simply too *schwerfällig* (**ponderous**). No issue of 1943 contained an article on music or art, but between 1944 and 1946 seven appeared on music and seven on art; some expressed concern for exiled German artists and musicians or reported on their activities. Philosophy was not treated until 1946, the last year of publication. Music did not have the propaganda value for the editors that literature offered, but the first article on music, Gerhard Masur's *Wolfgang Amadeus Mozart* by its very title reminded readers of Germanic accomplishments in music, as did only the surname, *Mozart* or the monosyllabic *Bach*. Masur expresses this concept better when he enthuses that the name of the Austrian genius calls to mind *die Süssigkeit des Lebens* (**sweetness of life**). Ironically the music of an Austrian, the enemy, could make the dark years seem less depressing. Masur asks: *Gab es Epochen der Verdüsterung und der Trübsal auf die nicht Licht gefallen wäre, Heiterkeit und Erlösung, wenn die klänge Mozarts über ihre Schwelle schwebten?* (**Have there ever been periods of darkness and sadness which failed to be brightened and cheered by the sounds of Mozart's music drifting over the threshold?** p. 25). Masur asks what makes Mozart's music unique and answers: *Mozarts Music ist die Musik der Liebe* (p. 27, on your own for a translation, hint *Liebe means* **love**). The concept of love appealed to Theile and Rukser because it could be related to their general humanitarian and pacifistic concerns.

Wolfgang Stresemann discussed the life and works of Alban Berg in the May/June issue of 1945. Berg, too, could symbolize germanic accomplishments, although Stresemann never stresses Berg's nationality, He emphasizes the reception of Berg's opera *Wozzek*, laments that he did not compose more and tells a little about Berg's life and place in music history, stressing his daring in writing a *Wozzek* and a *Lulu*. With the avowed aims of the *DB* in mind, however, one would be naïve not to suspect that Berg too held symbolical value for our German *Leaves*. Here was an additional intellectual, gifted, homesick and incensed. Their numbers were growing, and today all deserve to be remembered, honored and emulated. They set a standard, high, yet achievable, while the lowest forms of human beings could sink to Nazi standards effortlessly.

An introductory note to an extract from the memoirs of Fritz Busch (28, 1945) states that Busch was the embodiment of decency, far removed from Nazi thinking:

> *Die welt kennt Busch als einen der grossen Repräsentanten deutscher Musikalität, als unvergleichen Gestalter des Rein-Menschichen, so daß darüber nicht viel Worte zu machen sind. Aber soviel wir ihm als musischen Künstler schuldig geworden sind, nicht weniger haben wir ihm als dem Verkörperer des Deutschtums zu danken, das mit Hitler nichts zu tun haben wollte und darum trotz glänzender Anerbietungen die freiwillige Verbannung der Unterwerfung unter ein nichtwürdiges Regime vorzog (*p,34).

Translation: The world knows Busch as one of the greatest representatives of German musicality, as an incomparable creator of pure humanity, which makes it difficult to say more about it. Nevertheless, however great may be the debt we owe him as a musical artist, does not diminish our gratitude for his embodiment of German culture that would have nothing to do with Hitler and, therefore, he preferred voluntary exile to subjugation to an unworthy regime, in spite of the lustrous proposals it offered.

The several pages of Busch's memoirs taken from the section, *Elternhaus und Kindheit*, describe Busch's humble beginnings and his firm belief in moral principles. Why was this section of the memoirs chosen? Obviously to highlight Busch's admirable character and exemplary life.

Other articles evaluated modern music; they could not be construed as being supportive of any of the principal themes of the magazine. In the May/April issue of 1945 Ernst Toch, who was living in California and teaching music, defended modern atonal music as being representative of the times. *Jede Kunst spiegelt die wesentlichen Geistesrichtungen ihrer Zeit wieder* (**Each art form reflects the essence of what direction the spirit of its time is taking,** p. 13), Toch writes, and concludes, *die Entwicklung zur heutigen Tonsprache war naturgemäss, logisch und unvermeidlich* (**The development leading to the present day tone-speech was natural, logical and unavoidable.**) As part of his plan to expand the cultural aspects of his magazine, Rukser wrote to Wolfgang Stresemann in New York on July 25, 1943, soliciting an article on music. He explained the philosophy of the *DB*, described working conditions in Chile, and listed the kinds of articles needed.

> *Bitte erleichtern Sie uns auch die Orientierung durch weitere Mitteilungen. wir brauchen a) kritik—völlig ungeschminkte!—b) Informationen c)Mitarbeit auch bei der Gestaltung. Ich glaube mich nicht zu täuschen, daß Sie Musiker sind und daß ich im Hause Ihres von mir stets verehrten Vaters einmal eine Musik von Ihnen gehört habe? Aber sei dem wie immer: wir denken, daß jeder schöpferische Mensch von seinem Standpunkt aus heute etwas zu den grossen Fragen zu sagen hat und viel-leicht—wir, durch soviel Prüfungen geführten Deutschen sogar noch mehr als andere. Sprechen Sie sich bitte auch darüber mit Kaskel aus aber vergessen Sie bitte darüber nicht möglichst ausführlich an uns zu schreiben.*

TRANSLATION: Please assist us also with the orientation through further communication. We need a) critique—completely unembellished! b) information c) also help with the production. I still greatly respect your father and think I am not mistaken that you are a musician whom I once heard perform in his house. But, be that as it may, we think that today every creative person has something to say from his point of view concerning the big question and maybe—we, Germans who have been led through so many tests, have more to say than others. Also, speak about that with Kaskel,

> but please, don't forget as soon as possible to write us in detail about it.

Stresemann responded with an article entitled *New Yorker Musikbrief*, and patience was rewarded when his article on Alban Berg came two years later. The publication of the first is indicative of editorial interest in critical interpretations of the state of music in the 1940's. *Klavierstückene deutschsprachiger Komponisten in Südamerika (***Piano pieces of German-speaking composers in South America***, 31, 1946)* introduces the reader to the compositions of three young German expatriates. In presenting Guillermo Graetzer, Rudolph Holzmann, and Hans Helfritz to their subscribers the editors were helping these young composers to become better known and to build an audience outside of South America.

I have referred to Dr. Rukser's collection of paintings, yet, rather surprisingly, in spite of his being a connoisseur, art was not a favorite topic with the publisher/editors, nor was it completely ignored. Like the articles on music and literature, the essays on art added to the aesthetic appeal of the journal and offered the reader a change from the dominant political themes. In a time of exile the first article on art appropriately dealt with exiled artists. *Künstlerische Kräfte der Emigration.* (**Artistic Strength of the Emigration, 6, 1944**) by Max osborn asks some questions regarding the refugee artists who came to the USA.

> *In wie weit sind die in Amerika schon vorhandenen Energien vermehrt, ergänzt und dadurch bereichert worden?"* he wonders and adds: *Wie haben sich die neuen Elemente bisher mit dem Amerikanertum innerlich auseinandergesetzt und die enormen Anregungen aufgenomen, die ihnen zuströmten?*
>
> **TRANSLATION: To what extent were the energies already present in America augmented, increased and thereby enriched?...So far, how have the new elements internally come to terms with the quintessence of America and reacted to the enormous incitements which stream their way?**

Two further questions are, first: *Und wie wird ihr Auftreten auf Amerika wirken?,* and the second: *Was wird sich daraus ergeben?* (**And what will be the effect of their appearance in America. What will come of it?** p. 31) Osborn answers both with the information available to him in 1944.

He observed that Josef Albers of the *Bauhaus* and his wife had joined the famous Black Mountain college in North Carolina and Walter Gropius, in addition to his architectural work was lecturing at Harvard. Then, too, several renowned German colleagues who fled the Nazi homeland are included in the Article. Many readers will recognize Marcel Breuer, Ludwig Hilbersheimer, Hermann Meyer, Theodor Merill and Eugen Spiro. Osborn lists their places of residence and explains their new positions in the USA. He also writes about the new careers of well-known art historians, including Georg Swarzenski, Alexander Dorn and Karl With. osborn is gratefull to the states for accepting these persons and assuring the continuance of their careers. He feels that America was anxious to accept the artists. *Gleichwohl ist, kein zweifel.* he writes, *daß erst Amerika als das dem Künstler gemässe Tätigkeitsfeld zu betrachten ist* (**Furthermore, America must doubtlessly be regarded as the most accommodating place for artists to work,** p. 31). Today, nearly sixty years, later we can express an unequivocal affirmative response to Osborn's question concerning enrichment of America by the immigrants.

Tempting ammunition for a denunciation of the Nazis was provided the editors of the *DB* in this article but they made no propagandistic use of it. After all, the article spoke for itself. Presumably osborn's list of famous names, his mention of old and new employment of the artists and his few words on the Nazis, had for the two editors, the desired effect. Their double purpose in publishing some of the articles on art is evident. Readers of the *DB* were informed about several names in art and at the same time the cruelty and irrationality of the Hitlerites were exposed. An article in the November/December issue of 1945 expanded the theme of foreign art influence in the USA to include such European artists as Piet Mondrian. However In spite of the title, *Europäische Maler in den USA*, emphasis was given to German artists, especially those associated with the *Bauhaus*. E. Schlosz, author of the article, expressed his opinion of the strength of the *Bauhaus* influence in these poignant words: *Die junge amerikanische Malergeneration ist am vitalsten und stärksten dort wo sie sich der Bauhaustradition zuwendet,* (**The young American generation of painters is most vital and strongest at that point where it turns to the Bauhaus tradition,** p. 47).

For the *DB* it was the German influence that was most important in keeping German culture alive, and German artists were figuring prominently in a revitalizing of painting in the United States. Issues twenty-seven of 1945 and thirty-one of 1946 brought readers news of art in London. The first, *Londoner Kunstleben* (**The London Art World**) reported on the National Gallery and the war years. Kurt Badt happily explains that the paintings were removed to Wales and the gallery remained virtually untouched by bombs. The British,we are told, were using the National Gallery for another kind of art, since piano concerts were presented in the empty halls. A sigh of relief emanates from the pages at the news of the safety of the precious paintings.

The second article, also by Badt, reports on a Picasso-Matisse exposition held in mid-January of 1946. It seems that Picasso was preferred. Messieurs Theile and Rukser employed a unique means of expressing their gratitude to the whole of South America for welcoming them and fellow exiles. The two gentlemen reviewed Pál Kelemen's book, *Medieval American Art* (24, 1945) and became shocked and incensed anew at accounts of the disrespectful and widespread wanton destruction by the conquistadores of so much Indian art and architecture. Their appreciation of the work by Incan, Aztec, Mayan and North American Indian artists and architects is summed up in the following sentence:

> *So stehen heute noch die gesamten präcolumbischen Hochkulturen der neuen Welt und ihre Kunst vor unseren Augen als eine der grandiosesten und zugleich rätselvollsten Schöpfungen des Menschengeistes*, p. 49).

TRANSLATION: Today the complete pre-Columbian high culture of the new world and its art stands before our eyes as one of the most grandiose and at the same time puzzling creations of the human spirit.

Kelemen's enlightened work, a welcome piece of scholarship, brings the *unvergängliche Schönheit* (**eternal beauty**) of the art objects to the reader. This penetrating review of his book and evaluation of the indigenous art of South America helps to make the new world better known to the old. In retrospect it seems unfortunate that there were no additional articles on this subject, since the *DB* continually reflected editorial annoyance at German ignorance of South America. An obvious reponse, of course, is to point out that more could have been published. Additional articles similar to this one should have helped to alleviate the lack of knowledge, but how much could be published, especially when money is scare? We can do no more than thank the co-publishers for what they accomplished under the circumstances.

The *Leaves* looked at the medium of film more as propaganda than as art. In two articles, the film director, Hans Richter, Udo Rukser's brother-in-law, who was living in New York, analyzed first the Russian use of the cinema as propaganda then proceeded to Nazi, English and American propaganda films. Rukser had for some time been anxious to get Richter's article. Herequested help from Kaskell (Richter was helping Kaskell with the *DB*) in five letters in

1943: September 24, October 11, 25, 30, and November 8. Finally Richter's article was sent and divided for printing for the purpose of warning readers of the possible insidious propaganda effects inherent in the cinema. Lenin, Richter writes, *anerkannte sofort, daß von allen Euren Künsten der Film die richtigste sei, weil sie als politisches Mittel verwandt werden konnte.* (**Lenin recognized immediately that of all your arts, film is the right one because it can be used as political means,** 1, 1944, p.21).

The Russians' political films had a dual purpose. First, they were to awaken and strengthen the self-image of the oppressed Russian people and, secondly, to familiarize them with the function and purpose of the new political institutions in Russia. Readers are told that *Potemkin, Mutter* and *Sturm über Asien* served the first objective; *Generallinie* and *Erde* are two which tried to achieve the second objective.

In his second article Richter begins: *In allen Nazi-Dokumentar-Filmen wird Hitler als Gott eingeführt* (**In all Nazi documentaries Hitler is presented as God,** 2, 1944, p. 17). He points out the subtle devices used to glorify Hitler, including the sun breaking through the clouds when the *Führer* appears in *Sieg im Westen* (**Victory in the West).** Prior to the *Anschluss* (**annexation**) of Austria and the conquest of Czechoslovakia, Poland, Rumania, Norway, the Netherlands and Belgium, members of the governments of those countries were subjected to the viewing of films on Hitler, the power of the *Wehrmacht* and the Reich.

A warning to readers of the *DB* is clearly implied by Richter who concludes that *Das Ziel der Propaganda ist erreicht. Die Idee ist verkauft an die vielen ohne geistige Widerstandskraft, die stets bereit sind starken Worten zu glauben, wenn sie nur durch ein einziges Korn handfesten Beweisses erhärtet sind* (**The objective of propaganda has been reached. The idea has been sold to the many who have no powers of resistance, who are always ready to believe strong words even if they are substantianted by only one single kernel of hard evidence** 1, 1944,p. 17).

Karl Paetel wrote on the image of the Nazi in films (6, 1944). He found that *Lifeboat, Northern Pursuit* and *None shall Escape* give a more realistic portrayal than did earlier films. In these movies, according to Paetel, the Nazis are *Menschen*, which he explains as follows:

> *Menschen, bei denen die Reaktion ihren Gegner gegenüber-auch wo sie brutal ist—abgeleitet wird von Elementen des persöhnlichen Schicksals, der Erziehung;—manchmal gaben sie sogar einen echten Ton, wenn sie vom Glauben an den Nationalsozialismus sprechen*

Human beings whose reactions to their opponents—even when brutal—are drawn from elements of personal destiny, of rearing—sometimes they even sounded realistic, when they spoke of their belief in National Socialism, p. 42).

A fourth article on.. the subject of the cinema, *Die Roheit im Film* (**Brutality in Film,** 9/10, 1944) by Georg Pauly expresses consternation at the brutarity and violence that are common elements of so many American firms. Will the viewing of violence inspire increased violence?

Unfortunately we can not inform the critic that we still do not have an answer, but we suspect it to be responsible for violence and negative influence in general with increased exploitation of youth and negative elements through the addition of titillating sex scenes. Nothing is held back. That is what has happened in film and some kinds of music, we could explain, and long for the return of the *DB*, which could devote itself to a new cause.

Pauly was concerned at the affect of such films on mankind, especially on youth, and he expressed wonder at the lack of conscience of the film makers. Pauly laments the negative image of America these films are giving. All these articles recognize the potential power of the film in helping to improve *mankind*. A question implied in each, however, is how to keep this power out of the hands of those who would pervert its use. The *DB* never considered the cinema solely as artistic expression. it was not considered an art form like literature, music, and art Philosophy, other than political theory, was of little interest to the *DB*.

Articles on philosophical systems, on trends in philosophy, or on the lives of philosophers fill very few pages of the periodical. *Französische Philosophie seit 1940* (31, 1946) by D. Dubarle is a one-page analysis of recent developments in French philosophy. In the same issue Jean Paul Sartre's *L'Existentialisme est un Humanisme* is given a given a two-page review by S. Friedländer. Hanns Mayer's few words on *Deutscher Existenzialismus vor zwanzig Jahren* (**German Extentialism of Twenty Years Ago**) presents Jahnn's *Perrudja* to the reader as pre-sartre existentialism. Mayer asserts: *Zwanzig Jahre vor den Erfolgen Jean-Paul Sartres wurde in Hans Henny Jahnns Perrudja ausgesprochen—und Wie ausgesprochen—das es Verdamnis ist, Fleisch sein zu müssen, ohne Geist zu wollen.* (**Twenty years before the success of Sartre it was emphasized—and how emphasized! That having to be flesh without wanting spirituality is damnation,** 34, 1946, p. 56).

One other article on philosophy, *Die Bedeutung Diltheys für die Philosophie der Gegenwart* (**The meaning of Dilthey for present day philosophy,** 28, 1945) by Erwin Johann Rüsch, defends Dilthey against an attack on the philosopher by Eugenio Pucciarelli, professor at the University of La Plata in Argentina. No more was published on the subject of philosophy. Perhaps the spirit of the times was not thought to be conducive to freewheeling philosophical speculation.

The *DB* manifests a significant nonpolitical interest in travel. Articles, few in number, on various countries mitigate the admonishments, diatribes and preachings of others, even some of the *belletristic* writing, and tend to soften and give the reader a break. He is allowed to relax, turn to the *Blick in die Welt (***Look at the world)** section and take an armchair visit to Australia, India, Russia, Bali, Indonesia or England, which received greatest attention along with the American states, for the USA was still for many a *Traumland* of *unbegrenzte Möglichkeiten* (**a dreamland of unlimited opportunity**). Albert Theile commented on books which treated a part of the world he had visited. *Australien—vorgestellt durch C. Hartley Gratton* (**presented by Gratton, 2,** 1943). *Indien ohne Illusion* (3,143), and *Erinnerung an Bali* (**Remembrances of Bali,** 5, 1943) were three such reports augmented by Theile's own perceptions on the lands. Each article is objective, tending to see more of the positive than the negative in each country. Allowing for his youth, Theile was well-traveled which lent authority to his opinions in general. Few could equal his first hand experience.

Australia is described as rich and untamed; many German emigrant readers of the *DB* were looking for such a refuge. Upon reading Kate Mitchel's *India without Fable* on the poverty and (already then) general misery, Theile felt encouraged to write on the subject himself. Dutch suppression and mistreatment of the people of Bali, whose country according to the editor, *ist ein geplantes, mit dem Schweiss von Generationen verwirklichtes paradies.* **(…is a true paradise, brought to fruition through the sweat if generations.)**

And…there you have it. The article stresses the beauty, praises the planning and assures that only Switzerland equals it. I can not resist sharing my immediate reaction that a Swiss is always a Swiss, but, then, the mountainess little nation is truly beautiful. One wonders, did he include Swiss winters in his comparison? Familarizing readers with foreign nations was part of the magazine's effort to foster international understanding.The Soviet Union, England and Indonesia are shown in historical perspective with emphasis on those concerns which are, as in Theile's articles, peculiar to these countries.

And, now, this writer has finished first preparing you for an account of a virtually unknown but fascinating tale of World War II and then commencing to relate that account of a valiant and devoted small group, who from Chile struggled against the Nazism. How many more may exist, untold and quite likely, never to be told?

Ralph P. Vander Heide, Ph.D.

A TRIBUTE

Dr. Rukser and Albert Theile deserve kudos at a level beyond our ability to delivery them. Consider: they took on Hitler, the Nazis, entrenched evil and a propaganda machine stronger and more efficient than any the world had to date experienced, and what do we conclude about Hitler?

Somehow, through scheming, intrigue, cajoling, exhibiting fierce anger, immorality, mood swings, chicanery, disregard for all humanity and all the rest, we know about *Onkel Wolfie* who came to rule, with no limits on his powers, the greatest nation in Europe. He did it, but this writer will never understand how. Although I do believe I am making progress. The man came from nothing. In 1914 he was an undistinguished private in an undistinguished Bavarian infantry regiment who despised Jews with abnormal hatred and became a rabid Pan-German and anti-Communist.

Known for being lazy, he burst forth energetically to establish with only a few devoted helpers his *Nationalsocialistische Deutsche Arbeiterpartei* (**National Socialist German Workers' Party**). He bragged that his band of followers numbered fewer than one hundred, and that is one of the few absolute truths he ever told. So, again: How did he do it? Assuredly, the band of rabble grew and attracted ever more riffraff, the disreputable and the disgruntled. By 1924 the man of Chaplinesque likeness from Lenz, Austria, had caused a lot of fuss, his followers had increased by leaps and bounds, and he had been sentenced to jail for being an organizer of the abortive *Beer Cellar Insurrection (Putsch* in Munich on November 9, 1923. Putsches occur now and then in Germany. One can easily confuse this one with the *Kapp Putsch* of 1920 in Berlin. Hitler, as we know, was long not finished, not even slowed down much.

In fact this God to be said he would quit if the Munich insurrection were not successful. It wasn't, but there was no giving up. He had lied again to the *Volk* and was found, very slightly wounded, lying in the *Odeonplatz* (**Odeon square**) to avoid the bullets. His body guard had taken 3 or 4 bullets. Then the leader was arrested—not commendably heroic, but look what was to come because he ducked bullets. At least had he been killed due to manliness, the entire world would have been spared misery and Hitler been granted martyrdom, always those "what-if's."

To be completely fair, I am urged by my conscience to report that several, maybe all, historians point out that as a "runner" in WW I, the proud young Adolf demonstrated "bravery" in literally running messages behind the lines (or where ever).

I dissuade myself from challenging those respected researchers, but must inquire: Could this runner have been demonstrating a young man's devotion to a cause? Was it bravery or foolishness? I note a parallel with the burning of the *Reichstag* when the poor young Dutchman, Marinus van der Lubbe, was charged with setting the fire. He, the Nazi press wrote, was a most dangerous Communist. In reality the boy was a bit demented more in need of psychiatric help then an executioner. The fire was set by the SA and pinned on the handy victim.

Re-energized, Hitler simply enthralled the masses; he mesmerized them by screaming what they wanted to hear, including the opprobrious invective directed agains the"enemies" of the *Volk*. They cheered and the tyrant welded from these followers an organized and disciplined militia, not stupid at all. The militia awarded him their unconditional fealty.

By this time Hitler had learned to combine in himself the self-righteousness of the monomaniacal fanatic with the persuavie oratory of the revivalist and the cunning of the mass psychologist and spellbinder. Where did he learn that stuff? How did he do it? Many followers were very intelligent and politically savy persons, but Adolph (*Onkel Adolph* or *Onkel Wolf* Richard Wagner's grandkids called him) went ever forward. Readers may need just a short refreshing on the history at the time of his appointment as chancellor:

The *Reichstag* had been dissolved due to ineptness, bickering, intrigue and all with which we are so familiar in the world of politics, and with the way now clear, the aged and weary Field Marshall, Paul von Hindenburg, relying on whatever power he still had as president, could install the new government of "national unity," which would divide the Germans as never before. Historians enlighten us that the old gentlemanly soldier-president seemed dazed, utterly confused, as that evening, he stood gazing down at the *Volk* who were waving rather *pro forma* beneath his window in sharp contrast to the ecstatic welcome they were granting their new Austrian suppressor, who would soon have some of them slaughtered, for the immediate sequel of Hitler's win was a mass persecution unequaled in German history. The Communist party was abolished along with other abolishments, imprisonment, torture, and all the Nazis could conceive of.

Von Hindenburg's brain was stirred only by those inspiring military marches being played by some who marched with the *Brown* and *Black* Shirts, the *Hitler Jugend* and the thousands of citizens. The Field Marshal had been inaugurated as President (*Reichspräsident*) of the German Republic (Weimar Republic) on May 12, 1925. He had served the Motherland honorably.

Hitler, who would serve the Motherland dishonorably, also stood looking down, but from the window of his Chancellery, gloating with a smirk on his face, greeting his myrmidons who lustily and with arrogance and confidence sang the *Horst Wessel Lied*, the emotive military ditty, composed by the young dedicated Nazi, Horst Wessel, killed at age 23 by a Communist. At least the story had worth as anti-Communist propaganda. In truth it could be that Wessel fell on his rifle. On this evening it did not matter. Thousands waved their torches in sheer delight. Hitler had done it! Suddenly, all the struggle had become a *fait accompli*.

By 1932 he had lost his German citizenship, but by 1934 held absolute power in the country that had relieved him of it, and he could proudly announce that all those persons he disliked would now be *ausgebürget (literally* **out-citizened)** On August 12, 1934, President Paul von Hindenburg died at the age of 87. Almost immediately Adolf Hitler assumed personally the titles of *Führer* and *Reichskanzler* and abolished the President title. This audacious step had to be "legalized," but that was no problem because the popular endorsement of the "plebiscite" gave this "God" almost 90%.

From half-baked neurotic art student in Munich to army private to party organizer to having it all. From his army days it had taken only eighteen years. The last year was the most incredible of all, for when he addressed the *Reichstag* on January 30, 1934, he could look back on a year unequaled in German history (or most likely that of any country).

He had destroyed the Weimar Republic completely and substituted its democracy for his dictatorship, smashed all opposition political parties, driven out the unwanted and Jews from any offices they held. He had defederalized the Reich, wiped out democratic associations and labor unions, abolished freedom of speech and the press. Adolph Hitler, the guy with the dazzled mind, a complete nobody had become a hugh somebody. All aspects of life, the courts, the political and social lives, simply everything was *gleichgeordnet* **(coordinated)** under Nazi rule. Now for Germany *der Wille des Führers ist recht* **(the will of the *Führer* was the law** *)*. As is said, Go figure! No *geistiger Widerstand* **(moral, spiritiual opposition)** was evident in the homeland as it was among the refugees.

Our friends, the publishing twosome in Chile faced them (him). How we love such stories of Goliaths and Davids. It is hoped that we who know the story of the *Deutsche Blätter* will never forget the tireless labors, which resulted in a most commendable achievement and be sure to pass the story on to future generations.

As I now write about the *Blätter*, I am reminded of my childhood readings and *The Little Engine that Could*. The big difference is that I always cheered so hard for that little engine. I wanted him to make it.

Conclusions

This study has analyzed the mission of the *Deutsche Blätter* in the political, religious and cultural spheres, and found that the periodical treats various aspects of the (*traditional* or *preexisiting*) ever perplexing German Problem and studies *new* developments with regard to the concept of *new* which arose due to Germany's initiating the Second World War. Fervent hopes and plans for a revitalized and peaceful postwar Europe were a second vital message of the magazine. Equally important are the delineations of National Socialism, Socialism, and Communism.

A salient religious issue treated the degree of effectiveness of the Catholic and Protestant churches in attempting to prevent world war II and the closely related moral question which the war raised: Should churches in wartime abandon their universal commitment to all mankind in order to support individual national interests? The periodical attacked this course of action as immoral and hypocritical. The historical role of organized religion in bettering mankind forms a third religious concern of the journal.

Cultural subjects are German and Latin American literature along with articles on travel, music, art, and philosophy. These are found to be generally free of politics, and intended to offer the reader aesthetic appeal. The original mission of the *DB* was to remind the world of the German cultural tradition and to combat National Socialism; in stressing the cultural tradition of Germany the editors and contributors made a distinction between Nazism and the German people. Goethe, Schiller, Lessing, Kant, Albert Schwweitzer, Thomas Mann and less well-known humanists and intellectuals from the German lands are repeatedly called to mind and contrasted to the Nazis.

As the magazine developed, additional objectives emerged but the humanistic outlook became dominant. The future unity of the European countries and world-wide cooperation among nations became a central theme, and increasing emphasis was placed on blueprints for postwar Germany while the *Blätter* called for a spiritual and moral regeneration. A return to age-old and universally recognized virtues was urged upon the world. For the most part, only articles by contributors who shared the purposes and politics of the editors were printed, although minor divergences from editorial thinking were permitted, most notably on religious issues. Rukser and Theile rarely criticized the Catholic Church, but they printed strong criticism by others. While there was no identifiable *party line* to which writers had to conform, articles were expected to reflect the humanistically oriented perspective of the *DB*. With the exception of what we may term *belletristic* passages, all articles were subordinated to the objectives of the co-editors/publishers.

A shift in emphasis and tone is discernible between the early and final issues, but most readily observed is the reduction In the number of diatribes against Hitler and the Nazis, After Germany's defeat, such denunciations became unnecessary and were replaced by an ever-increasing number of schemes for a peaceful future and for democratic forms of government for the conquered land, The somewhat shrill tone of early issues was dampened by sobriety and logic.

Of the various plans and schemes for the *New Germany*, examined in the *DB*, those which provided for the physical, psychological and moral rebuilding of the vanquished nation were editorially favored, an understandable and logical reaction in light of the fact that the editors had striven to keep the German cultural heritage alive while Nazi deeds were causing the world to denigrate or discredit all Germanic achievements. With the end of the war Rukser and Theile agreed that Germany must resume its traditional cultural leadership; the plea became even stronger after 1945 and the tone more urgent.

With time, more and more space was devoted to literature. Early issues had contained little literature and this was frequently supportive of *DB* opinions and goals. The editors were most certainly aware that the emotionalism of some early articles would not have great attraction for readers in the more sober and somber postwar world.

The introduction of Latin American literature in the magazine aimed at new appeal and improved quality. Rukser and Theile knew that both the German and English speaking nations were for the most part ignorant of the excellent writing being created in Latin America and hoped to help alleviate this lamentabte situation by printing some of the best works and commenting on the authors. Had the *Blätter* continued publication, the inclusion (maybe *infusion)* of Latin American literature would doubtless have been one of its most appealing features.

Today, the question arises as to what extent the publication is dated or bound to the war years. An answer has to be based on the various subjects and issues it covered. In general, timeless components predominate. One obviously time-bound aspect of the magazine, however, is its concern with preventing Germany from provoking another war. Given the militaristic history of the nation from the time of Bismarck through World War II, the *DB's* anxiety was justified in 1945. Today, readers surely agree that Frederick Haussmann's suggestion (typical of several) of an international police force to watch over the German air force seems ludicrous, and the rantings about Pan-Germanism appear naive. Pan-Germanism, a formerly dreaded threat, and according to one article *the breeding pen of Nazism* has been of no concern for many years.

The journal's fear that Germany would be reduced to an agricultural state with no voice in the conduct of her own affairs, or in European and world politics, is also ludicrous as analyzed in the present day. The strong, industrialized, wealthy Germany we know in 2012 bears little resemblance to the vanquished, impoverished nation pictured in the *DB* or for that matter, literally pictured in those wonderful photo magazines of the era such as *Life* and *Look*. In becoming a leader in postwar Europe, Germany realized a most important hope of the magazine.

Vansittartism, the Morgenthau plan, high reparations payments and other harsh proposals for postwar Germany, once feared and denounced in the *DB*, are in 2012 of no concern in world politics. The periodical's passionate pleas for rejection of such plans are only interesting in their historical setting or as lessons for possible future peace settlements elsewhere on earth. Germany has achieved the philosophical ideal of those who wielded the pen (none better than contributors to the *Deutsche Blätter)* instead of the sword through overcoming its demons and building in concert with the rest of Europe (dare it be written?) a *Lasting Peace*. It is, of course, common knowledge that Germany has risen steadily since the end of WW II to become the leader among the countries of Europe.

To be a bit facetious it seems that all Germans read the articles in the *Blätter,* took the information to heart and became the dominant nation in Europe to the point where at the time of this writing Germany is questioning whether she still wants to be the savior of Europe. Some German politicians complain that national interests are neglected while the country has become over the years drunk with Europe. One notes the use of a new term, *lifers* in the European Parliament being applied to those individuals most devoted to the European cause; several of the *lifers* are Germans. Also, the current debt crisis in Greece and other problems has become a kind of crisis of German identity. I keep thinking of the message of our little magazine, which by now has become beloved: A united, peaceful Europe must be created and it above all must survive. I contend that this utopian Europe has been born, lived more than sixty-five years, and surely will survive (Remember the love of bridges and the *Kuchen*). Is it truly assured? I remember what Hitler cleverly accomplished. Return to the page that recounts the successes of just one year.

The numerous studies of the German character are also time-bound. Today, historians, Germanists and other scholars may be intrigued by the psychology of the German, but the fascination exhibited by the *DB* for explaining the behavior of Germans, especially their apparent bent for militarism, is no longer in vogue. As recently as ten years ago there was still much interest in the German psyche, but it has been superseded by other concerns, chief among which is making sure the Euro succeeds. If the Euro does not work, the union which the nations committed to it have formed will pass into history as a failed experiment….And, that is unthinkable!

Perhaps the most dated aspect of the *DB* are the reports of Nazi atrocities which characterized early issues. Modern readers are doubtless appalled at the crimes against humanity, but the emotionalism the accounts caused in the early 1940's can not be reproduced. With each year increasing our distance from World War II, the misdeeds become only dispassionate historical facts taught to the youth of the USA, who confuse the two great wars of their forefathers beyond belief. To anyone who does not agree, I say simply: So, go teach history in any school in the states.

The most important permanent value of the *DB* is its emphasis on humanitarianism, which is best defined as sincere concern for every human being, and on world peace. Nearly every article on world-wide cooperation, respect for small nations, alleviation of suffering, international peace and concern for one's fellowman applies today in a world of greater population with its new set of cruel dictators. The reminder of tolerance, kindness and world cooperation is always poignant..

The short stories, essays on literature and poems that appeared in the *DB* are timeless, for they have their own intrinsic aesthetic value independent of potitical and historical developments. Even those with a moral or propagandistic message continue to speak to modern readers, i.e to both enlighten and entertain, for, due to skilled editing and discriminating choices in what was printed, our forefathers as well as our descendants can share the interpretations of the human condition in general and as perceived in those war years when Germans eagerly followed a madman whom they commonly simply referred to as *Führer* (leader, but also *Gott* a plausible synonym). Are not such perceptive renderings the task of the outstanding practitioners of all the arts? And...did not the *DB* print only the finest literature, the writings (the thoughts preserved on paper) of scholars, thinkers and other intellectuals?

Facing organized religion, we conclude that some of the religious issues, though directly related to the war years and Germany, notwithstanding raise questions of timeless relevance. Be it Protestant or Catholic resistance to the Nazis, the broader question is should churches protest and resist war even when their national loyalty is jeopardized. Since the war many intellectuals, both non-German and German, have related the specific facts of the churches and Nazism to this broader issue. A salient example of the matter is Rolf Hochhuth's play of 1963, *The Deputy*, which accuses Pope Pius XII of concurring in the deportation of Italian Jews to Auschwitz. As might be assumed the work stimulated a heated controversy on the subject when it appeared. Of course, it too is now regarded as dated, but the point was well made and the pertinent question, which remains is most unsettling: Could something similar happen (or is it happening as I write?) in our modern world for which a new term has been coined, *ethnic cleansing?*

Furthermore, it has been determined that a shocking disparity existed, and, therefore, must continue to exist among the attitudes of bishops and cardinals toward Jews.

Articles which attempted to determine whether religion improves human behavior and fosters moral conduct are of permanent interest, as are those which insist on the separation of church and state. the *DB*'s concern for freedom of religion for all mankind will likewise always have relevance.

Of intrinsic desireability are also the discussions of travel, music, art and philosophy. An armchair trip to foreign lands can be as pleasurable today as in 1944. Essentially, the *Deutsche Blätter* will always be relevant and current. Unlike so many of the inflammatory *Kampfblätter* of the war years which are now of purely antiquarian Interest, the *DB* thanks to its concern with timeless values, high standards and its humanitarianism remains pertinent, informative and inspiring.

A SHORT FINAL WORD OF THANKS AND A REMINDER

The unequaled little publication that fought Nazism with its humanistic message in a time of world wide havoc has been part of my life for 37 years. I hope that the reader has been enlightened and entertained as much as was I upon discovering, studying and analyzing this unique relatively short-lived journal published and edited by two gentlemen and their handful of helpers. devoted to a cause. One should never forget that they virtually learned on the job or by doing. Burning devotion can assure commendable outcomes, and, indeed, perhaps (just perhaps) words can be as powerful as weapons.

Maybe *Reichsführer* Paul Josef Goebbels, infamous Minister of Propaganda of the equally infamous Third Reich, instead of ending his screeds by asking the German people if they wanted *Butter oder Kanonen*, should have given them the choice between *Worte oder Kanonen*. And if asked now? Since quality coffee, flush toilets, utilitarian, beautiful bridges and tunnels are taken for granted by the former Teutonic hordes (*Huns, Jerries, Krauts, Pagan Tribes, Master Race, etc.* as they were called*)*, they would surely choose the butter or maybe even the *Worte*, but not the *Kanonen*.

I dedicate this study to the memory of all victims of the Nazis, and as a reminder to future generations of what happened, rather easily. To cousin Dirk I say:

WELTERUSTEN, JONGE. MAG GOD JE ZEGENEN. WIJ VERGETEN JE NOOIT. MET JOUW VRIENDEN

REQUIESCAT IN PACE

APPENDICES

A—Alphabetical List of Contributors to the *Deutsche Blätter* with a Chronological List of Articles

Albert, Totila
Deutsche Nachdichtungen von vier Liebesgedichten Pablo Nerudas (5,1943)

Alvarez, Alejandro
Internacional (23, 1945)
La conferencia de Mexico y la de san Francisco (24, 1945)

Amorin Enrique
Der schwache Punkt (27, 1945)

Anders, Günther
Der Rückfall (32, 1946)

Andres, Stefan
Drei Gedicht (28, 1945)
Die Gorgonen (31, 1946)
Süditalienische Gegenwart (33, 1946)

Bab, Julius
Deutsche Stimme (3, 1944)
Lessing (7, 1944)
T. Manns Josephdichtung (27, 1945)
Edna St,. Vincent Millay, Versunkenheit (32, 1946)

Bacon, Francis
Von der Wahrheit (32, 1946)

Badt, Kurt
Londoner Kunstleben (27, 1945)
Picasso (31, 1946)

Bahr, Hermann
Der Botschafter Amerikas, Walt Whitman (9, 1943)

Baldus, Hermann
Franz Boas und Deutschland (29, 1946)
Curt Nimuenda jú Unkel (31, 1946)

Ballhausen, Friedrich
Die Bestrafung der Schuldigen (1, 1943)
Im Schatten von Morgen: Voraussetzungen für den Frieden (2, 1943)
Aufteilung oder Reichsreform (5, l944)
The Next Germany (6, 1944)
Die alldeutsche Gefahr (8, 1944)
Sumner Welles über Deutschland (24, l945)

Barth, Max
Deutsche Oden (2, 1943)
Ragnarok (11, 1943)

Bedregal, Yolanda
Kakteenbüten (25, 1945)

Bellon, Waldemar
Der internationale Mensch (7, 1944)

Benton, José Antonio
Die Onca (29, 1946
Brasilianische Legende (33, 1946)

Berger, Georg
Shakespeares „Kaufmann von Venedig" ist keine komödie (17, 1944)
Über Juden und Deutschland (34, 1946)

Bergengruen, Werner
Ferne Hoffnung (33, 1946)

Berlin, Heinrich
Gedanken zum Geschichtsunterricht (21, 1945)

Berlin, Philipp
Staat und Mensch (26, 1945)

Biermann, Berthold
Thomas Mann und Goethe (25, 1945)

Blumnthal, Otto
Swinburne (32, 1946)

Bock, Werner
Die deutsche Stimme (8, 1944)
zu seinem 75. Geburtstag (Carl Wolfskehl) (8, 1944)
Inflation im deutschsprachigen Schriftum südamerikas (27, 1945)
Der Torso (30, 1946)
Dienst und Armut (30, 1946)
Paul Zech (33, 1946)

Bondy, Curt
Das Jugenddorf (26t 1945)
Erziehungsarbeit im neuen Deutschland (31, 1946)

Borah, Tim
Neue deutsche Reimstandarte (24, 1945)

Borges, Jorge Luis
Im Traumkreis der Ruinen (8, 1944)
Gaucho-Literatur in Argentinien und Uruguay (27, 1945)

Bowers, Claude G.
Thomas Jefferson und Südamerika

Brasch, Hans
Creed (33, 1946)

Brecht, Arnold
Friedrich, Ebert und die Tragödie der deutschen Demokratie (26, 1945)

Broch, Hermann
An die Phantasie, für T. Man (25, 1945)

Brod, Max
Weltgescihte (5,1944)

Burckhardt, Jakob
Vom Ursprung der heutigen Krise (33, 1946)

Busch, Fritz
Elternhaus und Kindheit (28, 1945)

Conitzer, Gert
Auf ein von Bombensplittern getötetes Kind (32, 1946)

Constant, Beniamin
Lebendige Vergangenheit (11, 1943)
Über den Militarismus (4&7,1944)

Cordan, Wolfgang
Neue Gedichte (31, 1946)

Croce, Benedetto
Die Religion der Freiheit (11, 1943)

Curtius, E.R.
Stephen Spender: Geistliche Übungen (32, 1946)

Dallman, E.R.
Das Ende (26, 1945)

Dehmel, Richard
An mein volk (9/10,1944)

Diesenberg, Julius
Erziehung zur Demokratie (9/10, 1944)

Dietrich, Wolfram
Das deutsche Jahr (3O, 1946)

Donay, Eduard
Gott und ich (33, 1946)

Droste-Hshoff, Annette von
Mein Beruf (9/10, 1944)

Dubarle, D.
Französische Philosophie seit 1940 (31, 1946)

Dwinger, Edwin
Auch ein Weihnachtsabend (12, 1943)

Ehrenslein, Albert
Auch die Freunde (26, 1945)

Engelke, Gerrit
An die Soldaten des grossen Krieges (4, 1943)

Erdmann, Veronika
Träumetrümerlied (34, 1946)

Fischer, Hanns
Thomas Manns küntlerischesche Sendung (25, 1946)

Freund, H.A.
Das deutsche Vakuum (30, 1946)

Friedländer, S.
Das Wunder der Setbstverständlichkeit (28, 1945)
Jean-Paul Sartres Existentialismus (31, 1946)

Frölich, Paul
Heinz Behrendt, ein Nachruf (23, l945)

Garreton, Walker Manuel
Katholizismus und Gegenwart (27, 1945)

George, Stefan
Gedichte (5, 1944)
Gedichte (31, 1946)

Gide, André
Die Befreiung von Tunis (1, 1944)

Gollancz, Victor
What Buchenwald Really Means (27, 1945)

Graf, Oscar Maria
Die Feuertaufe (7, 1944)

Grünwald, Gertrud
Brief einer Deutschen (4, 1943)

Guzmon, Leonardo
Amerika und die Einwanderung (10, 1943)

Hannssen, E.S.
Das Psychische Kriegspotential (7 , 1943)

Hardt, Ludwiq
Aus der Grammatlc der Vortragskunst (33, 1946)

Haussmann, Frederick
Untergang Europas (3, 1944)
Europäische Schicksalsgemeinschaft (8, 1944)
Vansitarts Kritik (23, 1945)
Deutsche Wirtschaftsfragen (23, 1945)

Heilbut, Ivan
Saint Sulpice (23, 1945)

Heinlein, Federico
Neue Musikbücher (30, 1946)
Klavierstücke deutsprachiger Komponisten in s.A. (31, 1946)

Hebel, Johann Peter
Der Husar in Neisse(23, 1945)

Herzog, Erich
Weltgesundunq durch Arbeit (1, 1944)

Hesse, Hermann
Der Jüngling im Krieg (2, 1943)
Ode an Hölderin (6, 1943)
Die deutsche Stimme (12, 1943)
Oktober (28, 1945)
Rigatagebuch (30, 1946)
Zum Nobelpreis (34, 1946)

Heym, Georg
Der Krieg (7, 1943)

Heymann, Hans
Finanzierung des Friedens (2, 1944)
vom Nazi-Raubbau zur europäischen Friedenswirtschaft (7 1944)

Hiller, Kurt
Nachruf für Ernst Toller (9/10, 1944)
Salz und Galle, Gift und Pfeffer, Aphorismen (23, 1944)
Marx-Kritik in der Nusschale (25,1944)
Die Entscädigungsfrage (28, 1945)
Karl Kraus (33, 1946)

Hirsch, Julian
Rilke in England (3O, 1946)

Hofmannsthal, Hugo von
Denkwürdigkeiten (2, 1943)
Der Tod (6, 1944)

Hocking, W.E.
Tomorrow's Business (25, 1945)

Hölderin
Ein deutsches Schicksal (6, 1943)

Hove, Friedrich von
Wiederaufbau Europas—vor 125 Jahren (2, 1943)

Ibarbourou, Juana de
Bukolischer Abendspaziergang (32, 1946)

Icaza, Jorge
Gewitter in den Bergen (9/10, 1944)

Ilich, Max
Die Bestrafung der Schuldigen (7, 1944)

Jablonski, Walter
Dante an die Florentiner (6, 1944)
Keine Liebe wird umsonst gelitten (28, 1945)

James, William
Das Gegenstück zum Kriege (24, 1945)

Jaspers, Karl
Ansprache in Heidelberg (30, 1946)

Jünger, F.G.
Der Mohn (5, 1943)
Drei Gedichte aus dem "Halieutika" (10, 1943)

Kahler, Erich
Der Mensch und die Sachen (26, 1945)
Das Problem der Demokratie (29, 1946)
Die Verantwortlichkeit des deutschen Volkes (30, 1946)

Kahn, Fritz
Bibel, als Grundstein europäischer Bildung (2, 1944)

Kantorowicz, Alfred
Karl von Ossietsky zum Gedenken (9/10, 1944)

Kaskel, Josef
The Coming Age of WorLd Control (5, 1943)
Vansittarts Irrungen und Wirrungen (2, 1944)
Neue Wirtschaftspolitik in England

Kayser, R
Dem Gedächtnis Franz Kafkas (34, 1946

Kerschersteiner Georg
Arbeitsschulen (1, 1943)
Das öffentliche Unterrichtswesen im Volksstaate (1, 1944)

Kleist, Heinrich von
Über das Marionettentheater (30, 1946)

Klepper, Otto
Vorfragen des Friedens (33, 1946)
Die Kunst des Möglichen (34, 1946)

Koch-Weserr Erich
Politische Aphorismen (7, 1944)
Die Gegner des Nationalsozialismus (9/10, 1944)
Paneuorpa (25, 1945)

Koestler, Arthur
Die Gemeinschaft der Pessimisten (4, 1944)

Kruse, Ludwig
Wie nahe schlägt mir jedes Bruders Herz (11, 1943)

Laboulaye, Edouard
Über Religionsfreiheit (24, 1945)

Langerhans, Heinz
Maarschlied (7, 1844)

Lasker-Schüler, Elseu
Die deutsche Stimme (9/10, 1944)

Leifhelm, Hans
Erste Ausfahrt nach langer Krankheit (33, 1946)

Lessing, Juan
Das Individuum im künftigen Völkerrecht (7, 1944)
Der Mythos deutscher Unsiegbarkeit (4, 1944)

Lippmann, Walter
Mann Settlement (9/10 1955

Lips, Eva
Vielfalt des Lebens (7, 1844)

Lips, Julius
Exotische Gedichte (26, 1945)

Lochner, Julius P. 1
Gibt es ein „Anderes" Deutschland? (9, 1943)

Löwenstein, Hubertus Frledrich zu

Das eine Deutschland (5, 1944)

Magee, John
Höhenflug (24, 1945)

Mallea, Eduardo
Einsame, Zeitgemässe Aufzeichnungen (25, 1943)
Das Unsichtbare Land (32, 1946)

Mana, Gustav
Mut zur Utopie (1, 1943)
Deutsche Tragik (7 , 1943)

Mann, Thomas
Niemöller, (10, 1943)
Schicksal und Aufgabe (7, 1944)
Joseph und seine Brüder (24, 1945)
Erich von Kahler (28, 1945)

Marck, Siegfried
Manchester-Liberalismus oder freiheitlicher Sozialismus (25, 1945)

Masur, Gerhard
Rede über Mozart (3, 1944)

Mayer, Hanns
Deutscher Existenzialismus vor zwanzig Jahren (34, 1946)

Mersch, Christian
Gedanken zur Einwanderungsfrage (1, 1944)

Meyer, Uli
Hitlers Sieg,—eine Tragödie für Deutschland (2, 1944)
Klassenaufsatz (6, 1943)

Meyning, Fritz (Fritz Siegel)
Sicherheitspolitilt vor dreihundert Jahren (5, 1943)
Zum korporativen Staat (7, 1943)
Übergangswirtschaft (2,1944)
Das deutsche Problem von England aus gesehen (9, 1944)
Die letzte Schlacht (23, 1945)

Millay Edna St.Vincent
Versunkenheit (3, 1946)

Mistral, Gabriela
Die Silhouette der mexikanischen Indianerin (23, 1945)
Einzig bin ich nie allein (29, 1946)

Möller-Rosenthal, Katharina
Religion als Grundlage der Gesellschaft (4, 1944)

Moser, Margot
In Memoriarn Erich Kästner (4, 1944)

Nagel, Nikolaus von
Eine neue „Dolchstoss"-Legende (1O, 1943)

Neider, Charles
Das Irrationale bei Kafka (34, 1946)

Neruda, Pablo
Cuatro Poemas de Amor (5, 1943)

Neumeyer, Fred
Leonardo und das Kreuz (34, 1946)

Niemöller, Martin
An eine deutsche Frau (31, 1946)

Osborn, Max
Künstleriche Kräfte der Immigration (6, 1944)

Ossorio y Gallardo, Angel
Die katholische Kirche und die Zukunft (10, 1943)
Zweierlei Kathoizismus (9/10, 1944)

Overbeck, Sylvia
Wenn die Engel Schlafen (27, 1945)

Paetel, Karl O.
Ernst und Friedrich Jüngers politische Wandlung (10, 1943)
Stefan George (5, 1944)
Filmkritik: Nazis von aussen gesehen (6, 1944)
Der Führer (8, 1944)
Himmlers Janitscharen-Armee (9/10, 1944)
Staatsreich oder Revolution? (9/10, 1944)
Ballspiel mit Wahrheiten (24, 1945)
Randbemerkungen zur französischen Literatur (27, 1945)
Eine Umfrage bei jungen deutschen Kriegsgefangenen (28, 1945)
Ist die heutige deutsche Jugend eine verlorene Generation? (28, 1945)
Der Todesmarsch der Zehnmillionen (29, 1946)
Deutsche Jugend (31, 1946)
Deutscher Bücherbrief aus New York (31, 1946)

Pauly, Georg
Die Rohheit, im Film (9/10, 1944)

Pauly, Herta
Die Stellung zum Staat im kontinentalen und anglo-amerikanischen Protestantismus (32, .1946)

Pick, F.W.
Wolken über der ostsee (34, 1946)

Pimental, Francisco (Job Pim)
Aus den venezolanischen Freiheitskampf (Hierro dulce-sanftes Eisen) (25, 1945)

Piper, Otto A.
Das deutsche Hilfswerk (32, 1946)

Ranshofen-Wertlreimer, Egon
Die ewige tragödie Deutschlands (6, 1944)

Regler, Gustav
Die Ghettokinder (7, 1944)
Zehn Briefe an meinen Sohn (26, 1945)
Die Himmelsleiter (30, 1946)

Reyes, Alfonso
Goethe und Amerika (32, 1946)

Richter, Hans

Die Entwicklung des politischen Filmes (1&2, 1944)

Rilke, R.M.
Vorgefühl eines jähen und gewaltigen Sturzes (1, 1943)
Ungedrückte Briefe (6, 1944)
Gedichte in Deutsch und Spanisch (28, 1945)

Rolland, Romain,
Einleitung zum Roman "Clerambault" (11, 1943)

Rosengarten, W.
Frankreich blickt auf Deutschland (34, 1946)

Ross, Roberto
Die drei Alkalden (33, 1946)

Rukser, Udo
Right or Wrong—my Country? (1, 1943)
Recht ist, was dem Volke nüzt (2, 1943)
Europäische Phantasien (3, 1943)

Was können wir tun? (4, 1943)
Gibt es noch eine Rettung für Deutschland? (6, 1943)
Bolschewismus als Schreckgespenst (7, 1943)
Das moskauer Manifest (9, 1943)
Neue Methoden! (9, 1943)
Neue Methoden! (10, 1943)
Die moskauer Konferenz (11, 1943)
Der Leitstern des Friedens (12, 1943)
Neue Methoden (12,1943)
Zum neuen Jahr (with Theile) (1, 1944)
Das neue weltbild (3, 1944)
Polens Schicksalsstunde (3, 1944)
Minderheitenschutz—unerlässlich (7, 1944)
Nationalismus? Patriotismus! (8, 1944)
Über die Deutschen in Südamerica (with Theile) (23, 1945)
Internationaler Arbeitsdienst als Friedensinstrument (24, 1945)
Gerichtswesen und Demokratie (27, 1945)
Die Entwaffnung Deutschlands und ihre Folgen (30, 1946)
Die Erneuerung der Weltlandwirtschaft (3I, 1946)
Kontroll-Demokratie und Führerauslese (31 1946)
Europäische Notgemeinschaft (32, 1946)
zum Nürnberger Prozess (34, 1946)

Rüsch, Erwin Johann
Die Bedeutung Diltheys (28,1945)

Sahl, Hans
Der verlorene Sohn (6, 1944)

Salz, Arthur
Verfall und Erneuerung der deutschen Sprache (28, 1945)

Schenk, E.V.
Die Schweiz als europäisches Vorbild (6, 1943)

Schlosz, E
Europäische Maler in den USA (28, 1945)

Schmidt, Kurt
Rede vor jungen Sozialdemokraten (30, 1946)

Schmidt, Max
Indonesien (32, 1946)

Schneider, Otto
Walter Knoche (29, 1946)
Die Geburt der Planeten (31, 1946)

Schnitzlein, Hans
Schade ersatz? (30, 1946)

Schröder, R.A.
In der Nacht gesungen (26, 1945)

Schweitzer., Albert
Goethe (12, 1943)
Der Weg zur Regeneration der Kultur (29, 1946)

Silberstein, Franz
Kriegerische und friedliche Demokratie (2, 1944)
Ethos der Demokratie (3, 1944)
Vorstufen der Demokratie (24, 1945)

Silone, Ignazio
Die Wahrheit wird uns retten! (24, 1945)

Sinn, Edward
Frührerprinzip (4, 1943)

Sollmann, W,F.
Deutschlands politische Wiedergeburt (6, 1943)

Spender, Stephen
Geistliche Übungen (32, 1946)

Stresemann, Wolfgang
Alban Berg, zu seinem sechzigsten Geburtstag (25, 1945)
New Yorker Musikbrief (26, 1945)

Sternefeld, Ruth
Politische Krankheiten (5, 1943)

Steuerwald—Landmann, Anna
Und wir Frauen? (3, 1943)
Nach der Verbrecherliste die "Gutäterliste." (6, 1943)
Europäische Waisenhilfe (12, 1943)
Internationale Frauenbewegung, Weltfriedensbewegung (6, 1944)
Erziehung zur Gewaltlosigkeit (28, 1945)
Die in der Heimat und wir (31, 1946)

Swinburne, A.
Abschiednehmen, Beim Scheiden/Chor aus „Atlanta in Calydon" (32,1946)

Theile, Albert
Europa sucht sich selbst (1, 1943)
Die Welt als Einheit (7, 1943)
Erlebte Volkserziehung (8, 1943)
Über Romain Rolland (11, 1943)
Zum neuen Jahr (with Rukser) (1, 1944)
Über die Deutschen in Südamerika (with Rukser) (23, 1945)
Besinnung—worauf ? (31,1946)

Toch, Ernst
Glaubensbekenntnis eines Komponisten (24, 1945)

Uhland, Ludwig
Deutsche Oden(2, 1943)

Ulich, Robert
Über die kulturelle Zukunft Deutschlands (24, 1945)

Urzidil, Johannes
Die Sprache im Exil (32, 1946)

Valéry, Paul
Vier Gedichte (27, 1945)

Vatter, Ernst
Altamerikanische Kunst (24, 1945)

Viertel Berthold
Ode an Deutschland (33, 1946)

Vogelstein, Julie
Einführung zu „Warum lesen Sie nicht einmal wieder?" (4, 1943)

Vortriede, Werner

W. Butler Yeats (32, 1946)
St. Georges Prophetie im „Brand des Tempels,' (3I, 1946)

Waelbrock, Pierre
Internationale Nachkriegswanderung (26, 1945)

Waldinger, Ernst
Die deutsche Stimrne (2, 1944)

Walter, Thomas
Weihnachtsgebet eines Deutschen 1943 (12, 1943)

Weisskopf, F.C.
Unwahrscheinliche Wahrhaftigkeiten (4, 1944)

Wells, H.G.
Die Sankey-Erklärung der Menschenrechte (9/1O, 1944)

Werfel, Franz
Immer das letzte Mal (30, 1946)

Wiechert, Ernst
Der Dichter und seine zeit (6, 1943)
Der Kinderkreuzzug (12, 1943)
Gebet (30, 1946)

Winsnes, A.H.
Kaj Munk, ein dänischer Patriot (5, 1944)

Witten, Amo
Australien und die Refugees (5, 1944)

Wolfskehl, karl
Sänge aus dem Exil (25, 1945

Yeats, William Butler
Meerfahrt nach Byzanz—Nach langem Schweigen (32, 1946)

Zech, Paul
Der Nebelregen von Ouro muermo (7,1943)
Aus dem Zyklus „Neu-Beginnen" (7, 1943)
Aus dem Zyklus „Landschaften und Dinge des Chimú Lapacho (7, 1943)
Wer ist eigentlich dieser Paul- Zech?(11, 1943)
Sonette auf das Jahr 1944 (1, 1944)
Mirakel (4, 1944)
Dem immerwährenden Andenken der für uns Gestorbenen (6, 1944)
Die deutsche Stimme: Else Lasker-schüler (9/10 1944)
Indianische Tänze (23, 1945)
Strofen der Einkehr (23, 1945)
Die Tänze der ewigen Verwandlung (24, 1945)
Der Dramatiker Georg Kaiser (26, 1945)
Kurt Hiller (28, 1945)
Rainer Maria Rilke (28, 1945)
Die drei Gerechten: szenischer Prolog (34, 1946)

Zuckmayer, Carl
Die deutsche Stimme (aus "pro Domo") (9, 1943)
Carlo Mierendorff: portäit eines deutschen Sozialisten (6, 1944)

Zweig, Stefan
Die deutsche Stimme (3&8, 1943)
Begegnung zweier Europäer (5, 1943)
Episode vom Genfersee (2, 1944)

COAUTHORED ARTICLES

Im Schatten von Morgen (1, 1943)
Herbert Morrison
Kingsly Martin
Richard Law
Hu Shih
J.B. Priestly

Der Einzelne und die Gemeinschaft (3, 1943)
K'ang Yuwei
Kungfutse
Laotse
Lia Dsi
Mentse
Priedensziele in Asien (3, 1943)
Bertrand RusselL
Jawaharlal Nehru
l.tayling Soong Chiang
Teraknath Das
Wendell wilkie
Carlo Sforza
Henry A. Wallace
Joseph Stalin
Wickham Stead
Winston Churchill

Wie empfindet die Frau die Last der Kulturcrise? (2, 1944)
Gerti Geis
Katharina Möller-Rosenthal
Livia Neumann
Oda Olberg
Ruth Sternefeld

UNSIGNED ARTICLES

Deutsches Pantheon (1, 1943)
Was ist von der Nemesis in der Geschichte zu halten? (1, 1943)
Was wir wollen (1 & 2, 1943)
Der Freitheit einer Gasse (2, 1943)
Die antiliberale Bewegung in Deutschland und ihre Funktion (2, 1943)
Standpunkte,—-unsere und andere (3, 1943)
Polnische Mädchen (4, 1943)
Gewissensnöte (5, 1943)
Hölderin, ein deutsches Schicksal (6, 1943)
Aus der Verlustliste des anderen Deutschlands (7, 1943)
Morgen werde ich erschossen (7, 1943)
zum Sturz Mussollinies (8, 1943)

Ich will nichts von Europa wissen (9, 1943)
Die Sühne naht (1, 1943)
Lebendige Vergangenheit (1, 1943)
Pestalozzi und Napoleon (11, 1943)
Kampfgedichte die jetz gesungen werden (12, 1943)
Burgfrieden oder Bürgerkrieg? (1, 1944)
Hohe Politik im englischen Unterhaus (3, 1944)
Gott und Volk (4, 1944)
Neu-Deutschland Bewegung (4, 1944)

Aus Nazi-Europa (6, 1944)
Die Russen in Deutschland (7, 1944)
Ach Töten könnt ihr aber nicht lebendig machen (8, 1944)
Dumbarton Oaks 9/10 (1944)
Organisation der Untergrundbewegung (9/10, 1944)
Planwirtschaft in Frankreich (9/10, 1944)
Nazigreuel (9/10, 1944)
Sozialistisehe Solidaritit mit Spanien (9/10, 1944)
Unsere Verantwortung (9/10, 1944)
„1945" (23, 1945)
Kriegsgefangene und wir (23, 1945)
„Der Führer denkt für uns" (24, 1945)

Hitlers Zwingburg ist zerstört (24, 1945)
Hitler und seine Trabanten kapitulieren (25, 1945)
Roosevelts Vermächtnis (25, 1945)
Christliche Sozialisten zu den Friedensproblemen (26, 1945)

Der neue Völkerbund (26, 1945)
Früher war ich Nazi, jetzt bin ich für Ausgleich (26, 1945)
Zwei Briefe aus Deutschland (27, 1945)

Stimmen aus Deutschland (28, 1945)
"1946" (29, 1946)

Mutter, ach Mutter (29, 1946)
Programmatische Entschliessungen der Christlich-demokratische Union (31, 1946)
Suchende Jugend (31, 1946)
Wir (31, 1946)

Beiträge zum geistigen Wiederaufbau (32, 1946)
Istambuler Schriften (32, 1946)
Zur Mittelmeerfrage (32, 1946)
Deutschland-Briefe (33, 1946)
Abschied von Paul Zech (34, 1946)
Edward Y. Hartshorne (34, 1946)
Ribbentrop-Molotov Abkommen (34, 1946)

B—Flier Requesting Financial Aid to Bring DB to POW's an Unsere Freunde Und Leser!

Die "Deutschen Blätter" sind in den Lagern für deutsche Kriegsgefangene in den USA zugelassen worden, als erste deutscher Zeitschrift von ausserhalb! Damit bietet sich endlich die Gelengenheit, fast Eine Million deutscher Soldaten mit unserer unparteilichen und unabhängigen Zeitschrift bekannt zu machen. Wieviele von ihnen eingefleischtte Nazi sind und darum diese Blätter mit Mistrauen und Voreingenommenheit öffnen werden, wissen wir nicht. Um so mehr halten wir es für unsere Pflicht, dafür zu sorgen, daß möglichst viele Hefte unserer Zeitschrift in die Hände dieser Soldaten kommen, die, seit langem von der Welt abgeschnitten, entweder sich verzweifelt an jenes brutale Credo von Blut und Boden klammern, oder sich Rechenschaft zu geben trachten über die Ursachen, welche unsere Heimat in den tiefsten Abgrund gestürzt und unsere Volkskraft vernichtet haben. Denn sicherlich gibt es unter dieser Millionen Soldaten viele, die nach Klarheit verlangen, die nach Wahrheit dürsten der Wahrheit und Klarheit die ihnen das abgefeimte Regime der Lügenhaftigkeit, ungezählte Millionen mit Leiden und Tod verschont hätten; jene Wahrheit und Klarheit, die höchsten Adel unserer Überlieferung bedeuten; welche die schmähliche Besudelung des deutschen Namen mit unschuldigem Blut durch ebenso masslose wie ruchlose Verbrechen verhindert hätten..Darmit stellt sich uns eine Aufgabe, an deren Bewältigung wir nur mit Zaudern herangehen, denn wir sehen sowohl ihre sehr grosse Bedeutung wie ihre Schwierigkeiten und kennen das bescheidene Mass unserer kräfte. Aber wir dürfte sich heute einer ihm zufallenden Verantwortung entziehen? Zumal wenn es sich darum handelt, Hunderttausenden von Deutschen einiges über Mass und Wert, einiges über Schuld und Sühne, einiges über Knechtschaft und Freiheit zu sagen!Dieser auszeichnerrden Aufgabe hoffen wir mit Hilfe unserer Freunde und Leser gerecht zu werden, deren tätige Teilnahrne uns seit Jahren begleitet. Aber die neue Aufgabe bringtauch sehr grosse materielle Lasten. Denn es werden nicht viele Soldaten sein, die etwas für eine Zeitschrift ausgeben können. Wir bitten angesichts dessen alle Einsichtigen, uns bei der Finanzierung zu helfen. Auf die Hilfe eines jeden kommt es an. Wir haben zu diesem Zweck "Kriegsgefangenen-Abonnements, eingerichtet und den Preis für den Jahrgang 1945 auf $m/ chil. 80,- ermässigt. Jedem Heft wird auf Wunsch ein Kärtchen mit Namen und Adresse des Spenders beigefügt. Die Verteilung erfolgt in Verbindung mit unserem newyorker Redaktions-Vertreter, *Dr Josef Kaskel, 410 Riverside Drive, New York 25*, der seinerseits mit amerikanischen und deutsch-amerikansichen Hilfsorganisationen zusammenwirkt. Von der

Aufbringung dieser Abonnements wird es vielieicht abhängen, ob unsere Landsleute aus den Lagern eines Tages tief erbittert in die Heimat zurückkehren oder aber bereit zum friedlichen Wiederaufbau!

Santiago de Chile, Mitte Dezember 1944
Casilla 710.

DIE HERAUSGEBER DER "DEUTSCHEN BLÃTTER"
Udo Rukser Albert Theile

TRANSLATION: (ESSENCE) This is the first journal from the outside to be allowed in the POW camps. Therefore, this is a great opportunity to reach the one million German prisoners and bring to them the enlightened messages of the *Blätter* and wean them away from Nazi teachings. Only very few will have sufficient funds to pay for a subscription. The question is addressed concerning the acceptance of the *DB* by those who have deeply embraced Nazism (made it part of their flesh or *eingefleischt* Hitler's creed. On the other hand the millions of soldiers who are about to be released should have the magazine to help with philosophical issues vs. Nazism and for the reconstruction of Germany as well as for cleansing of the sullied German name. A long appeal is give for funding to help the periodical continue. Special payment plans are offered for this vital enterprise.

C—Flier Sent to German POW's

AN DIE DEUTSCHEN KRIEGSGEFANGENEN IN NORDAMERIKA
(TO THE GERMAN PRISONERS OF WAR IN NORTH AMERICA)

Verschiedenes Schicksal hat euch und uns nach Amerika geführt, aber die Ursache ist die gleiche,-es ist der Nationalsozialismus! Ihr habt für ihn gekämpft, freiwillig oder umfreiwillig, wieder strebend oder begeistert, in der meinung, der deutschen Heimat zu dienen. Wir haben ihn seit Anbeginn bekämpft, in der Gewissheit, daß der Nationalsozialismus das Unglück unseres Volkes wie der Welt bedeute. So hat uns das Schicksal als Flüchtlinge, euch als Gefangene in die neue Welt gebracht.

Wird es möglich sein, daß deutsche, die so Verschiedenes erfahren haben, sich über den Grund des Unglücks, das über die Welt hereingebrochen ist, verständigen? So schwer uns das scheinen mag und so gross die Vorürteile und Irrtümer auf beiden Seiten sein mögen: wir müssen es verssuchen. Denn nur wenn solche Verständigung gelingt, können wir hofen etwas dazu beizutragen, daß unsere Heimat aus dem schrecklichen Elend, in das Nichtswürdige und Wahnwitzige sie gestürzt haben, wieder herausfindet,- nicht um Herr oder Slave zu sein, sondern um als \/olk unter \/ölkern zu leben.

Diesem Ziele wollen diese Blätter dienen, die wir vor Jahren ins Leben gerufen haben. Aber solche Aufgabe verlangt zuerst und vor allem Selbskritik und schonungslose Aufrichtigkeit. Nur wenn wir die schwerigen eigenen Fehler erkannt und die entsetzlichcn Untaten eines unmenschlichen Regimes aus Überzeugung und nicht um des Vorteils willen verworfen haben, können wir daran gehen, die Folgerungen für eine deutsche Zukunft aus so schrecklichen Verrirungen , vederblicher Überheblichkeit und bodenlosen Dummheit zu ziehen. Das diese Zukunft in einer chaotischen Welt aubzubauen ist, erschwert diese Aufgabe unsäglich; aber dabeit haben wir uns selbst immer wieder zu sagen, daß dieses Chaos aus unserem Lande in die gekommen ist. Es ist zu ordnen, wird vor allem die ungeheure Verantwortung der Sieger sein, denen damit schier Übermensliches obliegt; und auch das deutsche Schicksal wesentlich von ihren Entscheidungen abhängen; wesentlich aber, nicht alleinI Denn wenn Deutschland nicht zum ewigen Krebsgeschwür am Körper Europas werden soll, dann die Sieger verstehen müssen, daß es einen Verlust für die Welt bedeuten würde, wollte man Deutschland ein für allemal mit dem Barbarentum Hitlers identifizieren und ihm darum die Möglichheitit friedlicher Entwicklung im Rahmen der europäischen Gesamtheit verkümmern. Wenn diese Einsicht

Bahn gebrochen hat, dann wird man uns brauchen, alle von uns, die guten Willens sind. In diesem Sinne glauben wir sowohl für den Frieden wie für die Zukunft Europas zu arbeiten, indem wir den heute heimatlosen Werten der grossen deutschen Überlieferung, dem bessern Teil des deutschen Wesens und dem, was wir an der Heimat lieben, gestalt und Stimme verleihen. Wir tun das ganz auf uns gestellt, ohne jede parteiliche Bindung ohne jeden Rückhalt: an Organisationen, in voller Unabhängigkeit, aber unter schwierigen Umständen und mit sehr bescheidenen eigenen Mitteln, die durch Spenden Einsichtiger ergänzt werden. Weden wir uns verständigen können, wir als Deutsche in Amerika? Die Flüchtlinge mit den Kriegsgefangenen? Das ist die Frage, die heute, im tragischen Moment unserer Geschichte Beantwortung fordert. Nur bei beiderseitigem, geduldigen Bemühen kann die Antwort im Sinne des Friedens und zum Nutzen der europäischen Heimat ausfallen.

Santiago de Chile, Mitte, Dezember 1944
Casilla 710

DIE HERAUSGEBER DER DEUTSCHEN BLÄTTER
Udo Rukser Albert Theile

TRANSLATION OF ABOVE—THE CORE MEANING

Different destinies have brought you and us to the Americas; however, the driving cause was shared: National Socialism. You have fought for it, willingly or not, maybe thrilled and devoted or struggling against it. The pamphlet goes on to point out the barbarities of Hitler and his crowd of followers, their hope and plans for the new Germay and new Europe, world peace and all the primary objectives of DB articles…Conclusion: The refugees and the prisoners together? That is the question, which begs to be answered in this traggic moment of our history. It is only through patient effort on both sides that we can arrive at an answer useful to all of Europe. Material from the former letter is included concerning the vital importance of rebuilding Germany properly, etc. We have to cleanse ourselves and get on the right track. We can not be seen by the victors as a great cancerous tumor on the body Europe. A patient and thorough establishment of peace if called for.

D—Flier Requesting Financial Aid for Children in Europe

FÜR DIE KINDER IN EUROPA

Langsam wendet sich das Schicksal in Europa und je mehr der Schleier gelüftet wird' den die Nazis über ihre "neue Ordnung" gebreitet haben, desto entsetzlicher is das Bild, daß sich uns enthült: Blut und Tränen, Hunger und Jammer überall! Aber nichts is so furchbar wie der Zustand der europäischen Jugend und nichts erfordert so rasche und gründliche Hilfe wie dies Elend. Denn wenn es drüben etwas zu retten gibt, dann ist es die Jugend, die auch unsere Hoffnung ist.

Bisher haben wir hier in Amerika kaum etwas tun können, jetzt aber gibt es zum ersten Mal auch für uns die möglichkeit zu handeln. Und diesmal haben gerade wir deutschen Nazigegner einer unerhört wichtige Aufgabe, weil eine symbolische ist: jene schrecklichen Wunden sind von Nazi-Händen geschlagen, darum müssen deutsche Hände unter den ersten sein, die Hilfe reichen!

Ob es unter Deutschen noch ein Gefühl für Menschlichkeit gibt, das wird und muss sich der Welt daran zeigen, ob wir bereit sind wirkliche Opfer zu bringen und wirkliche Hilfe zu leisten, um das von Nazis angerichtete Unheil wenigstens zu lindern. Es handelt sich also nicht um irgendeine Wohltätigkeitsaktion, von der man sich mit einem Almosen loskauft. Sondern wir haben menschliche Solidarität zu beweisen und das können wir heutzutage nur, indem wir so tief in die Tasche greifen, wie es nur geht.

Möge sich nicht dabei die erbärmliche Erfahrung wiederholen, daß nur die Ärmeren zu geben verstehen, die Wohlhabenden aber soviel Verpflichtungen haben, daß sie nichts übrig behalten, Jene Eltern, die noch das Glück haben, in die Augen ihrer Kinder sehen zu können, mögen den Blick hinüber schweifen lassen in die Alte Welt und auch jenen Millionen unschuldiger Kinder ins Auge blicken, die nichts als Not, Jammer und Elend kennen. Möge es nict dazu kommen, daß eure Kinder euch einmal vorwerfen müssen, etwas Wichtiges für sie ungetan gelassen zu haben, nämlich eine Tat der Menschlichkeit.

Mit welchem Mass ihr messet, mit dem werdet auch ihr gemessen werden! Überwinden wir die Trägheit des Herzens, helfen wir die Zukunft unserer Kinder sichern indem wir helfen, jene armen Kinder der Verzweiflung zu entreissen. Bedenket: unsere, vieleleicht nur unsere Hilfe könnte ihnen den Glauben an die Menschen wiedergeben.,

DIE HERAUSGEBER DER "DEUTSCHEN BLÄTTER"
Udo Rukser und Albert Theile

Geldspenden, auch die kleinsten, erbeten, durch Scheck auf die "Deutschen Blätter" oder durch Barzahlung in der Oficina 27, Huèrfanos 1039. Unsere Freunde bitten wir, jeder in seinem Kreise zu sammeln und mit Spenderlisten abzurechnen. Sämtliche Beträge werden durch Frau Carmen Cousiño de Eyzaguirre an das Chilenische Damen-Komitee: Salvad a los Niños in Santiago de Chile abgeführt.

TRANSLATION OF END NOTE: It explains payment methods. Readers are directed to collect funds jointly, then send off the money with a list of contributors to Mrs, Carmen Cousiño de Eyzaguirre at the Chiliean Ladys' Committee called Save the Children located in Santiago.

TRANSLATION OF FLYER (Essence): The general sense is to point out that sadness, suffering of children in Germany must be attended to. By whatever measure one measures, so will he be measured. Millions of children are afflicted. Perhaps the only help they will receive is ours. Blood, tears, suffering are everywhere. Children have been subjugated to Hitler's New Order, which must now be destroyed. If there is left in the German feelings of mercy, we have to now demonsrate it to the world. We have to dig in our pockets as deep as possible.

E—Anti-semitism of Hans Fritz von Zwehl and Reaction of Udo Rukser

RETYPED COPY OF LETTER OF APRIL 11, 1933: HANS FRITZ VON ZWEHL TO THE BRITISH *SUNDAY REFEREE*

(Dr. Ralph P. Vander Heide did not correct style or spelling in von Zwehl's English nor was *sic* used)

Ehrenbergstr. 10
Dr. Hans Fritz von Zwehl

Berlin-Dahlem

the 11th of April, 1933

To the Editor of the
" Sunday Referee",

17 Tudor Street
London E.C.

Dear Sir,

During a short stay in England I read in your number 2901 Bertrand Russell's article "History's Lessons for the Nazi" and highly appreciated the fair and open minded way it deals with the delicate question. As the author justly remarks it is very difficult for a foreigner to know exactly what is going on in Germany and still more so to understand it

You have never experienced a revolution chiefly led by Jews. You have not seen your valiant officers ignominiously insulted or even slain atrociously in their own country. Because a few highly cultured and distinguished Jews like Lord Beaconsfield and Lord Reading have rendered valuable services to your country you believe it makes no difference whether your civil servants are true-bred Englishmen or Jews. In fact that may be so long as you have no more than five per cent Jews in leading positions. Try a percentage as we had in Germany. In the law-courts 40 p.c., at the bar 60, in the press 70 and up to 100 p.c. on the stage and you will notice that the whole of your public life is no more <u>English</u> but has become something entirely different. There is hardly a German soldier who will not laugh you right in the face if you tell him that German Jews fought on the front in the same proportions as the rest of the population. The Jews anyhow who secured good positions in and after the war, never did. And disabled soldiers could not get a job as their places were taken by Jews. Since the war German Jews have undermind our morality and ruined our reputation abroad, exalting crime in their novels and plays, abusing our old army and sneering at the ideal of patriotism as a narrow-minded missionary might sneer at a native tribe's superstitions. You do not believe me? Well, friends of mine, German Jews, acknowledge these facts and deplore them. For the sake of self-defense we have to **reduce** Jewish influence. or, perhaps simply *reduce* to a reasonable extent, without any hatred or contempt, simply because it does not agree with us. You call that "persecution", If your house is full of strangers let in by some inconsiderate member of your family (alas! our former socialist government) and your poor relatives are standing outside, would you not ask the strangers to move on?

Vander Heide's Note: Please, *Herr Doktor*, von Zwehl, Please. Such ugly and intellectually sickening dialectics! This von Zwehel makes us wretch! We could of course say it is better to interpret his argument as progress. After all it is better to "reduce the influence of Jews" than to "reduce Jews." That is sick humor, of course, and not what the fawning Nazi parasite honestly believed. I, as hopefully do all readers of this book, consider it to be so vital that modern and future generations know that his words exemplify sadistic, goulish mockery and that *"elimination* of Jews" was his true desire.

TRANSLATION CONTINUES: According to our government's decree referred to in the same number of your paper no Jewish official or advocate who has served Germany loyally since 1914 or has fought for Germany and his allies can be turned out, the measure being applicable only to Jewish new-comers who had not served on the front. We do not mind an exceptional Jew keeping his position, but we will not stand any longer that practically the whole power in Germany is held by Jews with the exclusion of the other population.

Nevertheless cases of special hardship might arise. A few Jews might lose their positions they had deserved to keep. You feel sorry for them. So do I. But what about the disabled soldier who does not lose a job because he never had one to lose? A few days ago, in Edinburgh, I saw invalids from the great war begging in the streets. Brave Scots! They fought so heroically on that 21st of March 1918 when a revolver bullet struck me down. I feel more pity for them than for the German Jews.

I am, dear Sir, yours very sincerely
(-) von Zwehl
Barrister at the Appeal-Court in Berlin

RETYPED LETTER OF JUNE, 1933: RUKSER TO HANS FRITZ VON ZWEHL

(Dr. Vander Heide made an effort to arrange the typing and style like the originals.—very strange indeed, but that's how they look)

R/G
                      7. Juni 1933
                Herrn Rechtsanwalt Dr. von Zwehl,
                    Berlin W 35,
                        Ganthiner Strasse 7.

Lieber Zwehl:

Was Sie in Ihrem Briefe an die englishe Zeitschrift über die Beteiligung der Juden an Frontkämpfe sagen, hat mir keine Ruhe gelassen. Ich habe mich deshalb um zahlen bemüht. Von den rund 600.000 Juden waren 84.352 kriegsteilnehmer, davon 10.000 Kriegsfreiwillige. 78% waren an der Front, 12% sind gefallen, 29.874% wurden dekoriert, 2.022 sind zu Offizieren befördert. Ich finde, diese Zahlen sprechen vor sich selber, möchte aber doch noch folgende Grundsätze zur Bemerkung mache.

Ich halte es nicht nur für gefährlich, verallgemeinernd Kollektivurteile zu fällen, sondern, da es sich doch immer Werturteile handelt, auch ethisch für sehr bedenklichen. Unter den ethischen Gesichtspunkt hat jeder Mensch Anspruch darauf selbständig und für sich allein gewertet zu werden. Nur so kann festgestellt werden, ob und wie er vor der ethischen Forderung bestehen kann. Ich habe diesen Standpunkt gerade auch den Ausländern gegenüber vertreten, wenn sie irgendwelche unliebsamen Dinge, die in Deutschland passiert sind, verallgemeinern wollten. Ich bin nach wie vor davon überzeugt, daß dies due einzig richtige Basis ist.

                    Ohne mehr für heute,
                        mit den besten Grüssen
                          Ihr ergebener,

                            Rechtsanwalt und Notar

CORRESPONDENCE: UDO RUKSER/ HANS FRITZ VON ZWEHL-(TRANSLATED BY DR. RALPH P. VANDER HEIDE 1/28/09…Please note: The original letter in German is virtually illegible and, therefore, not included in this book. The arrangement on the page is true to the original—a bit strange.)

Sir. May 26, 1933
Attorney Dr. von Zwehl Berlin

Dear Mr. von Zwehl:
I beseech your help in the following case:

I have known the attorney, Elfriede Cohnen, Frankfurt/Main, For many years Gallusanlage,

And I have worked with her professionally. Miss Cohnen is of purely Aryan descent. While working with the Red Cross During the war (WW I) she lost a leg. She enjoyed an impressive criminal defense practice, and in that capacity selectively defended some Communists for which she received honoraria from Communist organizations. Politically she has personally long belonged to the center. Due to her defense of the Communists she was forbidden to continue practicing, and her efforts to be reinstated by the Ministry of Justice have been in vain because the selective defense of Communists has been declared a "crime against the people."
This case in my opinion is especially drastic!
Miss Cohnen proved her loyalty to the Fatherland through deeds and her personal blood offering. It is of fundamental legal significance should it now turn out that that her concept of *duty*, her defense of persecuted political opponents, was a trap. Because if this point of view truly prevails, it will mean the irrevocable end of the free advocacy system. **Typed script ends. In handwriting:** *Furthermore Miss Cohnen has also defended Nazis!*

Therefore, I beseech you to aide this completely innocent colleague, if through no other means than—an act of grace, possibly through the President of the Reich or the Ministry of Justice. **Illegible handwriting here—can not translate.**

With deep thanks,

Yours faithfully

NOTE: An effort was made to make the letters look like the originals in arrangement on the pages, etc. Some were very strange indeed.

F—Correspondence

THREE LETTERS RETYPED BY RALPH P. VANDER HEIDE, Ph.D. TO ALDOUS HUXLEY, CARL GUSTAV JUNG AND HERMANN HESSE ARE TYPICAL OF SEVERAL SENT TO *LITERATI* OF THE DAY.
RETYPED LETTER ONE:

UDO RUKSER TO ALDOUS HUXLEY
Dr. Udo Rukser   Quillota, Chile, April 2,
Mr. Aldous Huxley
c/o Mr. Chatto & Windus Editors
<u>LONDON</u>
Dear Mr. Huxley,

This is to tell you how deeply I am impressed by your work and how much I feel obliged to you. Really, I want to put it in a nutshell:

We all were Eyeless in Gaza, but after many a summer and putting Point counter Point we changed to See The Ends and the Means.

Well, you know that Beyond the Mexican Bay the world seems a bit different than over there and until now we did not get the full st?gt?c..? of the Brave New World. But people are doing everything to hurry up to the standard of the New Stupids, feeling ashamed to be awkward and old-fashioned with peace and liberal traditions.

But I am glad to say you, that there is a lot of people reading your books eagerly and moulding their minds with—taking comfort from the fact that there is an artist earnestly devoted to the very humanitarian ends. Maybe, you can imagine what this really means for us today.

Who is writing this, is a a German emigrant of some fifty years. I worked for humanitarian policy a good stretch of time. When Hitler rised to power, I refused to leave Germany in the hope, that there would be an opportunity for a change—not in the way of Ekki Gorsebrecht, but, talking to the people and then strengthening their minds—what succeeded to a certain agree in our personal cercle. But what could we hope after Munich? And in the year before all our british and french friends were fought back by russo-phobia so my wife and I after Munich decided to emigrate, in order to not become responsible for violence and war.

Recently, with my friend Albert Theile I started an anti-nazi monthly on a humanitarian basis. This review "Deutsche Blätter" is published in german language with the intention to fight back Nazi-propaganda from the german people living here. I will try to send you some copies of the first 3 numbers and hope you will not be afraid to find the illustrious name of yours in some pages. We dare not hope, that there may be a possibility to have some contribution of yours for this paper. But if you mean, that our efforts are not entirely unworthy of your appreciation and you would send us some lines about, this would mean a lot for us. We are going on now to form an honorary comitee for the review and invited Thomas Mann, Hermann Hesse C.G. Jung to give us this support. Is there any hope, that in some future you could allow us to inscribe your name too in this comitee?

We hope that these lines will find you in good health, with all ways better eyes! We apologize duly for out poor English and bag you to forgive the expression of out thanks, sympathy, and contribution:
Yours very sincerely

(Retyped and translated by Professor Ralph P. Vander Heide, Ph.D. June, 2012. It appears again in the appendix translated in its entirety)

RETYPED LETTER TWO:

UDO RUKSER TO CARL GUSTAV JUNG, APRIL, 1943

Dr Udo Rukser an   Quillota, Chile, den 4.IV.43
Herrn Professor C.G. Jung
Küssnacht b Zürich
Seestrasse 228

Hoch Verehrter Herr Professor, (Highly Esteemed Professor),
    Unterm 9. November 42 habe ich mir erlaubt, Ihnen laut Anlage zu schreiben.Ich füge die abschrift meines damaligen Briefen bei, weil man heute ja nie weiss, ob Briefe ankommen. Die Zeitschrift, über welche ich Ihnen damals berichtet habe, ist seit Januar dauernd erschienen. Die bisherigen 3 Hefte werden wir Ihnen auf mehrfache Weise, die wir für sicher halten, zusenden wie auch bisher schon versuche derart gemacht worde den sind in die Zeitschrift hier eine werkliche Mission. So hoffen wir unsere Arbeit ständig weiter zu führen und zu vertiefen. Daß uns dazu eine Beitrag gerade von Ihnen unschätzbar wäre, werden Ihnen verehrten Herr Professor, die bisherigen Hefte zeigen. Denn nicht nur der uns so ehrwürdige Name Jung erscheint dort immer wieder, sondern wir bemühen uns, wenn auch unter schwierigsten Verhältnissen, in der Leitung der Zeitschrift Jungschen Geiste zu handeln. Freilich möchten wir dem jetzt gern sichtbareren Ausdruck verleihen und

zwar folgdendes vor: Wir möchten eine Anzahl von wirklichen Europäern, denen wir uns besonders verpflichteet fühlen, bitten sich für ein Ehren-Komité unserer Zeitschrift zur Verfügung zu stellen. Wird enken dabei an Sie, an Thomas Mann, Hermann Hesse, Aldous Huxley, F.W. Foerster, Alexi Carrel, um nur die sichtigsten zu nennen, an die wir uns jetzt wenden. Daneben würden einige der hiesigen Humanisten treten deren Namen Ihnen kaum etwas sagen werden,

Wir sind uns darüber klar, daß es eine starke Zumutigung ist solche Bitte auszusprechen, zumal wenn Sie Unsere Hefte vieleicht noch nicht einmal gesehen haben. Aber wie so vielen noch nicht einmal gesehen haben. Aber wie so vieles. Muss die unerhörte Not unserer Tage solchen ungewönlichen Schritt entschuldigen.Und wenn er jetzt auch kaum mòglich ist, uns Ihnen Über den Ozean und alle Zensur hinweg vorzustellen, so bitte ich unsere Absicht doch vor allem als eine Huldigung aufzufassen, die wir Ihnen zu Schulden glauben und mit der wir Ihnen unsere tiefe Dankbarkeit und Verehrung ausdrücken möchten für so unendlich Vieles. Was wir Ihnen und nur Ihnen erdanken. Indem ich mir die Freiheit meine, die besten Wünsche für Ihr Wohlergehen zu sprechen, verbleibe ich in dankbarer Verehrung Ihr sehr ergebener.

Highly Esteemed Professor,

On November 9, 42, I took the liberty to write you concerning the enclosed. I am including a copy of that previous letter here because today one never knows if letters arrive. The magazine about which I notified you then has appeared regularly since January. We will send you by different means that we consider safe, the 3 issues which have appeared to date and also try to make clear that the magazine here is a true mission. Therefore, we hope to take it continuously further and deeper. It will become obvious when you see the three issues, that a contribution from you would be invaluable, esteemed professor, for not only does the honorable name, Jung, appear repeatedly, but we try, even under the most trying of circumstances, to direct the magazine in a „Jungian spirit." Clearly, we would like to distribute this now visible expression, and plan the following: We would like to have a number of true Europeans, to whom we feel especially indebted, to offer their services to our periodical's „honor committee," which we would place at their service. To mention some of the best known, we would list you, Thomas Mann, Hermann Hesse, Aldous Huxley, F.W. Forester, Alexi Carrel, just to mention some obvious names to whom we will now turn. Along with them a few of today's Humanists will be listed whose names will mean little to you.

We agree that to give voice to such a request is an unwarranted demand, especially when you probably have not even seen a single issue. But like so much these days, the proposal must be excused due to unprecedented need. And if it is now barely possible to introduce ourselves across oceans and through all the censors, I will request that our intention be considered an homage, which we believe we owe you and with which we would like to express our deepest thanks and veneration for so very much for which we thank you and only you.

Freedom that I love, the best wishes for your well-being to speak. I remain in grateful honor, your devoted,

NOTE: As do all languages, German has peculiarities which baffle us. These constructions, which I referred to in our mini lesson on German, surely influence how one interprets one's world. *Freiheit die ich meine* (**freedom that I love**) is one of those peculiarities. The verb *MEINEN* translates as **suppose, think, to be of the opinion that, reckon, guess, say, intend, to have in view** or **purpose** and idiomatically as you see above or here: *Meiner Meinung nach*=**in my opinion**).

RETYPED LETTER THREE:

Albert Theile to Hermann Hesse   1.11.1944

Sehr Verehrter Herr Hesse,
Wiederholt habe ich versucht, mit Ihnen in Verbindung zu kommen, aber die Nazi-zensur wird wohl meine Briefe unterschlagen haben. Jetzt, nachdem der Weg wieder frei, hoffe ich auf mehr Glück. Zunächst habe ich Sie von herr Takayama in Tokyo zu grüssen, der noch 1940 mit einigen Freunden, darunter Herr Takayama, gegen den japanischen Totalitarismus auftrat; gelegentlich erschien noch die Zeitschrift "Blutenstaub" war damals nicht eingegangen und hat Übersetzungen Ihrer Gedichte durch Katayama gebracht. Euere Gedichte, besonders eins, das Sie unter dem Eindruck des neuen Weltkrieges geschrieben, zirkulierten unter Freunden und waren mit der Machine abgeschrieben. Ihre Bücher waren selten und seh gesucht, die weitaus teursten von allen neueren deutschen Büchern. Narziss und Goldmund" kostete 80 Yen (Kaufkraft von 40 USA! Mit Ihren essays und Gedichte ging es ähnlich. Da auch in Japan die Studenten schmale Börse haben, ist viel abegeschrieben Worden, und wird in dieser Form gelesen; übrigens auch in Südamerika!
In der Sonntagsbeilagen des "Argentinischen Tageblatt" in Buenos Aires erscheinen von Zeit zur Zeit kleine Erzählungen von Ihnen; aber wir wissen nicht, ob es Nachdrucke sind. Hier ein Geständnis: wir haben von Ihnen im Weihnachtsheft des Jahres 1943 aus der Gedichten des jungen Josef Knecht

abgedruckt: zu einer Toccate von Bach. Doch heimlich dürsten wir…und Klage, und ich hoffe, Sie werden uns diese Freiheit nicht Übel nehmen.

In diesen Tagen las ich in der Neue Rundschau (Jahrgang 1934) "Das Glasperlenspiel" und der "Regenmacher" wieder. Haben Sie inzwischen das darin angekündigte grössere Werk abgeschlossen? Ist es erschienen? Wir möchten sehr gerne etwas von Ihnen bringen, neuere Gedichte, eine Erzählung, jedenfalls eine unveröffentlichte Arbeit.

Ich liesse Ihnen Hefte unserer Zeitschrift schicken; es wird weiter regekmässig geschehen. Hier lege ich einige Urteils bei obwohl ich weiss dies aus früherem Briefwechsel mit Ihnen; beim Lesen von "Glasperlenspiel" wurde es mir bestätigt. Ist Ihnen bekannt, daß Gilbert in Tokyo mich mit dem Entwurf einer solchen Zeichenschrift bis zu seinem Tode beschäftigt hat? Die Chinaschrift diente ihm dabei als Ausgang, Nur weniges ist von seinen Arbeiten erschienen, sein Nachlass von seiner verständnislosen Familie vernichtet worden. Unsere Zeitschrift, die durch ihren Kampf gegen den Nazismus eine betont politische war, wird im neuen Jahr vielseitiger werden, weltweiter. Wir hoffen mit unseren Mitarbeitern unser Teil zum geistigen Wiederaufbau unserer Heimat beitragen zu können. Werden Sie uns bald antworten?

Mit bestem Dank im Voraus und allen guten Wünschen und Grüssen

Verehrungsvoll der Ihre,
Albert Theile

TRANSLATION OF THEILE TO HESSE LETTER 1.11.1944
(Translated by Ralph P. Vander Heide, Ph.D.)

RETYPED LETTER THREE (See appendix also)

Most esteemed Mr. Hesse,

I have repeatedly tried to contact you, but the Nazi censors undoubtedly confiscated my letters. Now since the way has become free again, I hope to have more luck. First, I must give greetings from Mr. Takayama in Tokyo, who back in 1940 along with a group of friends opposed Japanese Totalitarianism. Occasionally, the magazine, "Blutenstaub" *(Pollen)* appeared. It wasn't yet discontinued and published translations of your poems through Katayama. Your poems, especially one, which you wrote under your impression of the new world war, circulated among friends and was copied with typewriters. Your books seldom appeared and were by far the most expensive of all new German books. *Narziss und Goldmund* cost 80 Yen (exchange rate 40 to a dollar!) With your essays and poems that was also the case. Because in Japan the students have little money, many books are copied and are read in that form, moreover also in South America!

In the Sunday supplements of *The Argentinian Daily Newspaper* in Buenos Aires one of your short stories appeared from time to time, but we do not know if they are copies. Here comes an ad

mission: In the Christmas issue of 1943 we copied from you out of *the Poems of the boy Josef Knecht: to a Bach Toccate*. Never the less we secretly thirst…and complain, and I hope you will not take it badly,

In the last days I read again in the *Neue Rundschau* (of 1934) *Das Glasperlenspiel.* and *The Rainmaker.* In the meantime have you finished the larger work mentioned there? We would very much like to publish something by you, new poems, a story in any case a unpublished work.

I had issues of our magazine sent to you; that will continue to occur regularly. I am enclosing some evaluations although I know this from earlier correspondence with you, it was confirmed when I read *Glasperlenspiel*. You know that Gilbert in Tokyo gave me the task until his death of developing such a magazine. The Chinese script served him as a beginning. Only a little of his work appeared, his unpublished work was destroyed by his ignorant family. Our magazine, which through its fight against Nazism was strongly political, will in the new year become much larger with more pages. We hope along with our fellow workers to be able to contribute to the moral reconstruction of our homeland. Will you answer soon?

With many thanks in advance and all good wishes and greetings,

With great respect, yours,
Albert Theile

The pronounced fawning tone rather jumps out at the reader, but the exiled publishers did what they had to do, to use another present-day expression. Help from Hesse was worth exhibiting a servile demeanor, if it could assure a positive response, support and some original pieces of literature.

G—Letter of Appreciation for the *DB* From a German POW

Retyped and translated by Professor Ralph P. Vander Heide, Ph.D. June, 2012. An effort was made to make the letters look like the orignals with strange arrangements on the pages, abnormally big spaces, etc. I remind repeatedly that I wanted to retain the original appearance, and it came out close. I am the first to find it weird, apparently not composed by a professional secretary.

Dipl. Ing.   (24) Pinneberg/Holstein
Eberhard Ulbrich   An der Mühlenau 31 den 15. September 1946
Verlag der "Deutschen Blätter"
Casilla 710 Chile

Während meiner Gefangenschaft im Lager Camp Carson, Colorado, USA, war ich Abonnent der Deutschen Blätter.
    Welchen Wert die Deutschen Blätter für uns Kriegsgefangene, vor allem auch die Antinazis unter uns, hatten, brauche ich Ihnen wohl kaum auseinandersetzen. Auch in unseren politischen Arbeitsgemeinschaften lieferten sie uns wertvolles Material zu anregenden Diskussionen.
    Obwohl die Hitlerherrschaft mit ihrer hermetischen Abschliessung nach aussen hin nun verüber ist, sind die geistigen Mauern um Deutschland noch längst nicht abgetragen; nun aus materiellen Gründen, zu einen grossen Teil wenigstens, unter den Nachwirkungen der vergangenen Jahre. Auch das wird Ihnen bekannt sein.
    Wir ehemaligen Kriegsgefangenen, die wir auch hinter Stacheldraht drüben in eine geistige weiter hineingestellt wurden, die die Aelteren unter uns schon fast vergessen und die Jüngeren niemals kennen gelernt hatten, empfinden diesen Zustand einer immer noch anhaltenden Abschliessung und die daraus folgende Enge des im wesentlichen auf sich allein angewiesenen geistigen deutschen Raumes als besonders bedrückend.
    Aus diesen beiden Gründen: der Wertschätzung der Deutschen Blätter an sich und dem Wunsch nach Erweiterung des geistigen Raumes, in dem wir zur Zeit hier leben, sei es auch nur schrittweise, entspringt diese Frage an Sie: Gibt es zur Zeit eines Möglichkeit, die Deutschen Blätter auch in Deutschland zu beziehen und unter welchen Bedingungen?
    Vielleicht ist es auch möglich, einige ältere Hefte zu bekommen. Auch damit wäre in der gegenwärtigen Lage schon viel geholfen. Ich habe bei meiner Entlassung nur eines mitnehmen können, das mir persönlich das lassenen Gepäckgewicht in Anspruch genommen. Hier aber fehlen das Material und

die Anregung; für mich umso mehr, als ich selbst zum Schriftstellerberuf hinübergewechselt bin.

Ich wäre Ihnen für eine Nachricht ausserordentlich dankbar, am meisten natürlich für eine solche, die in der einen oder anderen Form meinem Wunsche Erfüllung in Auswicht stellt.

Mit vorzüglicher Hochachtung,
Gez. E. Ulbrich.

TRANSLATION (FULL): I was a subscriber to the Deutsche Blätter during my imprisonment in Camp Carson, Colorado. I can not express how deeply we POW's valued the magazine, especially the anti-Nazis. Of course I hardly need to explain that to you. This was also the case for our work organization where the journal provided worthwhile material for lively discussions.

Although the reign of the Hitlerites with its hermetically sealed protection from the outside is now (9/46) behind us and finished, the intellectual walls around Germany are by no means removed; simply due to material grounds, at least to a great extent, under the influence of the past years. You are familiar with that also.

We one time prisoners, who were behind barbed wire over there, were behind wire intellectually also, which the older men among us have almost forgotten and the younger ones never were aware of, find this situation of being locked out to continue and the narrowness which follows from that, in an atmosphere that is in essence intellectually and spiritually German, especially oppressive.

It is from these reasons: the high evaluation of the DB in itself and the wish to broaden the intellectual environment in which we live here at the moment, though it be step by step, that my question for you arises: Is there any possibility at this time to receive the DB, if so, under what kinds of restrictions?

Maybe it is also possible to obtain a few old issues. Also that would help a lot in the present circumstances. Upon being released I could bring only a few items which took all the space allowed me. Here, however, there are no materials and no impetus: for me even more so, since I myself have switched over to the profession of writer.

I would be extraordinarily thankful to your for a reply, most of all, of course, for an answer that in one way or another would focus on the fullfillment of my wishes.

With highest respect,

H—Letter to Herbert Hoover

LETTER TO HERBERT HOOVER INDICATING CONCERN FOR THE "GERMAN QUESTION" AFTER THE *DB* CEASED PUBLICATION
(Retyped by Ralph P. Vander Heide, Ph.D. September, 2012)

Mr. Herbert Hoover   29-3-47
Stanford University
<u>Stanford Calif.</u>

Dear Sir:

    With the greatest interest we read the news about your Mission to Germany and your plan to make the American zone of Germany a going concern. Remembering the great work you have done always for the sake of peace and humanity we highly apreciate your actual activity, which we consider a powerful contribution to solve the most urgent problems.

    We, therefore, take the liberty to send you by the present a memorandum we have written about the German question. We will be very glad when there will be any opportuniity to have some information about your plan mentioned above. We need such material badly for our purposes.

                              With our anticipated thanks we remain very truly
                                              Sincerely DEUTSCHE BLÄTTER

I—*Runder Tisch* at Home of Joseph Kaskell

(DISCUSSION EVENING—ROUND TABLE), MARCH, 5, 1945

The list is a "who's who" of many, but by no means, all of the emigrant intellectuals who fled, often with very few possessions or financial means to the USA. They found exile in other countries as well, but I am dealing primarily with the states. The few I met or had some acquaintance with are listed in bold print. Think of all the stories they have to tell as do the engineers, the musicians, the artists, all the expatriates in all walks of life. My original plan was to include information on all of the names below. Some became well-known or famous here or at least some of the persons in the cinema industry or performance world did. I have decided to leave to you the satisfaction of your curiosity. With the advent of the Internet and immediate information always available, you readers can learn precisely what you wish to know. Forgive me, but it would be most daunting. Just a little help follows below from another short piece I did.

On March 5, 1945, an illustrious group of some ninety German exiles met in New York City at the spacious Riverside Drive condominium of Joseph Kaskell for a *Runder Tisch* (**discussion evening**). Part of this discussion time was allotted to the *Blätter*, for all agreed its message, whether of "classical humanism" or at times more reflective of Albert Camus's "pessimistic humanism," should be disseminated beyond the end of the war.

"Professor," "Author," "Dr.," "Director," "President," "Manager," "CEO," "Conductor" and more titles abounded. Paul Tillich, the theologian, was there along with Fritz Karsen, former Superintendent of Schools in Berlin, and the authors/journalists, Berthold Viertel and Max Barth. Other names included Julius Bab, dramatist and theatre critic; Gerhard Jacoby, professor and writer; Arnold Brecht, poltical scientist; Kurt Wolf, who was to found a publishing firm, as well as Erich Kahler, who authored some ninety books; Ivan Heilbut, the author, and the Stresemann brothers, Wolfgang and Joachim, whose father had served Germany as Chancellor during the Weimar Republic. For twenty-two years Wolfgang was the General Manager of the Berlin Philharmonic; Joachin, a gifted pianist, was to study law and economics and work for Chase Manhattan Bank in upper echelon positions—and more, on up to ninety such names, some already prestigious, who had fled the Nazified *Vaterland*. All were destined to make great intellectual contributions to their new "Motherland."

I am duly impressed when I think of the education level of these participants. Nearly all (I am guessing a bit here, but being familiar with the German system, I can feel confident in guessing) were educated at the higher level secondary schools, the **Gymnasien**. I can image high level political discussions, philosophy even higher mathematics being thrown in along with the obligatory *Kaffee und Kuchen*, more than likely prepared (or at least supervised) by Mrs. Kaskell herself. Indulge me a bit. I have let my mind run, but I know I am nearly "spot on" as our British friends say, and I would like to have been in attendance. Here are the guests:

(I used a bold font here to highlight the names of persons with whom I had some acquaintanceship.)

Mr. and Mrs. Erving H. Adler, 116 Park Lane So. Kew Gardens, L.I.,N.Y.
Mr. & Mrs. Siegfried Aufhauser, 87-42 Elmhurst Ave., Elmhurst, L.I.,N.Y.
Dr. Angelus, 114 E 95, llew York
Julius Bab, 14 Jessica Place, Roslyn Heights, L.I.,N.Y.
Dr.H.S.Baerenspring & Mrs. Hauptman, 243 Riverside Drive New York
Prof. Friedr. Baerwald, 106 W 74th St.I New York
Max Barth, 317 Wi 95, New York 25
Roy C. Bates, 303 W 106, New York
Mrs. Elisabeth E. Blencke, 338 West 77th, New York 24
Berthold Biermann, 51W 89, New York
Dr. Felix Boenhein, 315 West 57, New York
Ernst Döblin, 3746 85th St,Jackson Heights, L.I. N.Y.
Hermann Budzislawski, 328 E 50, New York
Mr. and Mrs. Henry Breslauer, 34-05 71st st., Jackson Heights, L.I.N.Y.
Prof. Arnold Brecht New School for Social Research, 66 W 12 New York
Dr. & Mrs. Hermann Dunker, 83-15 118 St., Kew Gardens L.I.N.Y.
Mr.& Mrs.George Eliasberg, 41 Kew Gardens L.I., N.Y.
Reverend Frederick J. Forell, 525 Central Park East, New York
Paul Froehlich, 8409 Talbot St. , New Gardens, L.I.N.Y.
Dr. Curt Glaser 102 W 73 St.,N.Y.
Dr. & Mrs. Kurt Grasheim, 667 Madison Ave.,New York
Mr. Paul Graupe, 112 Central Park West New York
Mr.& Mrs. Paul Hagen,211 E 25 New York
Dr. Ivan Heibut, 328 W96th St. New York 25
Dr. Paul Hertz, 68-29 Burns St, Forest Hills, L.I.N.Y.
Prof, Eduard Heymann New School Soc. Research, 66W. 12, NY York
Prof. & Mrs. **W.E. Hocking,** 398 E 79, New York
Prof. Honig, YMCA, 347 Madison Ave. New York
Dr. Gerhard Jacoby, 138 W 82, New York

Prof. Ernest Jacoby, Columbia University, New York 27
Dr. Erich Kahler, 1 Evelyn Place, Princeton, N.J.
Prof. **Fritz Karsen**, 250 Cabrin Blvd., New York 53
Dr. & Mrs. Gerald Krassa, 517 W 113 New York
Dr. Fritz Landshoff, c/o S. Fischer, 381 Fourth Ave. N.Y.
Dr. & Mrs. Ernest Lewy, 118 E. 70, New York
Prof. Julius Lips, 640 Riverside Drive, Apt. 11B, New York
Mr. Robert Lochner, NBC, 30 Rockefeller Plaza, N.Y. 20
Mrs. Hilde Lochner, Tudor City Hotel, E. 42, N.Y.
Hubertus Prinz zu Loewenstein, Newfoundland, N.J.
Karl Nierendorf, 53 E 57 N.J.
Karl O. Paetel, 68-43 Burns St., Forest Hills, N.Y.
Mr. & Mrs. Erwin Piscator, 56 West 10th N.Y.
Dr. Alfred Plaut. 33 East End Ave., N.Y. 28
Max Raphael, 229 E. 63rd st. Apt. 24, New York
Mr. **Hans Richter**, 134 E. 60, N.Y.
Mr. & Mrs. H. Schlesinger & Mrs. Dispeker, 48 E 66, N.Y. 21
Dr. & Mrs. Hans Schaeffer, 61 E 57, N.Y.
Dr. & Mrs. Rudolph Schlesinger, 25 Stoney Side Drive, Larchmont, N.Y.
Dr. Edmond Schlesinger, 415 W115, N. York
Erich Schmidt, 436 Central Park West, N.Y.
Mr. & Mrs. Rudolph Schreiber, 80 Bload St., N. York
Dr. & Mrs. Paul Schwarz, 230 Central Park South, New York
Dr. Anna Selig, International Study Center, 55 W 42, N.Y. York 18
Dr. Hans Staudinger, 71 Washington Sq. S. Apt 17 NY 12
Dr. Fritz Sternberg 116 W Ilth St., N.Y.
Prof. Gustav Stolper, 52 Wall Street, New York
Messrs. **Wolfgang & Joachim Stresemann**, 54 E 79, New York
Mr. & Mrs. Billly Suhr, 50 E 50, New York
Dr. Gottfried Treviranus, Hotel Savoy Plaza, New York
Prof. & Mrs. **Paul Tillich**, 99 Claremont Ave., New York
Mrs. Claira Thomas, 28 W 74. St., New York
Dr. Frans Ulstein & Miss Elizabeth Ulstein, 22 E 79, New York
Mrs. Maja Unna, 180 Sullivan St. New York
Mrs. Cecelia Odefey Valentiner, 37 E 75th, N.Y.
Mr. Julio Alvarez de Vayo, 180 Sullivan Road N.Y.
Berthold Viertel, 346 W 84, New York 24
Prof Oswald G. Villard, 20 Vesey St., N.Y. 7
Henry Waldstein, 404 W 115, N. York
Julius Weigert, 28 W 97, New York

Werne Wille, 305 west 82nd St., N.Y.
Prof. Kerl A. Witfogel, 420 Riverside Drive, New York 25
Dr. Gerhard Wodtke, 115 E 86, NY 28
Prof L.E. Wolferz, 547 W. 123 St., NY
Kurt Wolff, 41 Washington Sqr So.,NY
Dr. Alfred Wynder, 654 Lyons ave., Irvington, NY
Marianne Zerner, 76-35 113th St., forest Hills, N.Y.

J—photos: Hitler, Goebbels, Mann Jews, Borkum, Vander Heide, Rukser Theile

Hitler as Lohengrin, captured German painting U.S. army

ADOLPH HITLER, THE MURDEROUS PHENOMENON AND CALAMITOUS DICTATOR

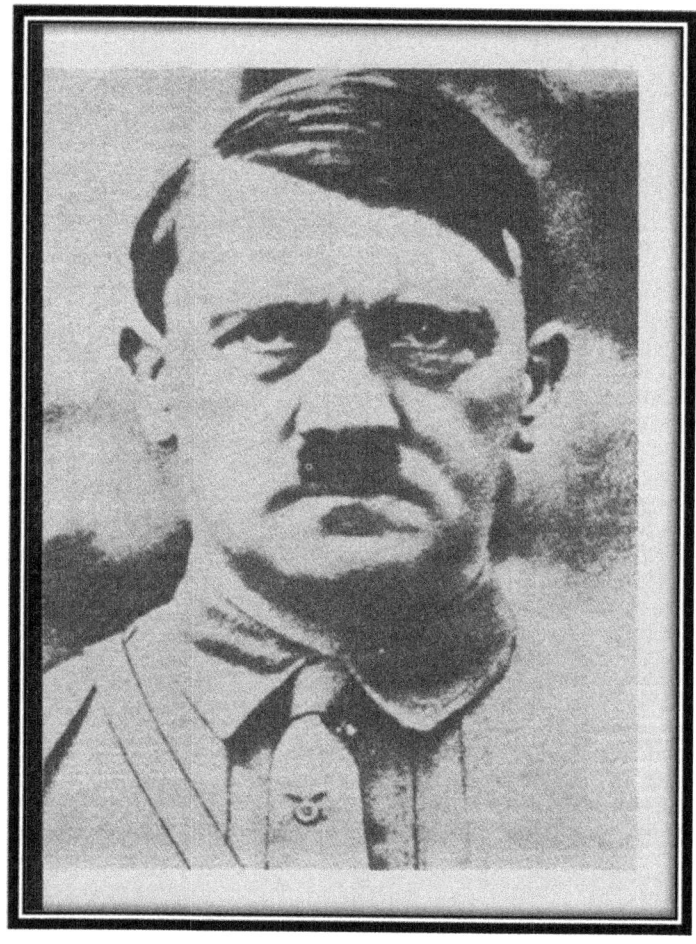

TYPICAL PORTRAYAL OF JEWS
GRUSS AUS BORKUM & DAS BORKUM LIED
WHICH SANG: "Der muß heraus" (repeatedly)

"ETERNAL JEW" AS SEEN BY DUTCH NAZIS

The Nazi occupiers deported the majority of the Dutch Jews to concentration camps, with the assistance of the Dutch police and civil service: the Netherlands had one of the highest levels of collaboration with the Nazis during the Holocaust. 75% of the country's Jewish population were exterminated, a much higher percentage than countries like Belgium and France.

WHO IS RESPONSIBLE FOR THE WAR...
THE JEW OF COURSE...WHO ELSE?

NOTE: BISMARCK AND BANNER: "FREE FROM VERSAILLES FOR FREEDOM AND VATERLAND"

YOUR SOLUTION:GERMAN NATIONAL

THE INFAMOUS EXTERMINATION CAMP NEAR MUNICH: DACHAU

JOSEF GOEBBELS, MINISTER OF PROPAGANDA AND PUBLIC ENLIGHTENMENT IN THE THIRD REICH

THE MENTALLY DERANGED ACADEMIC, JOSEF GOEBBELS. ONE OF THE FIRST TO USE RADIO, AIRPLANES IN POLITICAL CAMPAIGNS, GREAT MOTIVATIONAL SPEAKER. OUR LITTLE MAGAZINE FROM CHILE WAS UP AGAINST ALL OF THIS.

RESUMEN CASTELLANO

¡NO QUIERO SABER MÁS DE EUROPA!...

Una conversación típica con uno de aquellos alemanes que a la fuerza quieren romper los lazos que los unen con su pasado. Ellos se creen en América en una isla segura y consideran a Europa descartada, sin pensar en que esta clase de aislamiento había fracasado hace tiempo y que el mundo es también políticamente una unidad.

EL EMBAJADOR DE AMÉRICA:

WALT WHITMAN

Hermann Bahr ofrece en este ensayo no sólo la biografía de aquel gran poeta americano, sino también una apreciación completa de su arte. Para Bahr es Walt Whitman el heraldo de la democracia americana. La democracia, en concepto de Whitman, no consiste en leyes, sino que «viene del corazón». Por esa verdadera democracia clamaba Whitman: «I speak the pass-word primewal, I give the sign of democracy...» Ese clamor, jamás extinguido, no llegó a cumplirse todavía.

NUESTROS TESTIGOS: THOMAS WOLFE

Fragmentos de la última novela de *Thomas Wolfe:* «You can't go home again», que testimonian el estado interno de Alemania, apreciada y llorada por este escritor como por ningún otro novelista moderno de los EE. UU.

¡MÉTODOS NUEVOS!

En el segundo artículo: «¡Para el orden mundial,- un servicio de informaciones mundial!» reclama *Udo Rukser* informes semestrales acerca de todos los acontecimientos de significación general, de carácter político, social, militar y científico que permitan formarse un juicio sobre las tendencias existentes. De esta manera podrían proporcionarse a la Humanidad las bases para ciertas cuestiones, «se crearía la posibilidad de una opinión pública imparcial y bien informada». Sólo una opinión pública bien fundamentada puede tener la fuerza moral necesaria para imponer a los pueblos la «Ley de Solidaridad Internacional».

¿POR QUÉ NO VUELVE A LEERLAS...?

MEMORIAS DE CARL SCHURZ

De las memorias de Schurz, el gran estadista germano-americano, se reproduce aquí de ensayo su encuentro con Carlos Marx.

LA VOZ ALEMANA: CARL ZUCKMAYER

Del agotado trabajo de *Carl Zuckmayer* «Pro Domo», se reproducen aquí sus impresiones de la época inmediatamente después de la primera Guerra Mundial y su confesión de fe alemana... «Esta más grande Alemania, la del espíritu, del derecho, de la libertad, arde hoy en nuestros corazones con más fuego, con más dolor que nunca... Y más que en ningún otro tiempo el poeta tiene que ser su defensor, su conservador y su heraldo».

¿EXISTE UNA «OTRA ALEMANIA»?

Louis P. Lochner, que durante 21 años trabajó para la Associated Press en Berlín, contesta *afirmativamente* a esta pregunta fatal en su libro «What about Germany?» (véase el N.º 7 de las H. A., pág. 31). «Es una Alemania momentáneamente sumergida. No tiene voz porque toda exteriorización de su existencia le fué arrebatada... Es una Alemania todavía manifiesta su adhesión a los ideales de la civilización normal, al derecho humano e igual para todos... Una Alemania abochornada y humillada con todo lo que los nazis cometen en su nombre...»

EN LA SEGUNDA PARTE DE LA REVISTA

y bajo el título «Recortes» se publican un resumen del artículo de Henry W. Ehrman sobre el porvenir de Alemania, la respuesta a una publicación de Kingsburry Smith en el «American Mercury» de Nueva York. En la sección «Del Tercer Reich» se publican relatos sobre la situación de la mujer alemana, la «movilización más grande de la Historia», la agricultura nazi y los «Heimgekehrte Volksgenossen» (connacionales de vuelta al hogar). En la sección «Libros» se comentan algunos libros de arte, publicados últimamente en Suiza. Siguen noticias literarias internacionales y la sección «Revista de Revistas». Con una «Crónica Política» cierra el número noveno de las «Hojas Alemanas».

Mientras la desgracia no ataque el íntimo orgullo del hombre, éste conserva la fuerza de continuar la lucha y de cumplir su misión esencial, que es la de vivir con todo el ardor de que es capaz, como si su vida fuera la más importante que toda otra cosa para los destinos de la humanidad.

MAETERLINCK

A SUMMARY IN SPANISH WAS PLACED AT THE END OF EACH ISSUE OF THE DEUTSCHE BLÄTTER

**DR. RALPH P. VANDER HEIDE
LAKE BLED, SLOVENIA, JULY, 2012**

Ralph P. Vander Heide, Ph.D.

TYRANTS WHO WOULD DISRUPT FREEDOM MUST FIRST DESTROY BOOKS

DR. RUKSER, LAWYER, *LANDWIRT*, PUBLISHER, *"LITERAT"*

Literat und Landwirt

Solange Dr. Udo Rukser als Anwalt in Berlin lebte, war er den Kollegen als Herausgeber der „Zeitschrift für Ostrecht" bekannt. Jetzt wohnt er in Chile und beschäftigt sich nicht mehr mit juristischen Fragen. Nach Berlin ist er zurückgekommen, um in der ibero-amerikanischen Bibliothek Material für ein Nietzsche-Buch zu sammeln, an dem er seit fünf Jahren arbeitet. Vor einiger Zeit hat er ein Werk veröffentlicht, das die Universität in Venezuela inzwischen in die Reihe ihrer Lehrbücher aufgenommen hat: „Goethe in der hispanischen Welt". Er ist im Grunde ein verspäteter Schlußpunkt unter das Goethe-Festival, das die Universität in Santiago zum 200jährigen Geburtstag des Dichters veranstaltet hatte.

Dr. Udo Rukser

Dr. Rukser wurde damals in das Festkomitee gewählt und merkte bei dieser Gelegenheit, wie wenig doch über die Wirkung einer so überragenden Persönlichkeit auf den kulturellen Lebensbereich eines anderen Landes eigentlich bekannt ist. Dessen ungeachtet wurde das Festival natürlich ein Erfolg. Santiago erlebte in der Zeit sogar die erste spanische Iphigenie-Aufführung.

Bereits 1933 hat Dr. Rukser Berlin verlassen. Er stieß kurz nach der „Machtergreifung" in einem Prozeß mit der gesamten „Freisler-Equipe" zusammen. Er zog sich mit seiner Frau auf einen Hof am Bodensee zurück und wurde Landwirt. Seine Verbindung zu Goerdeler wurde Rukser schon vor dem Krieg fast zum Verhängnis. 1938 emigrierte er Hals über Kopf nach Chile.

Dort baut er jetzt auf seiner Hazienda zwischen Santiago und Valparaiso Orangen, Zitronen, Nüsse und Paltas, die in Deutschland wenig bekannten Butterfrüchte, an. Beinahe hätte er auch dieses Land verlassen müssen. Denn um der Stimme des „anderen" Deutschlands Gehör zu verschaffen, der Stimme, die die braunen Machthaber gewaltsam zum Verstummen gebracht hatten, gab er im Krieg die „Deutschen Blätter" heraus. Mit dem Erfolg, daß ihn die Nazis zum Kommunisten stempelten und seine Ausweisung verlangten, die seine Freunde gerade noch verhindern konnten.

L. H.

Curiously a letter containing three poems written by a German soldier, was found by an American soldier in Sicily who gave it to Dr. Vander Heide. Soldiers of any nation only want to return to loved ones in their homeland. We hope Walter made it, his anguish quieted, that he was not *gesneuveld!* Enjoy! and ask: WHY need it be? And, how many millions of soldiers have shared these sentiments?

DRANGSAL (**ANGUISH**)

Mein Herz es schlägt so fürchterlich
Zu Dir mein Kind, daß weist Du nicht
In meiner Brust so ganz verborgen
Pocht es am schönen Pfingstag morgen

So brach dann still zur Mittagszeit
Mein Dienst zum Wachkommando an
Die Zeit ging mir sehr langsam um
Drum liebes Mädchen sei nicht dumm

Nutz Deine schönen Festtagstage
Zum gang ins Grüne immer zu
O-könnt' ich jetzt zur Abendstunde
Bei Dir mein Kind in Deinem Bunde

Dann würde unsere Herzen sprechen
Dein süsser Mund vor Freude lächeln
Und fühlten uns so ganz allein
Im Himmel bei den Engelein!

My heart beats so wildly in my breast,,
Soley for you, my dear the best
You do not know how hard it pounds, deep inside,
And so forlorn on this lovely Easter morn

My turn at guard duty began midday
But the hours passed not rapidly
Therefore, dear girl, do not be silly
Make sure to use this day fully

Enjoy the day… stroll outside to
See the green of the country side
Oh—if only now as nightfall arrives
I with you could share our two lives

Then two hearts would speak for awhile
And your sweet mouth from joy would smile
We would feel ourselves alone as though in
heaven where angels atone

Translated by Dr. Ralph P. Vander Heide

THE FINAL WORDS OF MEIN KAMPF

Ein Staat, der im Zeitalter der Rassenvergiftung sich der Pflege seiner besten rassischen Elemente widmet, muß eines Tages zum Herrn der Erde werden.

Das mögen die Anhänger unserer Bewegung nie vergessen, wenn je die Größe der Opfer zum bangen Vergleich mit dem möglichen Erfolg verleiten sollte.

IN A TIME OF RACIAL POISONING THE STATE THAT DEVOTES ITSELF TO THE CARE OF ITS BEST RACIAL ELEMENTS WILL, ONE DAY BECOME RULER OF THE WORLD ("zum Herr nder Erde")

ADOLF HITLER,
1926

Ein Weltbürger des Geistes
Albert Theile zu Besuch in seiner Heimatstadt

Auf der Zeche „Schürbank und Charlottenburg" in Schüren begann er als Schlepper — der 1904 in Hörde geborene Albert Theile, der heute vor allem im spanisch-südamerikanischen und im arabischen Sprachraum als einer der großen Vermittler zwischen deutscher, orientalischer und lateinamerikanischer Kultur gelten darf. Nach langer Zeit weilte Prof. Theile gestern wieder einmal in seiner Heimatstadt.

Als ein echter „Selfmademan des Geistes" hat er sich vom Industriearbeiter über den „Begabten-Abiturienten" zum Kunst- und Geschichtswissenschaftler hochgearbeitet. Schon 1933 war für ihn die Emigration die einzige Alternative zum Hitlerregime. Er begab sich auf weltweite Wanderschaft, über Norwegen, Moskau und Japan führte ihn sein Weg nach Chile, wo er während des Krieges die „Deutschen Blätter" als eine unabhängige literarische Emigrantenstimme herausgab.

Schon in den zwanziger Jahren ergab sich u. a. die Beziehung zu dem anderen berühmten Hörder, dem Bildhauer Berhard Hoetger. 1928 wurde Theile Redakteur der von Hoetger inspirierten Zeitschrift „Die Böttcherstraße". Die Vielfalt seiner literarischen Tätigkeit seither dokumentierte ein von der Stadtbücherei zusammengestelltes Schriftenverzeichnis.

1952 kehrte der an der Staatsuniversität Santiago noch heute als Professor geführte Theile nach Europa zurück. Von der Schweiz aus redigiert er die beiden Zeitschriften „Humboldt" (für den spanischen Sprachraum) und „Fikrun wa fann" (Wissenschaft und Kunst) für alle arabischen Länder, die vom Auswärtigen Amt finanziert, aber völlig unabhängig Deutschsprachiges aus Ost, West und Süd exportieren und Bemerkenswertes aus den genannten Regionen zu uns hereinbringen.

Ein echter Weltbürger aus Dortmund, der sich auch als 65er eine politisch progressive Denkweise bewahrt hat. bs

VON HÖRDE BIS CHILE: Prof. Albert Theile. (Foto: Schaub)

ALBERT THEILE

A world citizen of the spirit and "self-made" Theile is one of the leading arbitrators among the Arabic, German, Spanish speaking countries and the orient. During WW II he published in Chile the literary voice of the emigrants "Deutsche Blätter."

HEFT 28 ENTHIELT:

Rainer Maria Rilke / Paul Zech
Verfall und Erneuerung der deutschen Sprache / Arthur Sala
Zwei Sechziger:—Erich Kahler / Thomas Mann—Kurt Hiller / Paul Zech
Das Wunder der Selbstverständlichkeit / S. Friedlaender
Erziehung zur Gewaltlosigkeit / Anna Landmann Steuerwald
Elternhaus und Kindheit / Fritz Busch—Europäische Maler in den USA / E. Schloss
Die Bedeutung Diltheys für die Philosophie der Gegenwart / E. J. Rüsch
Stimmen aus Deutschland:
Friedrich Meinecke / Walter von Molo / Frank Thiess
Ist die heutige deutsche Jugend eine verlorene Generation?
Umfrage unter jungen deutschen Kriegsgefangenen in den USA
Gedichte von Rainer Maria Rilke (auf deutsch und spanisch),
Hermann Hesse, Stefan Andres—usw. usw.

HEFT 29 ENTHIELT:

Der Todesmarsch der zehn Millionen / Karl O. Paetel
Das Problem der Demokratie / Erich von Kahler
Der Weg zur Regeneration der Kultur / Albert Schweitzer
Franz Boas und Deutschland / Herbert Baldus
Walter Knoche (†) / Otto Schneider
Die unterirdische Opposition in Deutschland während des Krieges
Wo steht die deutsche Intelligenz?
Glückwunsch an Gabriela Mistral
und vieles andere.

HEFT 30 ENTHIELT:

Das deutsche Vakuum / H. A. Freund.
Die Entwaffnung Deutschlands und ihre Folgen / Udo Rukser
Schadenersatz?! / Hans Schnitzlein—Riga-Tagebuch / Hermann Hesse
Rilke in England / Julian Hirsch—Neue Musikbücher / Federico Heinlein
Die Verantwortlichkeit des deutschen Volkes / Erich von Kahler
Dienst und Armut / Werner Bock
Ansprache in der Universität Heidelberg / Karl Jaspers
Rede vor jungen Sozialdemokraten / Kurt Schmidt
Gedichte von Werner Bock, Wolfram Dietrich, Gustav Regler, Franz Werfel, Ernst Wiechert
und anderes mehr.

HEFT 31 ENTHIELT:

Die Gorgonen / Stefan Andres—Besinnung,—worauf? / Albert Theile
Deutsche Jugend / Karl O. Paetel
Erziehungsarbeit im neuen Deutschland / Curt Bondy
Die in der Heimat und wir / Anna Landmann St.
Heimkehr / Paul Zech
Kontroll-Demokratie und Führerauslese / Udo Rukser
Neue Gedichte / Wolfgang Cordan
Stefan George's «Brand im Tempel» / Werner Vordtriede
Gedichte von Stefan George, deutsch und spanisch:
Übertragungen von Guillermo Thiele
Deutschsprachige Komponisten in Südamerika / Federico Heinlein
Picasso / Kurt Badt
Jean-Paul Sartre's Existentialismus / S. Friedlaender
Curt Nimuendajú Unkel (†) / Herbert Baldus
Die Geburt der Planeten / Otto Schneider
Die Erneuerung der Weltlandwirtschaft / Udo Rukser—und vieles andere.

END OF YEAR ISSUE—CONTENTS OF THE YEAR LISTED

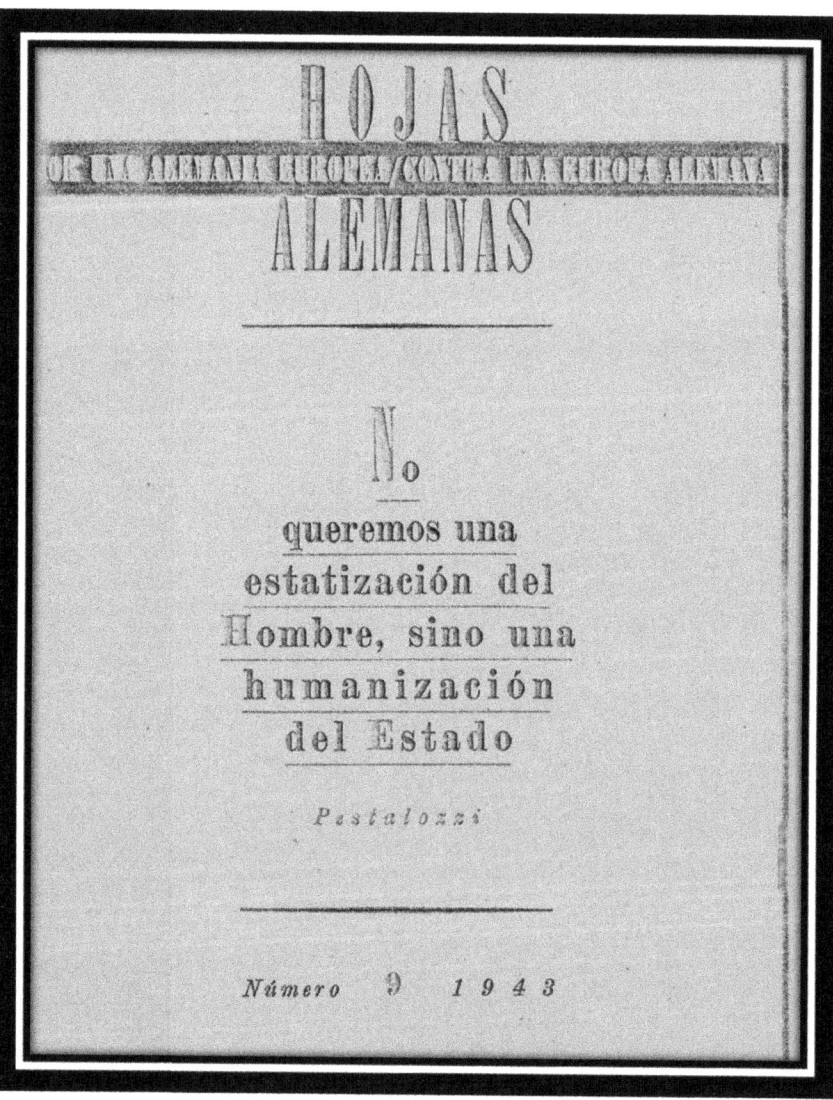

BACK COVER REINFORCED THE
HUMANITARIAN MOTTO IN SPANISH

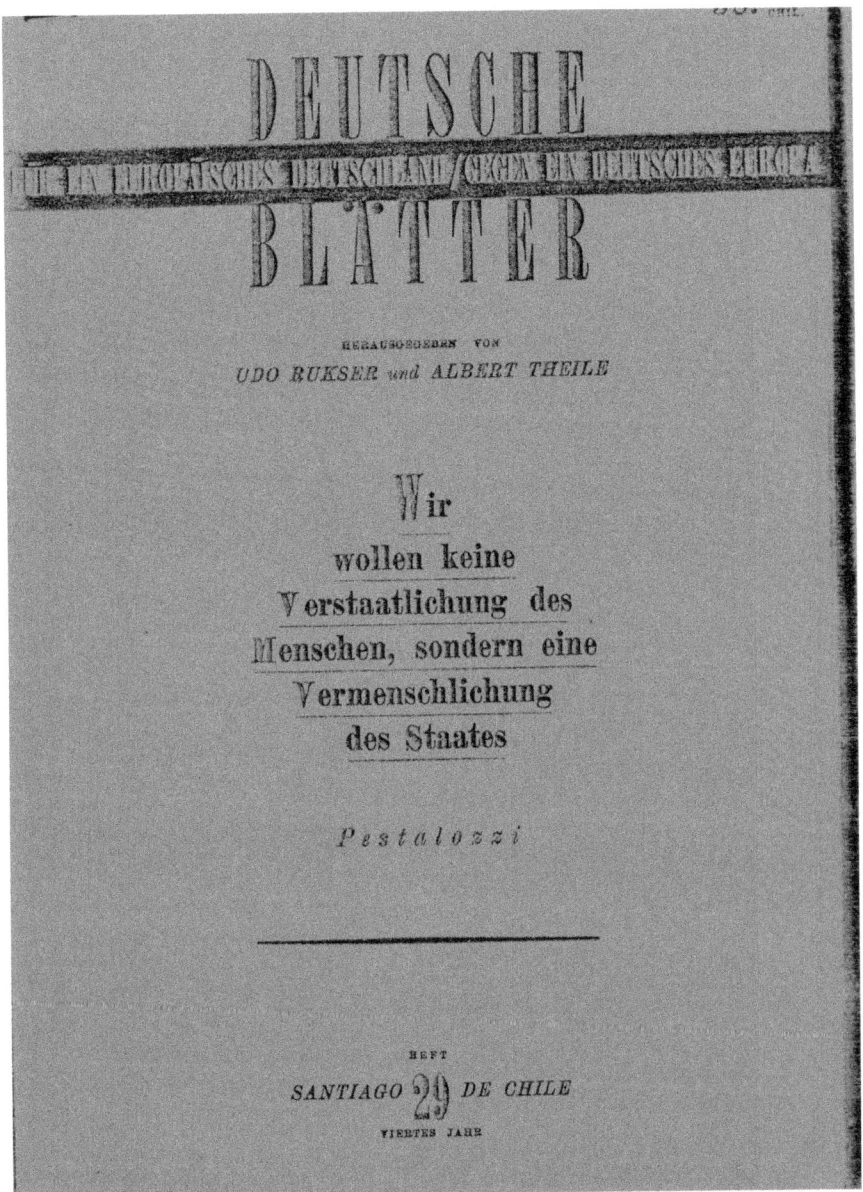

NUMBER 29 OF THE TOTAL 34 ISSUES OF THE *DEUTSCHE BLÄTTER*, THE INTELLECTUAL ANTI-NAZI PUBLICATION FOUNDED AND EDITED BY DR. UDO RUKSER AND ALBERT THEILE, AIDED BY A SMALL STAFF OF PERSONS DEVOTED TO THE CAUSE.

Ralph P. Vander Heide, Ph.D.

DEUTSCHE BLÄTTER
FÜR EIN EUROPÄISCHES
DEUTSCHLAND/GEGEN EIN DEUTSCHES EUROPA:
A CULTURAL-POLITICAL STUDY

by

Ralph Peter Vander Heide

A Dissertation
Submitted to the State University of New York at Albany
in Partial Fulfillment of
the Requirements for the Degree of
Doctor of Philosophy

College of Arts and Sciences
Department of German
1975

COPY OF TITLE PAGE OF ORIGINAL DISSERTATION
COMPLETED IN JUNE, 1975

K—Acknowledgments in Original Dissertation

I wish to express my gratitude to several individuals who helped me complete this Study: Professor Albert Theile for his informative letters concerning the *Deutsche Blätter;* Anna Steuerwald-Landmann for granting me interviews in Nürnberg as well as for her correspondence; Dr.werner Röder, Director of the Institut für Zeitgeschichte in Munich, for his assistance with materials; Dr. Erich Koszyk. Director of the Institut für Zeitungsforschung in Dortmund for permitting me to study the several letters and other materials presented to the institute by Udo Rukser; Dr. Marianne Oeste de Bopp for submitting to interviews in Mexico, for her letters and for encouraging me to write on the *Deutsche Blätter.*

My special thanks goes to Dr. Joseph Kaskell for sharing with me his personal insights and recollections and for putting at my disposal his personal correspondence, without which this study could not have been completed. Interviews with Karl O. Paetel were also invaluable.The members of my dissertation committee (professors J.M. Spalek, J. Beharriell, E. Schrader-Gentry, J.P. Strelka and A. Carlos) for their suggestions, especially Dr.Beharriel for improvements of style and punctuation.

Dr. John M. Spalek, my *Dissertationsvater* has been most patient with me and tireless in his many readings of the manuscript. His constructive criticism, perceptive corrections and encouragement have been most beneficial, vital. I can say only: Thank you, John.

My wife, Judy, has become an authority on the *Blätter* through assisting me with various aspects of my work. I owe her most thanks for proofreading and for reassurance that the study could be completed.

My parents, too, are thanked for years of encouragment and their unwavering faith in me. My father died last October with pride in his heart for my work. He conscientiously worked for the railroad for thirty-five years following years of farming and other work in mills and factories. Mother was a grade school teacher. I can not articulate in words my gratitude to them. However, I know they understood.

APPRECIATION HAS NOT WANED

Now, these many years later, I will express my deepest appreciation to all the above again. The value, in fact, is greater, since I have reached now the stage where I have that "wisdom of the years" people talk about. I am more aware than ever of the education, toleration, encouragement, insights, wisdom, time and all the rest they shared with me. I fervently hope that maybe I have helped mankind at least a little as they did me.

ALTERNATIVE QUOTATIONS ON SOME ISSUES OF THE *DEUTSCHE BLÄTTER IN 1945*

TRANSLATED BY RALPH P. VANDER HEIDE, Ph.D

Wird auch aus diesem Weltfest des Todes
Wird auch der schlimmen Fieberbrunst einmal
Die Liebe steigen?—Thomas Mann

(From this world festival of death,
From the evil feverish passion
Will love at last arise?)

Freiheit der Vernunft erfechten
Heisst für alle Völker rechten-Friedrich Schiller

(To propagate freewill
**Is to inspire justice for all nations*)*

Die Welt wird neugeboren, Gerechtigkeit und
Urzeit kehren wieder, und von dem Himmel
Steigt ein frisch Geschlecht—Dante Alighieri

(The world will be born anew,
Justice and old times will return,
And from the heavens a new
Race will descend)

A FINAL QUESTION: WHY WERE NOT ACTS SUCH AS THE FOLLOWING "THE LAST STRAW?"

To witness the prancing of SA soldiers through the streets of German cities, especially after so many fiendish acts such as *kristallnacht* (**crystal night**, literally or **night of the broken glass**) when so many store windows (Jewish merchants above all) were plundered, is, I am sure, terrifying and never to be forgotten. And prance they did, singing the melodic, inspiring *Horst Wessel Lied*.

I think it vital to probe the reasons for this highly civilized and cultured nation going mad. Citizens supported these wackos, and it seems to me that witnessing these singing goose steppers would be the last straw in making the decision to clear out.

Most of the military marches struck a cord within us, *Das Volk* was later to insist, which urged them to join in. The *Heimat*, das *Volk* and our inspired *Volksführer* were calling…So let us sing this moving *Lied* in memory of Horst Wesel who was killed, they agreed, and they sang:

Die Fahne hoch die Reihen fast geschlossen.
SA marchiert mit ruhig festem Schritt
Bald flattern **Hitler** *über allen Strassen.*

(**With flags raised high the ranks firmly**
Closed, SA men march with a confident, certain stride
Soon "*Hitler***" banners will be fluttering above all the streets.**)

NO *LIED* WAS COMPOSED FOR MY COUSIN OR HIS PLATOON.

THOMAS MANN

LIST OF SOURCES CONSULTED

(FOUR ADDED TO ORIGINAL LIST OF BOOKS)

Berendsohn, walter A. Bieber, Hedwig. *Paul Zech.* Dortmund, städtische Volksbüchdrei, 1961.

Die Humanistische Front. Zürich, Europa Verlag, 1946.

Bopp, Marianne Oeste. "Die deutsche Presse in Mexico," *Publizistik* May,/June, 1961, pp, 145-160.

Bopp, Marianne Oeste. "Die Exilsituation in Mexico." *Die deutsche Exilliteratur.* Edited by Manfred Durzak, Stuttgart, Reclam, 1973, pp. 175-182.

Cazden, Robert. *German Exile Literature in Arnerica 1933-1950.* Chicago: American Library Association, 1970.

Don Quichotte en Miniature (Grüße zum 65. Geburtstag am 23. November 1971 für Karl O. Paetel von Freunden in Deutschland und anderswo). Privatdruck,Nürnberg: Druckhaus Nürnberg, 1971.

"Drei berühmte Dortmunder in wort und Bild in der Stadtbücherei." *Bekanntmachungen: Amtliches Organ der Stadt Dortmund,* June 27, 1961.

Ernst, Fritz. *The Germans and Their Modern History*.Translated by Charles M. Prugh. New York: Columbia University Press 1966.

"Er übersetzte Gabriela Mistral." *Ruhr Nachrichten*, July 4, 1964, p.*2*

Fermi, Laura. *Ilustrious Immigrants*. Chicago: University of Chicago Press. 1968.

Foerster, Friedrich Wilhelm. *Europe and the German Question*. New York: Sheed and Ward, 1940.

Gomez-Gil, Orlando. *Historia Critica de la Literatura Hispanoamericana*. New York: Holt, Rinhart and Winston, Inc., 1968.

Greeley, Brendan, "The Good Germans." *Bloomberg Business Week*, Sept 26, 2011, p. 10.

Grosser, Alfred. *The Colossus Again*. New York: Frederick A. Praeger, 1955.

"Geistige Unfreiheit vertrieb Weltbürger." *Westdeutsche Allgemeine Zeitung*. July 5, 1974, p. 1.

„Zu Gast in der Heitmat." *Westfälische Rundschau*, June 6, 1969, p. 4.

Hinton, Thomas. "The Background of German Classisicism." *The Classical Idea In German Literature 1775-1805: An Introduction and an Anthology*. Cambridge: Harvard University Press, 1964.

Hüser, Fritz. *Albert Theile: eine unvollständige Übersicht über sein Leben und Schaffen*. Dortmund: Stadtbücherei, 1969.

Kant, Immanuel. *Zum ewigen Frieden*. Leipzig: Philipp Reclam, jr. , 1946.

Lehnert, Herbert. "Bert Brecht und Thomas Mann im Streit über Deutschland," *Die Deutsche Exilliteratur seit 1933.Vol. I: Kalifornien*. Edited by John M.Spalek and Joseph P. Strelka.Bern: Francke Verlag, 1975.

Lewis, Ward B. "Literature in Exile": Paul Zech. *The German Quarter;y, 43* (May, 1970), pp. 535-538.

"Literat und Landwirt," *Tagesspiegel*, February 2, 1961, p. 12.

Mann, Thomas. *The Coming Victory of Democracy*. New York: Alfred A. Knopf. 1928.

Mann, Thomas. "Deutschland und die Deutschen." *GesammelteWerke in Zwölf Bänden*. Band XI: *Reden und Aufsätze*. Oldenburg: S. Fischer Verlag, 1960.

Nietzche. Friedrich. *Beyond Good and Evil*. Translated by Helen Zimmern. New York: The Modern Library, 1937.

Paetel, Karl O." Das deutsche Exil." *Deutsche Rundschau*. 70 (May/June, 1937),pp. 93-103.

Paetel, Karl O. "Die Presse des deutschen Exils 1933-1945." *Publizistik*. 4 (July/August, 1959), pp. 241-256.

Pinson, Koppel S. *Modern Germany its History and Civilization*. New York: The MacMillan Company, 1954.

Seelisch, Winfried. "Das andere Deutschland: eine politische Vereinigung deutscher Emigranten in Südamerika." Unpublished Diplomarbeit, Otto-Suhr-Institut, 1970.

Shirer, Willliam L. "From Jesse Owens to the Summer of 1972." *Saturday Review*. March 25, 1972, pp. 40-44.

Sontheimer, Kurt. *Thomas Mann und die Deutschen*. München: Nyrmphenburger Verlagshandlung, 1969.

Sternfeld, Walter. "Die Emigrantenpresse." *Deutsche Rundschau*. 77 (April, 1950), pp. 250-259.

Steuerwald-Landmann, Anna. "Erlebnisse im Exil (Chile 1939- *1947*." *Fürther Heimatblätter 3* (1970), pp. 109-126.

Theile, Albert. "vorwort zur Reprint-Ausgabe." Nendeln, Liechtenstein: Kraus Reprint a Division of Kraus-Thomson Organization Limited, 1970.

Usher, Roland G. *Pan-Germanism*. New York: Grosset and Dunlap, 1913.

Vander Heide, Ralph P. *"Welterfahrung und Weltbewältigung bei Siegfried Lenz."* Unpublished M.A. Thesis, University of Utah, 1968.

Ein Weltbürger des Geistes." *Westdeutsche Allgemeine Zeitung,* June 3, 1969, p. 1.

Wertheimerr Mildred S. *The Pan-Gerrnan League 1890-1914.* New York: Columbia University, 1924.

Wille, Werner and Sperl, Heinrich. *Aufrecht zwischen den Stühlen K.O.P.* Nürnberg: Druckhaus Nürnberg, 1956.

"In Wort und Bild." *Werbezeitschrift Dortmund, July 1, 1969, p. 2.*

Zeitschriften und Zellungen des Exits 1933-1945. Bearbeitet von Horst Halfmann. Leipzig: Hausdruckerei der Deutschen Bücherei, 1969.

QUESTION ON THE BIBLIOGRAPHY

Why not several new source in the bibliography? Because I wanted to base the revision on my original work, but make it very personal, relate what I have experienced in many visits to Germany, teaching and reading the language, earnng a Ph.D. in Germanic Studies and having made the acquaintance of many Germans in all walks of life and living in their homes, which is not to say that I did not consult persons and the media as well. Movies, TV and now the Internet are a daily source of information. Compiling, organizing and focusing on the most important occurrences in Germany and her relationship with Europe and the world has been my objective and also to determine how prophetic those pieces in the *Blätter* were.

LETTERS

Most of the letters I consulted in 1974 and 1975 were archived either in Munich, Germany, in the section on German exile literature at the *Institut für Zeitgeschichte,* where I was guided and greatly assisted by Dr. Werner Röder, or were in the possession of Joseph Kaskell or Karl O. Paetel. I do not know where they may be since the death of Messieurs Kaskell and Paetel, although much of the information on the emigrants and their papers is in the archives of State University of New York-Albany campus (SUNYA) Where my "dissertation father," John Spalek, labored to rescue all he could. We visited Karl Paetel's widow to make certain that Paetel's writings were saved. Dr. Spalek is alive at the time of this writing, but long since retired. He is known world-wide for his work with *Exilliteratur*, and unquestionably, deserves kudos upon kudos for assuring preservation of so much.

Another source is the considerable number of papers given to SUNYA by Roy Curt Bates, although most of that is his own prodigious writings. Dr. Bates was born in Germany, practiced law and wrote a great deal for seventeen years, but like others had the good sense to flee to New York rather early when the jackboots began to march around. Like Dr. Kaskell he studied law and he, too, became an attorney for the second time. After that it seems he practiced law, continued to study everywhere, was possessed with mastering English, took a degree in library science and worked as an editor for Funk and Wagnalls. He officially changed his name, Kurt Bauchwitz, to Curt Bates, which I interpret as a defiant act. It says a lot about his feelings for the *Heimat*, especially when combined with his passion for using only English.

What an interesting lot those émigrés were who produced the *Exilliteratur*. The question arises: Without the forced exile would so many have become so much, so interesting, so unique? Are we not in debt to the new way of life and of viewing existence forced upon them (*Weltanschauung*)? I believe we can supply a positive answer about those who through living in two or more countries experienced more than one lifetime.

Last but not least, I should satisfy curious readers that I too have some of the original or photocopied exchanges of letters, which are numerous. Mine are from Thomas Mann, Aldous Huxley, Carl Gustav Jung, Theile and Rukser of course, Fritz Karsen, Edward Hocking, Joseph Kaskell, Hans Richter, Alejandro Alvarez, Stefan Andres, Hubertus Prinz zu Löwenstein, Fritz Siegel, William Shirer, and my own correspondence with Mrs. Mann, Theile, exile researchers, Mrs. Paetel, the T. Mann Institue, Dr. de Bopp and others.

My copies or originals came from various sources. Already in 1974 I found the materials in Dortmund to be in complete disaray, disorganized, torn, uncategorized, and, indeed plundered. The *Institut für Zeitungsforschung* (**The Institute for Newspaper Research**) proved to be of little value, and I have had no desire to return, although Dr. Erich Koszyk, Director, made every effort to help. I obtained perhaps three or four of my copies from Columbia University.

My original dissertation contained a "list of sources consulted" as well as a list of interviews and letters. I have decided not to list the seven pages of all those letters. Again all are not in my possession, but I consulted all in 1974-75, which sometimes meant a true perusal and at other times, a glance. The total number of letters I consulted is 561, and, of course, there are more somewhere or they have been destroyed. Loss and pillage account for how many I wonder. I remind the young readers that we had no computers back then either. Just the Rukser to Kaskell epistles alone number 62; the Kaskell to Rukser and Theile 96 (62 of which were addressed soley to his old friend Rukser) and Theile to Kaskell, 23. Need I say that is a tremendous amount of work they performed.

INTERVIEWS

I interviewed Joseph Kaskell, Karl O. Paetel, Albert Theile, Anna Steuerwald-Landmann, John Spalek, Joseph Strelka, Sonja P. Karsen (daughter of Fritz Karsen), Marianne Oeste de Bopp and Carl Gustav Jung in the USA, Mexico, Germany and Switzerland. Additionally, many persons in many lands, especially the Germans and Austrians in whose homes I have lived have granted me the most productive interviews, informal and quite likely over a glass of beer or sharing that *Kuchen und Kaffee* I keep writing about. No information is more valuable than what is revealed in a relaxed and intimate way.

I was also pleased to meet and get to know a bit some of Germany's postwar men and women of literature. Sigfried Lenz allotted me some of his time when I wrote a Master's Degree thesis on the literary production to date of the then young (1974) author, who now at age eighty-five recently was honored with the Goethe Medallion. It was overdue and so very well deserved. I spent some time with Uwe Johnson and Heinrich Böll, both now deceased as well as with others. The postwar writers such as the *Gruppe '47*, probably best labeled as a group that is not really a group, sought to come to grips with the very issues explored in the *Deutsche Blätter* as pinpointed here by Lenz in which he defines the mission and calling of a *Schriftsteller (***writer**, you know by now):

> *Zum Schriftsteller wird man weder bestellt noch gerufen wie etwa ein Richter. Er entschließt sich vielmehr freiwillig dazu, mit Hilfe des schärfsten und gefährlichsten, des wirksamsten und geheimnisvollen Werkzeuges—mit Hilfe der Sprache die Welt zu entblösen, und zwar so, daß niemand sich in ihr unschuldig nennen kann. Ein Schriftsteller handelt, indem er etwas aufdeckt:*

eine gemeinsame Not, gemeinsame Leidenschaften, Hoffnungen, Freuden, eine Bedrohung, die allen betrift.

Again, right on. Lenz said that this conviction stemmed from his life experiences. I say he has studied, experienced and written about the human condition, which is the life experience.

TRANSLATION: To be a writer one is neither assigned nor called, as is for example a judge. Rather, he has freely chosen, with the help of the sharpest and most dangerous among the most effective and most secret tools, i.e. with the help of language to expose the world in such a manner that no one in it can name himself guiltless. A writer acts when he discovers something: a common need, shared suffering, hope, joy, a threat which affects everyone.

In agreement with this study, we see language "the word," as a tool, secret perhaps, but effective in exposing the world. A writer's mission is to act, asserts Lenz, who has been reiterating his commitment for a lifetime, and to share the vagaries of existence. I do not believe the writers of today nor the German critics of literature among them, the perceptive Marcel Reich-Ranicki or his equals, Hans Werner Richter, Walter Jens or Hans-Albert Walter, need take a backseat when being compared to German *literati* of the past. Sometimes these modern wielders of the mighty pen have been very hard on their countrymen, even proffering questions about WW II to fathers who too often became immediately mute. I applaud them and I say, "good," it was needed.

May those who are still with us continue to examine and write about the human condition which Lenz masterfully defined, even in his early works among which *Das Feuerschiff* (**The Light Ship**—a Lighthouse Boat) immediately comes to mind. I apologize for not listing every name. However, I can assure all that they have together brought German liturature back from the edge of that abyss of which the *Blätter* warned and despaired.

From the bottom of my heart I thank all who have shared with me their most personal life experiences and their *Weltanschauungen*.

Copies of the Deutsche Blätter

ARE THEY OBTAINABLE TODAY?

I know little about available old issues other than my own. I have copies of all issues of the *DB*. In 1975 Haverford College in Haverford Pennsylvania and Columbia University in New York City had all the issues and the NY City Public Library had a few. It is quite likely that other universities have the *Deutsche Blätter* as well, but I have no knowledge of that. However, I recently learned that Indiana Univeristy has copies. I think it is not a complete set.

REPRESENTS: *HEIMAT, DAS VOLK,* PURITY
LEBENSBORN, YOUNG WOMANHOOD

German national soccer team on Nazi magazine cover

NAZIFICATION OF GERMAN SPORT

"Every German athlete should voluntarily participate in strengthening the military might of the German people."
—Hans von Tschammer und Osten, Reich Sports Office Director, April 30, 1933

Lightning Source UK Ltd.
Milton Keynes UK
UKOW04f0624151217
314491UK00001B/93/P